I ONLY TALK WINNING

I ONLY TALK WINNING

ANGELO DUNDEE

WITH MIKE WINTERS

FOREWORD BY
HOWARD COSELL

CONTEMPORARY
BOOKS, INC.
CHICAGO

Library of Congress Cataloging in Publication Data

Dundee, Angelo.
  I only talk winning.

   Includes index.
   1. Dundee, Angelo.   2. Boxing—United States—Trainers
—Biography.   I. Winters, Mike.   II. Title.
GV1132.D86A34   1985   796.8'3'0924 [B]   84-27474
ISBN 0-8092-5303-8

Published by Contemporary Books, Inc.
180 North Michigan Avenue, Chicago, Illinois 60601
Manufactured in the United States of America
Library of Congress Catalog Card Number: 84-27474
International Standard Book Number: 0-8092-5303-8

Published simultaneously in Canada by Beaverbooks, Ltd.
195 Allstate Parkway, Valleywood Business Park
Markham, Ontario L3R 4T8 Canada

To my wife, Helen,
for distinguished service beyond
the call of duty. Without her,
I would never have been able
to achieve.

CONTENTS

FOREWORD

Twenty-five years ago I remarked on television, "If I had a son who wanted to be a fighter, the only man I would entrust him to would be Angelo Dundee."

Since then I have never changed my mind. If anything, my opinion of Angie has strengthened.

I have lived with him through all of the years with Muhammad Ali, and his handling of that complex human being was superb from beginning to end. He understood Ali: the great champion's nuances, his principles, his uncanny ability to gravitate from social stratum to social stratum with engaging ease. He understood from the beginning what Ali's capacities as a fighter were, what Ali's moods were and how to cope with them, and how to prepare him for an opponent. But, at the same time, he knew never to interfere with or seek to influence the champion's deep-rooted private beliefs.

I was a factor in getting Sugar Ray Leonard steered into the hands of Dundee. I can tell you that the manner in which Angie charted Sugar Ray's career—fight by fight, opponent by opponent—is probably the most important factor in making Leonard the truly extraordinary fighter that he became. This was not easy, because there were major differences between Leonard's principal advisors and Angie. Angie had the strength and character to stick to his task so that the fighter could prevail in the ring. Though in a different way than in the case of Muhammad Ali, Angie's achievements with Ray Leonard were probably just as great.

Now, in this book, Angie tells everything about himself—his life, his character, the champions he has molded—with insights that he uniquely possesses. I know because I have been there from the beginning observing him, listening to him, learning from him.

When I turned my back on professional boxing on Thanksgiving weekend 1982, I left many good friends behind—many friends who fight for a living, whom I will always respect—and, of course, Angelo Dundee. My feelings for him will never waver—he is the best there is at what he does. And what I said twenty-five years ago, you can double or triple—he's the only man in boxing to whom I would entrust my own son.

He is special. So is this book.

Howard Cosell

I ONLY TALK
WINNING

CHAPTER ONE

LAS VEGAS, 1981

"It seemed as if my eardrums would burst from the shouting, yelling, and whistles that erupted from the crowd as we entered the ring. I felt I could taste the excitement and tension. It was an atmosphere I knew and loved. It was part of the magic that comes with a big-time controversial world title fight."

I did not give a damn what the media said. My guy was going to win, and win by a knockout.

Sure, I had watched Hearns fight Cuevas, and he was awesome, but Ray Leonard wasn't going to fight like Cuevas, and he was not going to fight the way he had fought Roberto Duran. A lot of people were going to get a big surprise.

I had been through the unbelievable hype of the "Thrilla from Manila," when Muhammad Ali and Joe Frazier fought their hearts out and electrified the world, but this fight, Sugar Ray Leonard going against Tommy "hit-man" Hearns, was something else!

A week before the fight the television cameras came to the gym in Miami to catch me before I left to join Ray at the training camp; even at that time I was confident about the result. I told the interviewer that Ray was going to win, and by a knockout, because he was the harder puncher. The interviewer's eyes glinted skeptically. Like most of the media, he could not believe that Leonard could out-punch Tommy "hit-man" Hearns. Well, they would sure as hell find out.

The atmosphere at the training sessions was fine. Ray, his trainer Janks Morton, and I got on well together—we always had. It was Mike Trainer that gave me a hard time. Still, the gym was my domain. Trainer was a lawyer and ran the business side of

Ray's company, and right now we were getting ready for the biggest fight of Ray's career; Trainer kept off my back and did not interfere.

The Roberto Duran–Sugar Ray fight in Montreal was big, the return fight in Vegas was even bigger, but this fight against Hearns was for the unification of the world welterweight title. That made it something extra special. The WBC (World Boxing Council) champion was Ray Leonard, and Hearns was the champ of the WBA (World Boxing Association). The winner would be the first undisputed welterweight champion for many years. May the best man win—that would be my man!

There is no need to tell me that anything can happen in boxing, because I know—believe me, I know. Ray would win as long as he did not let his emotion rule his head, as he had against Duran in Montreal. He had to be a cool, calm, thinking fighting-machine.

Hearns was some tough character: six feet two inches tall, three inches taller than Ray, and he possessed a long left lead that whipped out like a striking cobra. Hearns could punch, too; his fight record proved that. This guy would take some beating, but we could do it if Ray stuck to our fight plan.

Time after time I had watched videotapes of Hearns in action. Admittedly, because of his record of quick knockouts, there was not a lot to watch, but every piece of information helped. I even studied photographs of the guy, looking for any sign of weakness.

For nearly two years the media and matchmakers had been trying to get me to let Ray fight Tommy Hearns, but I did not want him. They said that I was ducking him, and maybe they were right. I was waiting for the right time—that is, a time that was right for us.

I had watched Hearns stop Pedro Rojas in Detroit. Tommy had looked too big and physical for Ray, but that had been two years ago and the time was not right.

As Hearns progressed I knew that eventually Ray was going to have to confront him. I stalled; the time was still not right. Hearns's popularity grew and grew. I watched and waited. I arranged for Ray to fight against a big, tall guy to get him ready for the tall, muscular Hearns. Ray fought the lanky Marcos Geraldo in Louisiana and tore him apart; Ray was getting ready.

After Ray had gone through the baptism of fire from the two Roberto Duran fights, I knew he was ready for anyone, and that most certainly included Thomas Hearns.

I concentrated entirely on the forthcoming fight. I closed my mind to the contractual problems I was having with Mike Trainer. All I wanted to think about was Sugar Ray Leonard beating Tommy Hearns. The time was right.

Only Caesar's Palace could have the inspiration to convert a hotel parking lot into a fabulous open air arena with all the hundreds of requirements and facilities needed to stage a televised world title fight. It was a monumental task. There was no way to escape being caught up in the excitement that this fight generated. Everyone connected with the promotion was acutely aware of his responsibilities. It was a sobering thought knowing that the fight would be seen on live and closed circuit television practically all over the world. As far as I was concerned, I knew we were ready. There would be no excuses. We were going to win.

It was time to go. The noise from the crowd was deafening as we made that short, but so, so long walk from the dressing room to the ring. My adrenalin was flowing like it had when I had made similar walks with Muhammad Ali.

I was back in Caesar's Palace, a venue that had given me both success and failure. What would it bring me tonight?

It seemed as if my eardrums would burst from the shouting, yelling, and whistles that erupted from the crowd as we entered the ring. I felt I could taste the excitement and tension. It was an atmosphere I knew and loved. It was part of the magic that comes with a big-time controversial world title fight.

I took a deep breath, exhaled, and immediately calmed down. I forgot about the crowd. I hardly heard the noise. I was completely switched on to the job in hand. My years of experience were paying off. All the knowledge I had picked up working with eight world champions would be needed now. This was not the time for nerves; it was time to concentrate on the here and now.

I watched, as Ray held a staring contest with Hearns in the middle of the ring while the referee gave them their fight instructions. Ray looked relaxed; it was a good sign. He had done his training with the kind of dedication that I had come to expect from him. I knew that he was ready, and I also knew that once the bell went for the first round, Ray would stand alone. All my encouragement, advice, and tactical knowledge would only be an aid to Ray. He would be the guy dishing out the pain and soaking up the punishment. Everything would depend on the skill, bravery, and will to win of Sugar Ray Leonard.

We were coming to the end of the fifth round; I wanted it over. I didn't like the look of Ray's left eye. I could even see the swelling from the corner where I waited anxiously for the round to end. I glanced at Janks Morton. His big, heavily muscled body was tight with tension. He wiped his perspiring forehead with a slow deliberate stroke, never taking his eyes off the two protagonists in the ring. He would hide his anxiety from Ray, but I knew he would be worried sick over the angry bruise that had appeared under Ray's eye. It would be a tragedy if the fight was stopped because of Ray's eye, yet I would be the first to agree to that decision if there was any danger of permanent damage. Another immediate worry was that the bruising and swelling would get worse and impair Ray's vision, and trying to fight Hearns with only half vision was not a course of action I would recommend.

Ray had looked good in the fight up till now. He had been cool and calculated, and had done all we could have asked of him. As we had planned, Ray was making himself a most difficult target to hit, moving laterally in either direction, which exposed Hearns's slowness when he moved to the left. Ray's superb reflexes enabled him to slip punches and score with counterpunches, but Ray had by no means taken a commanding lead. To be honest, I thought that Hearns was ahead on points, but until the swelling appeared under Ray's eye, I had no doubt in my mind of the eventual result. Now, I was worried.

As soon as the bell went for the end of the round and Ray was sitting on the stool, I began working on the eye. I had one minute to do what had to be done, and as I scrutinized the bruising, I fervently hoped that it would be time enough.

Call it luck, judgement, or plain good fortune, but an episode that happened months before in New Jersey was to play an important part in the final result in the Hearns–Leonard title fight.

While on a visit to New Jersey I was introduced to a Dr. Michael Sabia, a charming and articulate guy who was a big fight fan. He told me of his studies into the prevention of cuts and the healing of skin tissue that had been damaged or cut during a bout. At the end of our conversation Dr. Sabia gave me a gift of a product he had devised to contain and disperse bruising. He called his product "Enswell"—which is a pretty apt name! It was made of stainless steel, for temperature retention. It was about three inches long and half an inch thick. It looked a little like a modern, flat cigarette-lighter. I had a hunch about it and decided to have it with me on the night of the Hearns–Leonard fight.

I sponged Ray's face, washing away the sweat, and then gently dried him with the towel. I examined the bruising. It was under the left eye on the cheekbone. The cheekbone! Ray had sustained a slight injury during training; one of his sparring partners had got a little clumsy and had inadvertently hit Ray on the cheekbone with his elbow. At the time we did not make a big deal out of it, because it wasn't serious, but it had obviously made that area sensitive. Hearns had landed on the exact spot. Damn!

I delicately covered the swelling with a thin layer of vaseline. I reached into the bucket and took out the "Enswell" that had been lying between two ice packs. I placed the stainless steel on the swelling. The metal retained the cold temperature of the ice pack and was soothing and numbing to the bruised area.

I began applying a little pressure, smoothing the bruise away from the potentially dangerous area which was the upper part of the lower lid: if that bruised, the eye would close.

The bell sounded for round six, there was no more time for repairs. I believed I had contained the bruising temporarily. "Go to work, Ray," I said. I didn't mention the eye. Why worry Ray? "Let's go for it," I said, as Ray went back on to the battlefield.

Hearns was hurt. Was Tommy going to tumble? Ray had moved into top gear and was catching Hearns and hurting him. Tactically the fight had turned around. Hearns was moving away and Ray was the aggressor. Even the atmosphere in the arena had somehow changed, the crowd knew that Ray was out-punching Hearns and they could not believe it. In between each successive round I worked on the eye. Rounds six, seven, and eight passed. The eye, although ugly and painful, was holding out. In between each round I used "Enswell." Ray still had full vision, but time was not on our side. From the ninth round through to round eleven Ray looked tired and had slowed down. Tommy was getting back into the fight. Both men had their second wind; they were two supremely conditioned athletes. There would be no let-up.

Ray slumped onto the stool at the end of round twelve. He had lost his pep. It had been a frustrating round. I could sense the fight slipping away from us. We needed a knockout to make certain. Who knew how the judges would score it? Even if Ray won the next three rounds it was going to be a close call. I had to motivate him. "You gotta do it now, Ray. You're blowing it. You hear me? You can take him out. You gotta do it now." I had to get him back into high gear. I knew Hearns could be taken. The bell went for the thirteenth round.

Ray came alive. He was the complete fighting machine. He

caught Hearns with a long right. Hearns was in deep trouble. Ray chased him, there was a flurry of punches, and Hearns was falling through the ropes. The referee decided it wasn't a knockdown, and Tommy managed to last out the round, but I knew Ray had him. As the bell sounded Ray ran over to Hearns and began punching. He was in overdrive. Energy charged through him, making him feel stronger and fresher than when he had started the fight. Ray was oblivious to the ninety-seven degree temperature. He had the power that comes when you sense the kill, the knowledge that you are going to win. Ray swarmed all over Hearns, who was in desperate trouble. Hearns was helpless as he lay on the ropes, bravely refusing to quit. Finally the referee stepped in between the fighters, saving a courageous Hearns from further punishment. The fight was over. Sugar Ray Leonard was the undisputed Welterweight Champion of the World. He had earned more money for one fight than any other fighter in the history of boxing. He had also taken over from Muhammad Ali the title of the most charismatic and popular fighter in the world. Ray was now a superstar champion.

I embraced and congratulated Ray before he was surrounded and overwhelmed by a bunch of photographers, reporters, television interviewers, and well-wishers. I was exhausted, drained. For an instant I took in the frenetic scene going on in the ring—the jubilation and despair. I watched dispassionately.

Suddenly I wanted to go home, to find my wife, Helen, who was waiting for me in the hotel, and get the hell out of it. I wanted to escape all this bedlam. I needed to sort my mind out. I was fully aware that on this night I had played a part in a famous victory that would live forever in the annals of boxing history, but I was not in the mood to celebrate. Even so I supposed I would go through the motions; it was all part of the game.

I went over and paid my respects to Tommy Hearns, who was heartbroken. I knew how he felt. Ferdie Pecheco was interviewing Sugar Ray for television. I stood by Ray's side and listened. Ray held a towel over the badly bruised eye as he gave his accurate comments on the fight. I was turning to go when a restraining hand on my arm stopped me. A voice whispered in my ear. "Ferdie wants an interview."

Ferdie Pecheco, "the fight doctor," a friend who had worked with me through the Muhammad Ali years, turned towards me and began the interview. He ended by saying that I had been right in saying before the fight that Leonard was the better puncher. I smiled and began to leave as Ferdi said, "Congratulations, Angelo, on a brilliant victory in a brilliant career."

How far I had come! "A brilliant victory in a brilliant career!" He was talking about me! I knew, no matter how successful I was or became in the future, I owed so much of what fame I might have to my association with one man, Muhammad Ali.

Of course, when he and I first met, he was Cassius Clay, but that was way back . . . Willie Pastrano and I were going to Louisville. . . .

CHAPTER TWO

LOUISVILLE'S LUCKY FOR ME

" 'What the hell are you doing, Johnny?' I shouted at him as I held open the waistband of his boxing shorts and lifted his stomach, enabling him to breathe easier. 'Don't you want your new home? . . . That guy Charles is trying to take your home away. You're gonna lose your air-conditioning and picket fence. That sucker is taking it away from you. . . . Are you gonna let him?' The bell went for the ninth round. I stuffed his mouth-guard into his mouth and pushed him off the stool, propelling him to the center of the ring."

It had meant getting up a little earlier, but it was worth it. The morning was beautiful. From my desk, I picked up the air tickets that I had forgotten to take home with me the night before. I locked up the empty office and in under two minutes was back in the car with my wife, Helen.

"Sorry, Doll," I said, meaning that I was sorry to have taken us so much out of our way.

"Forget it. You have a lot on your mind," Helen answered, meaning she understood about me forgetting to take the tickets home with me, and it was true, I did have a lot on my mind. I had a wife six months pregnant; no air conditioning in my home—and in Miami, that ain't funny; I had been losing my money betting on the ball games; and on top of that, two fighters I was involved with were fighting each other. Yea, I had things on my mind!

As we drove across the Julia Tuttle Causeway, from Miami Beach to the airport on 36th Street, I said to Helen for at least the third time that morning, "Gee, Helen, this is God's Country." For me it was true, I loved it. I was a sucker for the warm blue water of the bay, the impressive skyline of Miami Beach, the palm trees, the causeways that opened up like some mechanical toy to let the large yachts and ships pass through. I loved the whole darn number.

We lived at 1080 North West 130th Street in a thirteen thousand dollar, three-bedroom, two-bathroom house. It was our third move since 1952. If you could ignore the fact, which I couldn't, that the house had no heat or air-conditioning, it was a nice house. In fact, all the neighboring houses were nice—trouble was, they all looked alike. Don't get me wrong, I was pleased to be living there, but each time we moved we went further away from the Miami Beach Convention Center where Chris, my elder brother, had his office.

I worked for Chris. My position in the business was difficult to define. I wasn't exactly a partner and I wasn't exactly an assistant. I was, at least by my own definition, what is commonly known as a "gofer." In other words, Chris would say to me, "Hey Angie, go for this" or "go for that." Do you know what I mean?

I used to help with the typing, sell tickets for the boxing or wrestling promotions, and sometimes deliver tickets and perhaps pick up an extra ten or twenty dollars from a grateful fan. Whatever needed to be done, I would do it. Hell, I didn't mind. I was earning a living, and remembering the past, I didn't complain. To be honest, the last four or five years hadn't been at all bad. I had been involved, on and off, with Carmen Basilio since 1952, and when in 1955 Carmen had beaten Tony DeMarco to take the World Welterweight Championship, I had been in Carmen's corner. I had slowly built up a reputation as a guy who knew what he was doing, and I had got my feet wet as a manager. Offers for my services were coming in—the only problem was, I wasn't making any bread. The main trouble was that the fighters were not making much money, so my percentages or salaries didn't add up to much. I was getting a little from a little, which is, I admit, better than nothing from nothing, so, being a married man I played it safe and stayed as a "gofer" for Chris. It wasn't the most glamorous position in the world, but who was I to complain? Besides, I was learning.

I thought that having a base in Miami and working out of my brother's office would cut down on the traveling, but it seemed as if I was always going somewhere. Sure, it was nice to get away from the office, because once I was away with my fighter I felt like somebody. It was "Goodbye gofer" and "Hello Angelo Dundee."

I need not tell you that all this traveling made life tough for Helen, but she didn't complain. We both believed that it would get easier as I became more successful. It goes to show you how wrong you can get!

On our way to the airport Helen was driving as usual, and as usual our three-year-old son Jimmy was sleeping in his baby chair secured in the back of the car.

"Did you take your sweater with you?" Helen asked me in her unmistakable southern drawl.

"I sure did, honeychile," I answered in a bad imitation of her accent.

I was going to Louisville, Kentucky. I had been there before and I liked it. Friendly people, a good hotel, great fight fans, and an excellent Italian restaurant—what more could you ask?

Unfortunately, Louisville in February could mean low temperatures, and Helen did not want me catching a cold and being laid up in bed. We could not afford it. A little sick maybe, but ill—no way. Hell! I had a pregnant wife and a son to support.

Helen and I always tried to arrive at the airport early so that we could park for a few minutes and rap. It is funny, we always had plenty to talk about, but never enough time to relax and really talk.

I leaned across to the back of the car and kissed the sleeping Jimmy. That baby always slept in the car. At night in his crib—nothing. In the car—sleep!

"Bye, doll, I'll call you tonight." I kissed her on the lips and gently touched her on her belly, feeling the swell of the new baby.

"Helen, I believe you are getting fat," I joked with her. "I like it."

"Thank you, kind sir." She fixed me with her glittering brown eyes. "This is the second time you have ruined my figure."

"I know, doll, but it's such fun ruining it." We laughed and kissed again—it is that kind of marriage. "Bye honey, I'll phone you from the hotel tonight," I reminded her, as I left the car, off to meet my man, Willie Pastrano.

I walked the short distance from where we had parked to the old, beaten-up terminal. Faye, Willie's wife, dropped him right outside the entrance. He didn't like to walk anywhere. You can imagine how he loved training and "roadwork"!

I saw him immediately. Two very attractive stewardesses were looking up at him with expressions that could only be described as lustful. He was a big, good-looking guy with black wavy hair, a smile like Errol Flynn, and the personality to match. Willie was a great athlete, but keeping that guy in shape was a pain in the butt. We had been together since 1952 when he was just a sixteen-year-old kid. I guess you might say that he and Ralph Dupas, who also joined me as a sixteen-year-old, sort of grew up under my tutelage.

Willie and I had a lot in common. We were both of Italian extraction, we both loved Italian food, and we were both married, although Willie never let his wife interfere with his idea of marriage! I once asked him what Faye would do if she caught him fooling around. He was quite serious when he answered that it was a compliment to Faye; he missed her so much he had to have substitutes.

From a sixteen-year-old lightweight, Willie had developed into a small but fully-fledged heavyweight. I say small, he was six feet tall, but by today's standards that would be considered small, and by Johnny Holman's standard he was certainly small. Johnny was his opponent, and Johnny was six foot six inches tall—and I mean tall.

It was an important fight for Willie. He needed to beat Johnny to keep in contention for a title shot. The pressure was on Johnny, too. After all, this was the first television fight from Louisville, and a good win in front of all the viewers could turn his career around.

Johnny had knocked out the former World Heavyweight Champion, Ezzard Charles, in April 1955. Unfortunately, in the return fight in June of the same year, Johnny lost the ten-round bout, on points. On paper the Pastrano—Holman fight looked to be a real tough affair. As far as I was concerned, Willie would dance home an easy winner, and I should know—I trained both guys.

I had been working in Johnny's corner when he had stopped Charles; that was some experience. The fight gave me the opportunity to use, first hand, applied psychology.

We were in the eighth round and Ezzard Charles was all over Johnny. I do not think Johnny had won a round. No matter what I said to him in between rounds, I couldn't motivate him. He was lethargic and seemed to be just going through the motions. What could I do to psyche him up? I remembered that during the training buildup for the fight we used to sit and rap, and Johnny never stopped mentioning his new home. He was so proud of the air-conditioning and his white picket fence.

At the end of the round Johnny slumped onto the stool and I began working on him both physically and mentally. "What the hell are you doing, Johnny?" I shouted at him as I held open the waistband of his boxing shorts and lifted his stomach, enabling him to breath easier. "Don't you want your new home?" His eyes, more alert now than they had been all night, locked into mine. "You hear me, Holman?" My voice was getting even louder. "That guy Charles is trying to take your home away. You're gonna lose your air-conditioning and picket fence. That sucker is taking it away from you. You gotta stop him. He's taking your home. Are you gonna let him?" The bell went for the ninth round. I stuffed his mouth-guard into his mouth and pushed him off the stool, propelling him to the center of the ring.

It was as if a new man had entered the ring. Johnny threw every punch in the book at an amazed Ezzard Charles. The end came quickly. Ezzard, completely unsettled by the ferocious attack, got nailed by a right cross and down he went. The fight was over and Holman had stopped Ezzard Charles. You have to respect the power of suggestion.

When Johnny first came to me, he had a bad record of defeats behind him. His manager was talking "quitting time." I think I helped him. The record book will show his series of wins under my training. Mainly I gave the guy some confidence in himself. It didn't do me any harm either. I was voted Trainer of the Year after the Holman–Charles fight in Chicago in 1956. The forthcoming fight with Pastrano was a television deal, and I knew the power of the medium. It was making "stars." Look what it did for Mary Tyler Moore—and she can't even box!

I liked Johnny. That was my problem; I liked both guys. At the 5th Street Gym in Miami, during training sessions Johnny and Willie used to work out together, and let me tell you, Willie would slap Johnny around. Of course, I realized what happens during a friendly workout isn't any guide to what will happen in a real-life fight situation, but I was trainer to both fighters and I didn't think it would be a good fight or a good result for Johnny. As it worked out I was right and I was wrong!

Johnny's manager disagreed with me when I told him my opinion.

"What are you talking about? Johnny's six inches taller than your guy. You're only worried about losing a payday with Johnny because you can't work both corners at once."

What can you say to a stupid, lousy remark like that? Anyway, Johnny trained up north without me and I concentrated on getting Willie really sharp, but as I mentioned before that was no easy thing to do.

For example, during the period Willie was building up from a lightweight, which is 135 pounds, to a heavyweight, which is over 175 pounds, I told Willie to drink plenty of milk. After a slow start and lots of friendly persuasion, he began to get into the habit, and everywhere we went he seemed to have a carton of milk with him. Now, normally, and especially in those early days, I am not a suspicious man, but I began to notice that every time Willie finished a carton of milk he seemed to be a happier guy. Once after training, Willie was dutifully drinking his milk, and I said, "Hey Willie, I'm thirsty, give me some milk."

"Angie, you won't like it, it's warm."

"That's OK. I like it warm." The seeds of suspicion growing, I reached for the carton. Willie didn't look too pleased. He began shaking the carton. He said with a fake sincerity, "What do you know, I think the carton is empty."

"Gimme the goddam carton," I said, taking it from him. I took one quick swig. My suspicions were confirmed. I stared at Willie. Willie stared at me. Then, with an apologetic smile on his face he said, "Hell, Angie, it tastes better with whisky in it. You know I never did like milk."

Flying with Willie was always fun. Willie was scared of flying, so naturally he made his usual queries about the "prop" engines, and I, as usual, assured him they were perfectly safe and running just fine. The stewardess who served us was rather homely, so I didn't think there was much chance of Willie trying to seduce her in the restroom, although I wouldn't have bet on it.

Normally I would have enjoyed smoking a cigar, but I didn't want Willie picking up any more bad habits. We ate on the plane, not that the food was so hot, but at least I could monitor what Willie ate. I tried to keep the mood relaxed, because I knew that the tension would begin to build as we reached fight night. I do not like to talk to the fighters about the upcoming fights outside of training hours, but this fight was more difficult than usual because Johnny and Willie were pals.

"I know Johnny is your pal, but this is not personal, it's your job," I told him.

Before we landed we took out our sweaters from our hand-luggage and put them on. 1 didn't want to catch a cold and I most certainly didn't want Willie laid up in bed with the sniffles. I expected Louisville to be a little chilly—it was.

Bill King, the promoter of the fight, was there to meet us. We quickly jumped into the car asking for the heat to be turned up; after all we were from Florida, where if the temperature drops below seventy degrees—man, that's cold.

Bill was in a happy mood. When the tickets are selling at the box office, everyone's in a happy mood. It was still only late morning so we went straight to the gym, where Bill had arranged a local press reception. I always prefer to arrive in the daytime so that I can size up the place, know where I'm at. Find out where the park is. In Louisville there was a little park down the road from the gym where Willie could run. Later on in years, when Willie came back to Louisville, he would always do his roadwork in that little park. A lot of fags used to hang around that area, and Willie would joke and kid with those guys and they became big fans of his. Getting Willie to do his roadwork was nearly as bad as getting him to drink milk without whisky. Left on his own he would do his running on a postage stamp. Still, Willie was a great boxer. If I wanted to see a runner, I'd go to a track meet.

I knew Willie was in good shape. I ought to know, I trained him. He was sharp, and he looked it as he worked out in the gym. The press boys were impressed, and so was Bill King.

"He looks perty good, Angelo. He sure as heck is fast for a heavyweight," Bill said in his peculiar accent. I lapped it up. I was proud of Willie's superb condition. I heard one pretty girl reporter from a local radio station remark that Willie was a good mover. I made sure Willie never got the chance to try out any of his moves on her. I like good press relations . . . and I've nothing against sex, but not just before a fight.

I was in my element. There was no conscious analyzing why I felt so happy and relaxed there in the gym with my fighter, surrounded by people from the news media. It was a good feeling. I never thought, "Hey, Angie, you feel good," I just did. Only now can I really stand away objectively and appreciate it.

The news guys in Louisville were all big fight fans, and I found it no problem to talk with them. My early days in New York had prepared me to relax with newspapermen, and I had many friends in that profession.

Sure, I had bad experiences with reporters. Sometimes I felt the reports before and after a fight were slanted, and way off base, but I realized that the news media is a vital part of the fight game and we need them as much, if not more, than they need us. From my first experiences in New York I learned great respect for the influence and assistance the press could give a fighter, but I wasn't too crazy on how some of the fighters and managers handled it. I didn't like to hear a fighter say, when being inter-viewed, "Ask my manager; I do the fighting, he does the talking." I didn't go for that. It seemed rather belittling. I did not want Willie, or any fighter I handled, to come over as a dummy, and at the same time cast me in the role of the sharp, fast-talking, anything-for-a-buck type of manager. I let my fighters talk, let them soak up the glamour and publicity. It was a new concept, but in later years that simple concept revolutionized the fight business.

I guess there must have been other good hotels in Louisville, but I always booked into the Sheraton. There were a couple of good restaurants in the hotel, and the staff all seemed to be fight fans. Willie and I shared a room, twin beds naturally—I liked the guy, but not that much!

Four days to fight time, and all we had to do was work out an hour a day in the gym, and about the same amount of time on roadwork either at dusk or bright and early before breakfast.

Most trainers prefer to do their road-running in the morning. I have nothing against that, but I believe there is a good case for doing it in the evening—they fight at night, don't they? Still, I usually leave it to the preference of the fighter, and this trip we opted for mornings. I was pleased, because that meant early nights, and Willie Pastrano would go to bed like a good boy and not be out swinging till the early hours of the morning.

Two hours' work a day was the whole deal, yet I was as busy as a bustling bee. I would check out all the Italian organizations. I would drop in at the *Louisville Journal,* and the radio and TV stations would hear from me as I would be trying to arrange pre-fight interviews for my fighter. Why? I wanted to publicize my fighter and I wanted to sell tickets. Willie was headlining and a fighter, like a theatrical star, had to be a "draw." Promoters would not pay big bucks for a fighter if he did not draw a big gate. Believe me, a lot of very good fighters, even champions, couldn't get a big payday because they didn't draw in the crowds. Jersey Joe Walcott, Jimmy Ellis, and Bob Foster were three great fighters who had trouble getting fights and getting big paydays for that very reason.

Bill King was in seventh heaven; the tickets were selling like crazy. He was a good promoter and he had done his job in publicizing the "fight," but every little bit helped. He is still in Louisville to this day, but he no longer promotes boxing. A pity.

The fight was getting closer and the tension was building up, but Willie seemed unaffected. I believe in letting my fighters train right up to the day before the fight. Hopefully careful preparations have taken care of any weight problems. There is a danger of weakening a fighter when he is forced to shed one or two pounds on the day of the fight. Willie had no weight problem; he had no problems at all.

Willie, in his last workout at the gym the day before the fight, looked one hundred percent.

"He is as sharp now as he'll ever be," I said to Bill King who was watching the session.

"He sure is, but let me tell you, Angie, I saw Holman work out and that guy is looking good too."

When Willie had showered and dressed, Bill asked us if we would lunch with him. I have to tell you, this guy Bill King was a heck of a good guy. He had an interest in the local horse track, and we were his guests there too. Willie was introduced over the loudspeaker and received a great ovation. Bill even named a race after him—"The Willie Pastrano Classic."

Willie couldn't make the lunch because he wanted to get back to the hotel room to watch himself on a lunchtime interview show that had been recorded the day before. I reminded him to have a plain meal for lunch and to lay off the milk!!

I lunched on tagliatelli alla crema, followed by veal pizzaiola, followed by an unmentionably large portion of cheese and celery, washed down by Frascati wine, expresso coffee, and a large *grappa. I* wasn't boxing tomorrow night!

Feeling slightly guilty I didn't mention food to Willie, who was stretched out on his bed watching the final seconds of the talk show.

"How are you?" I asked.

"Just great." He grinned at me. "I am one hell of a handsome Wop."

Willie and I settled down to watch television. We normally ate around six-thirty, so we had about four hours to kill. Willie sat in front of the television set and began searching for a program he liked. I sat on one of the two bedroom chairs, full and relaxed. I had no interest in the television. I was trying to visualize the way the fight would go tomorrow night. Johnny Holman could punch, but Willie was fast. As I saw it, Willie would jab and dance away out of trouble. His rapier-like left hand would keep Johnny off balance. Yes, I had it right. Johnny wouldn't touch Willie.

My mental plans and counterplans were interrupted by the ringing of the telephone. Willie ignored it. He was too immersed, hunched over the television set, checking out every available television channel, still looking for one he liked. He liked "horror" shows. In fact, he used to sketch violent scenes. He would draw this guy holding a dagger dripping with blood over some other guy or gal—and that was one of his nicer drawings. He was good. He was very artistic. It's rather strange, in my long involvement in the fight game I have met many boxers who drew or painted. You never think of these macho guys being artistic, but many are.

I picked up the phone. "Hello, this is Angelo Dundee."

"Hello. My name is Cassius Marcellus Clay. I am the Golden Gloves Champion of Louisville. I won the Atlanta Golden Gloves; I won the Pan American games. I'm gonna be the Olympic Champion, and then I'm gonna be Champion of the Whole World. I'd like to meet you."

I stared at the telephone in disbelief. "Who is it?" Willie asked.

"Some nut. He wants to meet me," I answered.

"Send the sucker up. The television's lousy. At least it will break the monotony."

"Well, Mr. . . ." I couldn't remember his name. He helped me out.

"Mr. Cassius Marcellus Clay, Mr. Dundee."

"Yea. Well, Mr. Clay, I can give you about five minutes or so. Willie has to take a nap."

"Thank you, sir. Is it OK if I bring my brother up too?"

I placed my hand over the receiver. "He has his brother with him," I said to Willie.

"What the hell," Willie said, "send them both up."

When they entered the room, not only did they enter, they filled it. They were big boys. Both over six feet three inches. They were slim, but you could tell by looking at them that they were well muscled.

I introduced myself and Willie, and Cassius introduced himself and his brother Rudy. He was very polite. Rudy was carrying a painting and a bust of some guy. It was modeled in clay, I think, I never did find out, but it was quite impressive. At first Cassius did most of the talking. He was a very likeable guy, and he spoke with obvious sincerity.

"I've seen you on television, Mr. Dundee. I saw you with Carmen Basilio, and I saw the Holman–Charles fight too. The fight I really enjoyed most was when Mr. Pastrano beat Al Andrews in Chicago. You sure do have one sweet left hand, Mr. Pastrano." Cassius's handsome face broke into a beaming smile.

Willie sat there grinning, trying to appear modest. He ate it up. The five minutes came and went; we were still talking. Willie and Rudy discussed the painting and the bust, and Cassius, when he did make a comment on that subject, knew what he was talking about. But mainly we talked boxing. I guess Willie and I took over the conversation and the two youngsters listened. The time flew, and I was enjoying myself. Well, there is nothing as interesting as hearing your own voice, on your favorite subject, to a captive audience!

After four hours, the boys left. I didn't ask them to, they had to get home. "Nice guys," Willie remarked. "Have you ever heard of Cassius?"

"No, but with his record he must be useful," I said. I didn't mess with amateurs and I only got to know them if they turned professional. "Nice guys," I reiterated. "Let's eat," I said grabbing my jacket.

"Yea, I'm hungry." Willie took a quick look in the mirror, ran his hands through his hair, grabbed his jacket, and made for the door. "Nice guys," he said to himself.

After I made my nightly call to Helen, Willie and I sat down to a steak dinner. Afterwards we went for our customary walk. Believe it or not, the walk after eating is part of my training schedule for my fighters. I do not like them to go to bed on a full stomach. I do not feel good if I do it, so I figure how can they.

Cassius Marcellus Clay was forgotten. We had the fight tomorrow night. We had other things on our minds. On the walk out we talked about our fight plan, but on the walk back I subtly changed the subject and we were rapping about home life; you know the kind of thing—the wife, the mortgage, and when could we afford a new car. I wanted my fighter relaxed. I didn't want him laying in bed, unable to sleep because he was worrying about the fight. We were in bed by ten o'clock. We both slept like babies.

The big night had arrived. The arena was packed. The full house created its own excitement, and the novelty of having television cameras angled around the ring gave the noisy crowd a sense of occasion. The extra lighting brought in by the television crew pinpointed the ring, making it the focus of everyone's attention. I thought at the time that this is the way to present boxing. Little did I dream that within seven years I would be one of the leading players on a stage presenting boxing halfway around the world to an audience of hundreds of millions.

Our changing room was small but it was clean, and by comparison to some of the rooms we had been in, it was a palace, and heck, it was brand new.

"How are the bandages?" I asked.

"A little tight," Willie replied. I snipped at the bandages with my scissors to loosen them. He nodded his head. They were OK. A knock on the door, a voice shouted out that it was time to go.

"Keep moving, he won't touch you," I said, slapping Willie on the shoulder. "Let's go."

The bell went and the fight was on. Everything was going according to plan until the end of the round. Willie had made Johnny miss and miss and miss again, but then Johnny didn't miss. Right at the end of the round he caught Willie with a left hook right on the nose, but before Johnny could follow it up the bell ended the round.

Willie sat slumped on his stool and I frantically began working on his nose. It was broken and bleeding badly. I applied some adrenalin chloride 1–1000 onto a cotton swab and squeezed it into the nostrils to stop the bleeding. Quickly I washed the blood from his face and gently applied a thin layer of vaseline over the nose.

"Can you breathe OK?" I asked.

"Yea, I guess so." Willie looked at me from the corners of his eyes. "I thought he wouldn't touch me?"

I slapped his cheek and said, "He didn't touch you, he hit you." He grinned. I put in his gum-shield. The bell went for the second round. "Dance, Willie, dance," I said.

He did. For nine rounds he was immaculate. In and out, dancing away, scoring points with his impeccable left hand. He was the classic boxer. I felt sorry for Johnny. It was like trying to hit a shadow. First Willie was there and then he wasn't.

It was a great fight and the packed house loved it. It was no surprise to anyone when at the end of the fight Willie was declared winner on points by a unanimous decision.

The crowd was exhausted, Willie was exhausted, and so was I. That night we had supper with Bill King and a couple of the television production staff. Everyone was in a party mood except Willie. Well, with a broken nose, you don't really feel like whooping it up. We cut out and went to bed.

The fight had taken the most money in box office receipts in the history of Louisville, so Bill had been delighted to pay me our purse after the fight. I had settled with Willie the following morning, and after deducting expenses and my percentage there wasn't an awful lot of bread left for Willie. I took one third, out of which I gave half to Willie's old manager, leaving me one half of a third, from which I had to pay Chris for my share of the Miami expenses. Great!

On the plane back to Miami, I told Willie that the first thing we were going to do was see a doctor and get his nose fixed.

"You know, Angie, I ain't gonna get rich doing this," Willie said as he carefully touched his nose.

"You and me both, Willie, but what else do we know?"

Willie was thoughtful for a moment, "I was thinking about that young kid Cassius, just starting out. I wonder if he realizes how tough this game is? He's a black guy; it's going to be even tougher for him."

"Yea," I answered, "but, if he's got the bug what can you do? He wants to be a fighter."

"Yea. Do you think he'll ever make it?"

"Who knows? Maybe. Who the hell knows anything in this game?"

CHAPTER THREE

SOUTH PHILLY

"A local promoter offered Joe a 'pro' fight. It was a chance to make a few dollars, so Joe jumped at the chance. However, there was one big hitch; Pop didn't want any son of his fighting for money! In our house, one thing you did not do was argue with Pop, so Joe decided that if he intended to fight, the only thing to do was not let Pop find out. How? Joe would use a different name. What name? . . . Dundee."

Because trolley buses ran along Morris Street, where I lived, ball games were not too popular. Parents didn't like the idea of kids rushing blindly into the middle of the street chasing a ball.

A neighborhood game that we kids played was called "pussy stick." I should point out that fifty or so years ago the word "pussy" had not yet taken on the slang meaning it has today. Our game had nothing to do with the female anatomy—it had nothing to do with pussycats either.

A small stick was placed on the sidewalk, then you hit it with a larger, heavier stick which hopefully made the lighter stick fly up from the sidewalk. While the stick was airborne, the idea was to hit it as hard as you could, with the heavier stick, and see how far it would travel. The kid who hit it the furthest won the game. Please do not ask me why this crazy game was called "pussy stick." I didn't invent it, I just played it. Besides, I was only a kid!

It was my turn to bat. On my first hit the little stick flew upwards, and my second shot sent it flying through the air. It hit Freddie, who was standing back a piece watching us kids play, on the shoulder.

Freddie was a big kid, at least two years older than the rest of us guys; he could have been thirteen. He turned and glared at me. I did not like Freddie. He often picked on me and made fun of me because I was fat. Freddie picked up the stick that had struck him and snapped it in two. He was mad.

"Hey, punk! You trying to be smart?"

"No. I just hit the stick," I answered. He had already moved towards me and stood threateningly over me.

"You did it on purpose, didn't you Fatso?" He pushed me.

"Hey, cut it out," I said, backing away. I hated being called "Fatso," but I was too scared to do anything about it.

"What's the matter, Fatso?" Freddie said as he pushed me even harder. He continued to push me around as he kept on talking. "You hit me with the stick, it's only right that I hit you." He punched me on my ear; it was meant for my nose but I moved my head in time. The other kids had gathered around, and although they were on my side they did not interfere. They were scared of Freddie too.

I knew I was going to have to fight back, but I was hoping that if I did not retaliate he would realize that the whole deal was silly and unfair, and he would leave me alone. It never works that way with a bully. He hit me again and hurt me. I started to fight back. I gave it my best shot, but I was a fat little kid who knew nothing about defending himself. I got a licking.

The front door of our house on Morris Street was never locked. I walked into the kitchen where Mom was cooking as usual. She turned and saw me. "Figlio mia, che cause su chese?" Roughly translated it means, "My son! What's happened to you?" She pulled me to her and I clung to her, allowing myself, at last, the privilege of crying.

My brother Jimmy either heard or sensed that something was going on. He came into the kitchen, and his curiosity turned to concern and then to anger as he listened to my story. He rushed out of the house in search of Freddie.

Mom released me from her embrace, which enabled me to follow Jimmy. Mom didn't like us kids fighting, but she liked bullying even less.

Jimmy had found Freddie. Jimmy may have been a little older, but they were the same height and Freddie looked heavier. Jimmy was very slim, but strong and fast. I watched them fight with a feeling of gratification, because Jimmy was knocking the hell out of my tormentor. I also felt ashamed that I had got licked, and that I was a fat kid who couldn't fight. All my brothers could fight, at least I presumed they could. I knew that my brothers Frankie and Jimmy could, and my eldest brother Joe had been a professional boxer, so I knew he could fight. He was grown up, so he didn't really count. As for brother Chris, the brother I had only seen maybe two or three times in my whole life, he was a "god" and obviously could do anything. It was only me, Angelo, who couldn't fight. I was the fat little brother who got hit upon.

That night, lying in bed with Jimmy, I mentioned to him that I didn't know how to fight, and would he teach me? Brother Frankie, who shared the back bedroom with Jimmy and me, overheard the conversation. He sat up in his bed—as he was the eldest he had the other bed to himself. "Jimmy, take Angie to the fire station tomorrow after school, and we will both help him along. Now, go to sleep, I'm tired."

I loved my brothers, I loved sharing a room with them; it was fun and it also gave me a feeling of belonging and security. This sense of belonging ran through all us kids growing up at 829 Morris Street. We had love and affection for each other, and we had parents who loved us and taught us to love one another. I had two wonderful sisters. Growing up with them taught me to respect womanhood—not that my Pop would have allowed me, or my brothers, to be anything else but respectful. My sisters Mary and Josephine have always been a blessing in my life.

As I look back to my childhood years in South Philly, I am filled with happiness from the memories of that home, flowing with love, on Morris Street.

My family was not like the caricature Italian family of the movies. As far as I know, there wasn't a gangster in the whole family, including cousins. We never ran barefoot through the ghetto market, stealing goodies from vendors' carts. My Pop would have whacked us if we had. We were an ordinary, hard-working, God-fearing family. Perhaps that old cliche applied to us: "They were poor, but they were honest."

No one seems to know the exact date of the Mirenda family's arrival in America, but arrive they did, round about the turn of the century.

My father, Angelo Mirenda, accompanied by his mother Maria, his wife Philomena, and their son Joseph, landed at the docks of New York and somehow, most likely through the friendship of other immigrants, found themselves living in Philadelphia at Carter Street, the south side of the city where the previous Italian immigrants had already formed a ghetto.

Within a remarkably short time, and without being able to

speak the language, Angelo found a job working on the tracks of the railroad, a job he held for over forty years, leaving only because of ill health and old age.

Angelo slowly learned to make himself understood in his new language, but Philomena never mastered English and spoke only Italian until the day she died. Maybe she never learned English because she never mixed with English-speaking Americans. All her neighbors and friends were Italian immigrants, and they naturally found it easier to speak in their native tongue. It was the children of these immigrants who learned to speak like "real Americans," invariably forgetting, in the process, their original native language. The Mirenda household spoke Italian, but the Mirenda children spoke "American."

Writing English was a feat that Angelo Mirenda never mastered. During his first few years in America he would fill in, to the best of his ability, enough forms and documents to sink a battleship. The name Mirenda evolved into Mirena, or depending on the deciphering of Angelo's writing or the mood of the government official, Mireno.

The Mirenda/Mirena/Mireno family had immigrated from Calabria, Southern Italy, for the usual reason. It was the search for a better life, the chance to work and earn enough money to keep the family in food and other necessities, and of course, the golden lure America offered all immigrants—freedom and the opportunity to improve and succeed.

Angelo Mireno—as he eventually called himself—moved to 829 Morris Street, a house he would own until he died. In this house, his wife Philomena gave birth to six sons, but one would die as a baby, and three daughters, one of whom would also not survive babyhood.

There would be a twenty-two year gap separating the youngest from the eldest child. Starting with the eldest the children were: Joseph (Joe), Christopher (Chris), Mary, Frank, James (Jimmy), Angelo, and Josephine.

Angelo Mireno had no worries on how to raise a family. He had his principles and, as a good Catholic, he believed that he would have no problems in distinguishing what was right from what was wrong. There would be discipline and respect, and he would make sure his home would be run under those guidelines.

He was strong and healthy. There were responsibilities to face: he had a family to support. Hard work didn't frighten him— support his family he did.

For many years things were not easy for Angelo. No matter how hard he worked there was never enough money to go around. Joe worked from the age of fourteen and, like all the children would do in later years, brought all his wages home to Mom, who would then dole out pocket money. Chris left home at the age of fifteen. He wanted more than South Philly could offer him, and he had the courage to go out into the world and seek the life he wanted. Angelo and Philomena were heartbroken, but as the years passed, their anguish turned to admiration and pride for the son who left their nest so prematurely.

About two years before I was born, my brother Joe was approaching the age of nineteen. He was a finely built young man, with the strength and durability of Pop.

Most of the local boys kept themselves in good shape. The local meeting place for guys who wanted to work out was the Mason Hall AC Gym, on Seventh and Morris. Joe began sparring with some of the talented amateur boxers who used the gym. He looked good, and started entering a few amateur contests. He was doing real well and getting a local following as an amateur, but amateurs do not make any money, and Joe wanted to make some bread.

The inevitable happened. A local promoter offered Joe a "pro" fight. It was a chance to make a few dollars, so Joe jumped at the chance. However, there was one big hitch; Pop didn't want any son of his fighting for money! In our house, one thing you did not do was argue with Pop, so Joe decided that if he intended to fight, the only thing to do was not let Pop find out. How? Joe would use a different name. What name? The name he eventually chose was Dundee. So, Joe Mirenda/Mirena/Mireno became Joe Dundee.

Why Dundee? I have tried to figure it out, but you must remember I was not born yet, and my brother Joe has now passed away. When he was alive I never thought to ask him, I just accepted it.

Choosing the name Dundee was not sheer chance; it was not a name picked at random from the telephone directory. I did some investigative work and I think I have figured out how it came about. It is kind of complicated but I'll lay it out for you.

There have been three famous Dundees, not including my brother, in the fight game. None of the three was born with that proud Scottish name.

There was Joe Dundee, born Samuel Lazzaro, who became the

World Welterweight Champion by beating Pete Latzo in 1927, and there was his brother Vince Dundee, born Vince Lazzaro, who became the Middleweight Champion of the World on October 30, 1933. Both brothers were born in Italy, although they grew up and fought in the United States. Need I tell you, Italy is quite a way from Scotland.

Now why did those two great fighters choose the Scottish name Dundee? In the early nineteen hundreds it was not advantageous to have an Italian-sounding name. The early Italian immigrants were, like most of the other immigrants, not held in very high esteem by the host population. They lived in Italian ghettos, held menial jobs, spoke with a funny accent, ate spaghetti and ice a de cream, and were considered by many average Americans to be "gangsters" and members of crime societies.

So I guess you can understand that it was no favor to have a difficult-to-pronounce Italian name on the marquee outside the arena. The Italian fight fans knew the Italian fighters, even if they called themselves O'Brien, Goldberg, or Fu Man Chu. A lot of Italian fighters settled for shortening their names, like Gugliemo Papaleo, who ended up Willie Pep, Featherweight Champion of the World.

As for why eldest brother Joe adopted the specific name of "Dundee," I think the answer lies in another Italian fighter by the name of Joseph Corrara. He started boxing in 1910 and often had fights in Philadelphia, where he became very popular with the Italian fight fans and especially my brother Joe. Joseph Corrara had over three hundred pro fights, and he eventually won the Junior Lightweight Championship of the World in 1921 by stopping George Chaney in five rounds. Now the point of the story about Joe Corrara is that he boxed under the name of Johnny Dundee.

Why did Mr. Corrara choose the name "Dundee?" Well, Corrara had two managers: Jimmy Johnston and Scotty Monteith, and you can't sound more Scottish than that. Are you getting the picture? I guess we can figure that Scotty Monteith and Jimmy Johnston suggested that Joe Corrara become Johnny Dundee, and as my brother Joe was a big fan of Johnny, Joe Mirenda known as Joe Mireno became known as Joe Dundee, professional boxer.

Joe Dundee's boxing career did not last very long and he never made the big-time, but he had about nine fights, and by the time Pop got to know about it, Joe was out of the business.

Without realizing it, Joe had started a new dynasty. Chris

adopted the name, and his success in the fight game promoted the Dundee name. Even before I joined Chris in New York in 1948, Jimmy and I were using the Dundee name, soaking up some of the glamour associated with our brothers Chris and Joe.

In later years, when I tasted the fruits of success, it was the name Angelo Dundee that made the press. I changed my name legally, so now the Mirenda family had blossomed into Mirena, Mireno, and Dundee—it sounds like a legal firm. Now my son Jimmy carries on the name Dundee for me; if he and his lovely wife Cathy are blessed with children, I hope it will be a name that my grandchildren will be proud of.

Pop would be home around five o'clock from Fort Mifflin where he was working on the railroad track. Mom would be busy setting the table for supper, and Jimmy and I would be working out at the fire station but not forgetting that we had to be home in time for supper.

We had fun at the fire station; the firemen would joke around with us. They called me "Tootsie." I don't know why, but it was always said kindly. Sometimes, very rarely, we would get home late, and Pop would get very angry. "When food is on the table, show your mother the respect to be there to eat it," Pop would say. It seemed to have more meaning when he said it in Italian. On Saturdays, Jimmy, Josephine, and I were supposed to scrub the floors. Jimmy somehow or other had taken on the role of foreman, but I would be as busy as hell, on my knees, with the scrubbing brush, soap, and water. Josephine would try to help, but she preferred to play with the soap. If we skipped out on the Saturday and hadn't done our chores, and if, on that rare occasion, I was home late for supper, Pop would get out the strap, and that was real bad news.

The strap was a piece of wood with nine leather tails attached to one end. Pop had carved the other end to make an easier grip. When you received four or five whacks from Pop with the strap you knew about it. Pop did not fool around, and you did not fool around with Pop.

One time, after Joe had quit boxing and had got married to Rose, he went on a binge and stayed out all night. When Pop saw him the next day, he slapped him hard across the face for not showing his wife or his parents respect. Joe was in his twenties at the time. As I said, Pop did not fool around.

I believe that Pop's discipline and Mom's warmth, combined

with the love they had for their children, made us a very close and caring family. We were close both emotionally and physically. I do not mean we were physically alike, which we are, but I mean we lived in close proximity. Chris, and then I, were the exceptions. No one else moved away; they only moved into their own homes within a block or two of Morris Street. (Today, in Watkins Street, South Philadelphia, within the space of six houses there are three Mirena families, and another family within one block.)

Joe was an established married man living in his own home by the time I was eleven. His boxing career long behind him, yet still somewhat of a local hero, he had never thought about moving away from the neighborhood. Chris, on the other hand, was a local hero because he had moved away. To leave the neighborhood was an act of adventure. When Chris first made his mark in the fight game his local reputation went soaring. On the infrequent occasions when Chris made a visit home he was treated like a visiting dignitary, especially if he was accompanied by one of his famous boxers like Wolgast.

To understand this adulation for any local celebrity, you have to understand the thinking of the Italian immigrant. In those early days in the twenties and thirties the children of the original immigrants had no knowledge or allegiance to their parents' homeland. Close family ties and lack of money made it difficult to travel or move away. Their whole life was centered around their local neighborhood. For most of my relations and friends, South Philly was the whole picture. You didn't leave the family nest. You worked locally, married locally, and died locally. The whole neighborhood celebrated when a local kid became a lawyer or doctor, and in those days that was not often.

Boxers, yes; singers, yes; academics took a little longer. As for other immigrants, the ring and the stage were the two ways out into the big world. One kid with whom I went to school made the break because he could sing a bit. His name was Mario Lanza—yea, he could sing a bit.

The local population would follow the fortunes of any entertainer, sportsman, athlete, or celebrity whom they knew to be of Italian extraction. We could identify with them; we knew that they had come from the same background as us kids, and we watched with pride and a little envy.

Maybe now you can understand the excitement that a visit from Chris caused. He knew famous people, he managed famous fighters, and he had actually had his name in the newspapers! I was impressed more than any neighborhood kid. After all, Chris was my brother; he was family.

From the age of six, when I attended Saint Nicholas' Church for religious instruction, I walked to school. After St. Nick's I attended Tasker School until I was eleven, and then until I was thirteen I went to Kirkbride School. Now I was a student at SPHS—South Philadelphia High School. I was still walking!

All the schools were within a two- or three-mile radius, so walking was no big deal. I did not mind the walking; it gave me time to daydream.

Until I reached my thirteenth birthday I used to daydream about being a fireman. Although I lost my desire to become a fireman, I never lost my admiration for those guys who do such a tough, worthwhile job, and I never lost my affection for the old regular coal-driven fire engine, with its magnificent steam funnel and my favorite toy, the fire bell.

My outlook had changed as had my appearance. As a teenager, I was a skinny young guy, looking a lot like my brother Jimmy, and my daydreams had become so varied and frequent, I could never remember what I had daydreamed about.

The only advantage of daydreaming was that it got me off running errands for Mom. She would send me to Kunz's cake store for some coffee cakes, an errand that should have taken five or six minutes. For one reason or another it would take me twenty minutes. It was not that I purposely daydreamed. I would just bump into kids that I knew and we would start rapping until I lost track of the time and forgot what I had been sent to get. Jimmy took over the running of errands, but he got even when it became time to scrub the floors! I scrubbed, he directed.

I liked high school, and I worked hard, although I was no great shakes as a student. It was kind of funny; I did my studying and always thought I would do well in the exams, but I only did about average. Maybe I daydreamed more than I realized.

Like the rest of my pals I did not know what I wanted to do when I left school. I knew that I had to get a job, because that was what all good young Italian-American boys did. There would be no hanging around street corners for me; I would find a job.

Pop never encouraged me to follow in his footsteps and work on the railroad. I guess he knew just how hard and unprofitable it was. Although he never, well, hardly ever spoke of it, I believe Pop would have loved to have owned a vineyard. Unfortunately, there were not many job openings tending grapes in South Philly! My pop was resourceful. He didn't let little problems like the wrong soil or cold winters spoil his dream. He bought grapes from a fruiterer at the 9th Street Market and made his own wine at home. The cellar was his vineyard.

With a little help from whichever son was handy, the grapes would be squeezed and allowed to ferment for a week. After draining they would be transferred to another barrel. At the correct time, which only Pop would decide, he would squeeze the pulp in a wine press and re-barrel the unmatured wine. There would be a waiting period of a month, then the wine was ready to drink. I must be honest, it wasn't at all that bad.

One thing about my home, there was always food on the table, and more often than not, wine to drink. I know we were not rich, in fact we were poor, with continual money problems, but Mom always seemed to have lots of delicious food waiting for us eager kids to eat. Mom was a happy lady, and there was never a time that I can remember when she did not have time for a hug or to share a laugh with me.

Just before she served supper I would slip into the kitchen without her knowing, and untie her apron strings. We would laugh, and she would shout in good humor at me as I would plead for a taste of the food before she served it.

After dinner, Pop would ask me about school. The family would sit around the table and talk, speaking Italian and invariably all at the same time.

It was a common practice for friends and relations to drop in. More food would somehow materialize for the guests, like crackers and bitter cheese, circles of spicy salami, and a selection of cookies. On reflection, it was no wonder that I had been a fat little boy. I had one very bad habit at the dinner table—I couldn't leave it! Jimmy would say jokingly, "Angie eats like a bird, a vulture!"

In my last year at high school, I began to get a little concerned about my future. College was out of the question, because I was not clever enough to win a scholarship with a grant, and there was no way my parents could afford to pay. Besides, the concept of leaving home and going to college was a little "way out." My lifestyle indicated that I should get a job and put money on my mother's table.

Not to go to college was no big deal; I decided to take a typing course, which might prove beneficial when I left school. In the meantime, I needed to get a job that I could do after school hours to make some money. Finding an evening job was no problem; one of my buddies, who played alongside me on the school football team, told me of a job opening at Pat's Steak House, which was, and still is, a very popular eatery. It was counter service only and the majority of the orders were "to go." You would often see the folks standing around outside the place eating their sandwiches.

I worked behind the counter making the steak sandwiches. If I had stayed working there for twenty years I would never have made a "cordon bleu" chef. A fast sandwich maker, maybe!

Three or four nights a week, after school, I would walk over to Pat's and go to work. You gotta be thinking that I ate at work, a nice big juicy steak. Wrong! Brother Frankie would bring me a plate of pasta from home; Mom would make me macaroni or spaghetti. I may have been working at Pat's Steak House, but I still ate home cooking. The job lasted two months; I got tired and bored, and so did Frankie from bringing me my pasta!

My schooldays were coming to an end. I had an idea in the back of my mind of what job I would try for after I graduated, but that was in the future. I needed a part-time job to see me through to graduation.

Since quitting Pat's Steak House, I had not worked again after school. I knew I would need some money once I graduated, as I wanted to buy some new clothes. I wanted to look right when I entered the grown-up world, and I did not like to ask Pop for money if I could get out and earn it myself.

I started a weekend job at a neighborhood shoe-shine parlor. Besides the cleaning of shoes, the establishment had a back room where they cleaned hats. The boss told me that I could be a great hat cleaner. I had potential. Great! The fumes of the cleaning fluid burned my eyes and made me feel sick, and the steam used in the blocking and shaping of the hats made me dizzy. Needless to say, I never reached my full potential.

The boss at the shoe-shine parlor was only paying me seventy-five cents for the weekend, and you can tell I hated it. I told Mom, and when she heard how much the guy was paying me she agreed that I would be better off quitting. She called the guy a cheapskate and said that I could learn a lesson from him: "Do not be penny wise and dollar poor."

It was July 1938 when I graduated. On my next birthday I would be seventeen. My Mom, her hair as usual in a bun, her lovely warm brown eyes moist with held back tears, was proud of her youngest son. Dad was too. I knew that he felt it was a special occasion because he had waxed the ends of his moustache.

I was filled with a confidence and energy reserved only for the young; it was a summer full of excitement and promise. Soon enough I would be working again. Next time, the job would be for real.

CHAPTER FOUR

I'M A BIG BOY NOW

"The most important thing in my life at that time was to meet Rosie. I had done a little smooching in the back of Al's car, and had a few kissing sessions on back porches, and, once or twice I had felt a girl's breast, but always over their dresses and sweaters. Hell! I was a virgin. It looked like I would stay that way until I married, but now—Rosie!"

Working was not so bad; in fact I enjoyed it. The only beef I had was that I had to get up so darn early to get there.

When I first began working at the naval aircraft factory five years earlier back in 1938, the factory had been located in Philadelphia, but later they had relocated the factory at Johnstown. In traffic it was at least a sixty-minute drive away, which meant I had to get up earlier.

Thank the Lord for my lovely younger sister Josephine, who used to wake me. I would struggle out of bed without waking Jimmy, who could sleep through an earthquake, and get all that washing and dressing bit done, then wait downstairs in the family room for my driver to call. I would sit on the sofa and wham I would fall asleep again. "Hey Angie, wake up. Do you hear me? Wake up, your driver is here," Josephine would shout, shaking me until I woke up. When she said "your driver," she did not mean that I had a chauffeur or my own personal driver. She meant that my "lift" had arrived—the guy who had a car and picked up a few of the guys he worked with, and drove them to work. We all chipped in a few dollars to pay the gas, and in South Philly the guy with the car was called "the driver."

I was a terrific passenger; as soon as I got in the car I would fall asleep again. The only conversation I had was "Thanks, pal" to the driver when we got to the navy yard.

33

I had done well at my job. I held the title "inspector," and I believed that I had earned it. Because of the type of work that I did, I could have gone into the navy and been stationed right where I was, but I thought that would be chickening out. When I got my call-up I would see duty wherever they wanted to send me.

The Japanese attack on Pearl Harbor had awakened in me, as with the majority of the American people, a fierce patriotism, and I was eager to do my share in the winning of the war. Jimmy was being inducted into the air corps any time now, and I would join him when the time came. I would have liked to imitate his choice of "air gunner," but I knew Uncle Sam would not waste my work experience. I would carry on working on the maintenance side, keeping the planes flying.

At the naval aircraft factory I worked on prop-engine navy planes; I would check out wiring fatigue. As the war progressed I began to work on the B17, the aircraft that was being used on the majority of the American bombing raids.

I will not bore you with technicalities, but for me it was of great interest. I felt I was contributing to a worthwhile job.

As Jimmy's induction into the forces became more imminent, I would often think about the effect the war was having on my life, and my thoughts would invariably go back to the time when I had left high school. Who would have thought then, that within four years America would be involved in a war on a worldwide scale?

At the age of sixteen all I was thinking about was starting work and earning my own money. I knew that I would have to work hard at whatever I did. There would be no escaping paying my dues—I learned that early, while I was still in high school. I had taken the Italian language as a subject that would earn me a credit for graduation. Heck! I could speak the language like a native. My Mom and Pop spoke it every day at home. It's a cinch, I thought. That's one credit I can count on. Wrong! It was the only darn subject I failed in.

I thought I knew it, so I never bothered to study up on the grammar, and Italian grammar is no pushover. I knew somehow that there would be no pushovers for me; what I got out of life I would have to work for.

After my graduation I did not want to commit myself immediately to a steady, long-term job, so when an opening came up for an assistant to the court recorder I grabbed it. My typing course at school paid off. I would type transcripts and legal reports. I only stuck with the job for a short time, but it improved my typing and it did wonders for my vocabulary. When I eventually started on the naval aircraft job, I did so with a quiet sense of confidence; I knew I could type, my spelling was above average, and I knew at least two legal terms—one in Latin, even!

The naval aircraft factory was different from anything I had known. The whole setup was "big," with so many people involved in the running of it. My superiors decided to put me on a training course and I moved from clerking to aircraft inspection. I felt good about it; I enjoyed the day-to-day challenges, and I liked the idea of working for the government.

My best pal since high school was Al Piluso. His mom sort of adopted me; she treated me like another son. My mom liked Al and always made him welcome at our home. It was a nice setup. I'll tell you one thing, we didn't have to eat out too often, not with moms like we had.

Al and I joined the Rio AC Club football team. Al was quarterback and I was an end. A bunch of us guys from the team used to hang out together; we were known as the "Rio boys."

I gotta admit our object in life was pretty uninspired. Outside of our respective jobs all we looked for in life was a deep suntan, a good muscular body, meeting girls, and playing football (not necessarily in that order).

We took our football seriously, and I made certain I kept in good shape. I worked out and boxed regularly with Jimmy at the Mason AC Gym. I began to put on muscle, and, although I was a little short for an end, I was a hard son of a gun.

In one game, the opposing quarterback tried to come round my side and his protection was sadly missing. I nailed him and he fell badly. Even before we checked, I knew he had broken his leg by the sound of the crack I heard. I do not know how the guy felt, but I felt awful. There was nothing I could do; it had been an accident.

I saw him weeks later watching one of our games; he was on crutches. I went over to him and apologized. He understood and we shook hands. It made me feel better; there is no escaping injury in sport, but I hate the thought of an athlete maliciously hurting a fellow sportsman.

Once I had joined the football team, life may have been predictable but it sure was fun. My week was all worked out: Sunday night I normally stayed home; Monday night I would go to Passyunk and Moore Streets and play darts; Tuesday through

Saturday I would go dancing. Did I really go dancing five nights a week? I guess I did. You had better believe I liked dancing. It wasn't to meet chicks, although there ain't nothing wrong with that, expecially if they can dance. I just wanted to dance.

Over the years, until I went to New York to work for Chris, I would enter dance competitions, and more often than not I would win a medal or a cup. A John Travolta I wasn't, but I was a pretty good dancer. All I needed was the dance floor, a good band, and a partner who could dance.

Talking of girls—my dance partners were girls, if you didn't know—South Philly boys had so much respect for neighborhood girls it was boring. To start with, nearly every girl's father or mother knew somebody who knew your father or mother. More often than not you would discover that the girl you had just met was your second cousin by marriage on your mother's side, or she was a distant relative, three times removed, on your father's side. Italian parents were very strict with their daughters, and Italian fathers did not take too kindly to guys who wanted to fool around with their little girls. It was marriage or nothing, so with local chicks, it was nothing.

When we went to parties, it always ended up with the guys in one room drinking beer and talking about football, baseball, or boxing, and the girls in the kitchen making sandwiches and coffee and talking about whatever young chicks rap about.

Maybe the system was not so bad, the guys were taught respect, and I'll tell you, in my day, it was safe for a girl to walk home after dark.

So things being what they were, I reached the year 1940. I was eighteen and still an innocent and naive young man.

It was fall, and a bunch of us went down to Passyunk and Moore Streets, where there was a seafood joint, a kind of "raw bar" which was a regular hangout for us.

"OK, let's go for a large order of the oysters. The guy that eats the most don't pay. The rest of the guys pick up the tab." Nick was laying down the ground rules that we all knew already. We had been playing this screwball game for months now, but Nick was like that, he was an organizer.

At the raw bar counter, I smothered the oysters with pepper and tabasco sauce until they nearly jumped up off the plate. We started eating, an oyster each, one after another. The first plate was emptied, no one dropped out. Another plate of oysters, I duplicated the "shtick" with the pepper and tabasco, only more so. We began eating. I started off first. My mouth was burning, but I was hanging in. One by one the guys swallowed their oysters, and one by one they dropped out screaming for water. I finished the plate. I never paid, ever.

"You got a stomach like cast iron, Angie," Nick said enviously.

"My family comes from Calabria, we can eat anything—we had to," I answered, grinning at the guys.

"You seeing much of Rita?" asked Andy, the eldest of the gang. He was nineteen. "Angie would like to, but Rita won't take off her dress," Andy gagged before I could answer the question seriously.

"Knock it off, Andy. Rita is a nice chick."

"Sure. That's the trouble, Angie, they're all nice chicks here," Andy said. I knew what he meant and I agreed with him.

"Hey, Angie, have you scored with Rosie?" Nick asked me.

"Rosie? Rosie who?"

"Who cares Rosie who. Do you hear that, Andy, Angie wants to know Rosie who." Nick and Andy began laughing as if I had just given them a great Jack Benny line.

"Hey, guys," I said, "What's the gag?"

"No gag, Angie. We're just surprised you ain't met Rosie yet. She lives on this farm in New Jersey, and boy is she a good looker. The thing is, Angie," Nick's voice softened and became conspiratorial, "Rosie likes a piece of action. If you play it right, you are in for one hell of a good time. Right, guys?"

Andy and Al, who had remained silent so far, nodded their heads slowly, but definitely in agreement. "Maybe Rosie wouldn't go for Angie," Al said.

"What do you mean? You're supposed to be my pal," I said. "And why the hell ain't you told me about Rosie?" I added.

"I thought you had made it with her. Really," Al said. He turned to the other guys, "Could you guys fix Angie up? You did it for me."

"Yea, come on, Nick. If you fixed up Al, what's wrong with fixing me up?"

"OK, OK, I'll see what I can do."

The most important thing in my life at that time was to meet Rosie. I had done a little smooching in the back of Al's car, and had a few kissing sessions on back porches, and, once or twice I had felt a girl's breast, but always over their dresses or sweaters. Hell! I was a virgin. It looked like I would stay that way until I married, but now—Rosie!

"Tell me straight, guys, is she a looker?" Their uniform affirmation convinced me. "When are you guys gonna fix me up?"

Nick gave me the word four days later. It was all arranged for Friday night. They had chosen Friday, because it could turn out to be a late night, if not all night! Mama mia! We had no work Saturday.

There were four of us in Al's Ford. Nick and Andy in the back, with me sitting in front with Al, who was driving. We had left South Philly when it was already turning dark. By the time we reached the New Jersey countryside the night was blacker than hell.

The conversation was raunchy, you know what I mean, the kind of things guys talk about when they are alone, and they are talking about girls.

I was assured that Rosie was one sweet looker: a blonde with sexy blue eyes and legs like Eleanor Powell. I was as excited as a virgin bride on her wedding night, which kinda made sense! We stopped the car about thirty yards from the farmhouse, which was in the middle of nowhere. In the dictionary, under the word "deserted" there is a photograph of that place!

"You gotta be quiet, Angie, you don't wanna wake up her old man," Nick said.

"What do you mean 'her old man'—she's married?" I tried to sound controlled.

"No, dummy. Her pop. You don't wanna wake her pop. Look, just don't make too much noise while you're enjoying yourself. D'you know what I'm saying?" I could see Nick's leer in the light from the dashboard. He went on talking. "OK, pal, you're on your own. You got money for cab fare?"

You guys ain't going, are you? I mean, come on, stick around for a while. See how I make out." I did not want them to leave.

Al reassured me. "OK, Angie, we'll hang around for fifteen minutes. If you ain't back, we will catch up with you tomorrow. Have a good time."

The thirty yards to the old wooden front door seemed like thirty miles. I did not want the guys to see that I was nervous, so I put on a swagger that I hoped made me look confident. I probably looked drunk.

The car had been swallowed up in the darkness, but I knew the guys could see me because above the farmhouse door was a light which went on about five seconds after I had gently knocked on the door. I stood there, my heart pounding, trying to look cool and calm.

The door swung open. A big man, wearing a plaid shirt and dungarees, stood in front of me filling the doorway. He was holding a large shotgun and it was pointed straight at me.

"Alright, boy, you just stay there. Don't you move a muscle, don't even think about it. D'you hear me?" I wanted to say "Are you kidding?" or "Come on pal, what's all this about?" All I could manage to get out was "Yes, sir."

"Is this the feller, Rosie?" Standing behind the man with the gun was a cute blonde with her hair in pigtails. So that was Rosie!

"I don't know, Pa. He looks like the one." I couldn't believe this was happening. "Hey! What's all this about. What does she mean I look like the one?"

"Don't you get smart with me, boy. Some sneaking bastard come here last month and knocked up my daughter, and I'm gonna find him and I'm gonna put some goddamn buckshot up his goddamn arse."

"Well, it ain't me. Tell him, Rosie, tell him you ain't never seen me before, ever."

"I don't know, Pa. It was dark. I'm not certain. I don't remember too well. I remember his voice, the sweet-talking bastard. He sounds like the one."

She meant me! "What are you talking about? I've never seen you before in all my life. I don't sound like the guy, I can't, 'cause I ain't the one. I'm from Philly."

"You keep your voice down, boy. Anything else you remember, Rosie?"

"Well, he was wearing polka-dot shorts. I remember that."

"Well, it wasn't me. I never wear polka-dot shorts. Never. Honest."

"Alright, boy. We'll soon check that out. Drop your pants."

"What are you talking about, drop your pants! Are you crazy or something?"

"D'you hear me boy? Drop your goddam pants, or I'll take a chance that you're the one and let you have a barrel-full of buckshot right now."

I stood there with my pants around my ankles, proudly showing off my pale blue shorts. "There, I told you. It ain't me, I never wear polka-dot shorts, I'm a pale-blue man."

"What do you think, Rosie?" The man lowered the gun and turned to face his daughter. In one movement, I drew up my pants, and without waiting to fasten them, I turned around and ran for my life.

As I ran towards the waiting car, I expected at any moment to feel the charge of gunshot hit me in the rear. When I reached the sanctuary of Al's Ford, the guys greeted me with howls of laughter and a round of applause. I had been set up.

The guys told me later that the guy with the gun was a pal of Andy's brother and worked at a gas station. Rosie was played by the guy's sister-in-law and she actually lived at that farm—with her husband!

It had been quite a show, and I had been part of the cast. The next time I drove down to the farm I was part of the audience and I watched some other poor sucker play the Rosie Game.

There is a postscript to the Rosie Game episode. After my initiation into the honored circle of suckers who had played the game, the guys decided that those of us who were still virgins had to get laid. So the guys that had something to lose besides money—there were fifteen of us—put five dollars each into the pot, and with the enormous sum of seventy-five dollars we hightailed it down to Atlantic City. After some tough bargaining we did a deal with an accommodating hooker who took away our money and virginity with the ease and expertise of the real pro.

Nineteen hundred and forty-three had reached the last quarter of its life, and I, at the age of twenty-two, was hopefully still in the first quarter of mine. I was a grown man about to embark on a new and dangerous adventure; I was only days away from being inducted into the armed forces.

Jimmy had been inducted months ago and was now an air cadet. Mixed with the enormous pride I had for him, I suspect there was also a tinge of envy. In some perverse way I wanted to face the dangers, do my duty, and make people look at me with awe and respect, but at the same time I did not want to go at all! Do you know that feeling, "You wanna go but you wanna stay"? Well, that is how it was.

One of the main reasons I wanted to stay was Rita Carlone. She was dark, small, and very pretty. I was deeply infatuated with her. I use the word "infatuated," but that is playing it down. I believed at the time that I was head over heels in love with her.

Our romance started simply enough. Rita was a good dancer, so when I saw her at the Bombay Gardens or the Barclay or any of the local dance halls, I would always ask her to dance. We made a good team. I talked Rita into partnering me in a dance contest at the St. Paul's dance hall, and to our surprise and delight we won. That did it! We became dance partners. We would spend our time rehearsing our dance steps and more and more we entered contests. Rita was so pretty and looked so bewitching as she gracefully moved across the dance floor in my arms, that I believed she more than helped us win so many cups and medals. We were on a roll. All our spare time was spent together, and everybody took it for granted that we were going steady. I guess we were.

As dance partners, we naturally had to understand and tolerate each other's temperament. Entering contests was a scary experience. All those people watching you! Would you goof up and ruin it for your partner? People act differently under pressure; Rita and I learned to live with our respective changes of moods. I was always trying to be light and bright, beating the tension with laughs, but Rita was quiet and inclined to worry. Our opposite personalities seemed to complement each other and our relationship developed. The months went by and we fell in love. Simple!

I stopped hanging out at the Rio club, although I still turned out for the football team, and I became more friendly to the other guys who were going steady. Fortunately, my best pal Al Piluso was going out with a nice chick—called Rosie, would you believe—and often we would make up a foursome: Al, Rosie, Rita, and me. We would take in a movie, or just hang out at the Melrose Diner where we would drink coffee and rap. On rare occasions we would drive to Atlantic City in Al's Ford. Whatever we did we always enjoyed ourselves.

Rita and I had our dancing and each other. We were a self-contained little unit. It was a nice easy relationship. Our families approved, which saved us a lot of aggravation. My pop knew the Carlone family only very slightly, but both our families were of a similar background, hardworking, Italian immigrant stock. I had a warm affection for Rita's mother, who was always kind and encouraging to me. She was like a second mom. Whenever I went to her house, food was put on the table and I had to dissuade her from cooking me meals. It seemed logical that Rita and I would get married, at least it did to me. We were young, Italian, and in love; in South Philly that meant marriage.

With my impending induction into the service on the immediate horizon, a rushed marriage did not seem a good idea. Rita and I decided to become engaged and wait until our future looked more settled. Somehow I managed to find the two hundred dollars for the ring, and Betty Corlone, Rita's mom, threw us a small engagement party.

Putting off the wedding was received with mixed feelings. My family agreed, but Rita's mom and pop were not too sure about it. I think they wanted their daughter safely married, even if her husband was stationed thousands of miles away. I could see their point of view, but I did not really want the responsibility of a wife while I did not know where I would be sent, or if I would ever return, although I would have got married there and then if Rita had wanted it. Rita thought it wiser to wait; she would wear my engagement ring until I returned.

We were so young. Rita was only eighteen years old and I was only months past twenty-two. Our experience of life didn't add up to anything. What did we know about love and marriage? We had been programmed by the movies and the South Philly culture. All through my teens, Mom and Pop and most of my relations would advise me to find a nice Catholic girl, preferably Italian, and get married and have kids. I know Rita went through a similar experience and received the same advice. Whether or not we were really in love with each other, we were prepared to believe that we were; it was a nice feeling.

My last few days before I reported for basic training were miserable. Mom and Pop were sad and worried. They would have two sons in the war. The war news wasn't good, and I could not lift their spirits; you could not get laughs from the casualty figures.

Rita was on a downer too. She was sweet and affectionate but she could not hide how depressed she felt. I tried to make light of everything, but the whole thing was getting to me. I did not want to leave South Philly; I didn't want to go to war. Sure, me and a million other guys! You can't say no to Uncle Sam. In late October 1943 I reported for duty.

CHAPTER FIVE

THE YANKS ARE COMING

"(The captain) leaned back in his chair, hand on his stomach. . . . 'I would like to train you and send you to Italy as one of our agents.' He leaned forward and pointed an accusing finger at me. 'I can't order you, Mirena. You have to volunteer, understand? I am going to give you twenty-four hours to think it over. You got the picture, huh?' "

The problem with having a lively imagination is that you can be sadly let down. I was joining the American Armed Services, and I imagined myself being immediately transported to an important far-flung theater of war. A strategic South Sea island, perhaps a European city under seige. I would arrive, in full battle dress naturally, and begin to win the war. It doesn't work that way does it? Haven't you heard of an "induction center"?

The military powers, in their wisdom, sent me all the way across the Ben Franklin Bridge from Philadelphia, Pennsylvania, to Camp Kilmer, New Jersey, to the induction center, where they took two weeks to cut my hair, fix me up with a uniform, and decide what to do with me. As far as I am concerned, the only memories of Camp Kilmer, New Jersey, I want to keep are the laughs I got when I told the other GIs of my previous experience in New Jersey when I had played the Rosie Game. A lot of GIs who had never been to Jersey before, or maybe since, will always think of me with my pants around my ankles showing off my pale blue shorts when anyone brings up the subject of New Jersey.

When I learned I was being moved out for basic training, my overworked imagination took over again. I visualized a barren desert where I would survive living under canvas, or some pine-covered mountain top, hundreds of miles from the nearest town, where in the cold of winter I would exist in an igloo. But no! I was sent to Miami Beach, and I am not complaining, believe me.

I think Philadelphia is a lovely city with the warmest, nicest people you will ever want to meet, but I still fell in love with Miami. Oh boy, those palm trees! They did things to me. And the weather . . . November in Miami is the nearest to perfect weather I have known. I guess you could say that I was rather taken with Miami.

Basic training was no big deal. I was in good shape and I liked the exercise. On reflection, I think I enjoyed the whole basic training bit, although I did occasionally get that old homesick feeling. I called Rita and tried to talk her into coming down to visit, but she had just started work at my old hunting ground, the naval aircraft factory. She couldn't get time off at the moment, but she was working on it.

My off-duty time was spent at the USO Club, where I went bowling with some of the guys. I turned out for the boxing squad and won a few fights at welterweight at the Flamingo Bowl. In my unit there were a few jokers who were not overly fond of big city boys, especially if the boys happened to be Jewish or Italian, but they knew that I could handle myself, and the bullies kept out of my way. Being known as a kid who boxed was a nice advantage in the unit, so I didn't mind the off-duty time I spent in training, and besides, I got steak instead of spam.

I was sorry when basic training was over. I didn't want to leave Miami, but always knew it would only be a matter of time before I would be shipped out. Maybe now I would be sent to some mysterious and exotic place. Paris? Algiers? Honolulu? Hardly! I was sent to typist school in Muskogee, Oklahoma. (I must admit it does sound exotic!) In between studies I watched the university basketball team, played a little touch football with some of the other GIs, and drank a lot of beer. Gee, it was tough! Before I settled into this demanding life I was transferred to Barksdale Field, Louisiana, for aircraft maintenance instruction. My brother Jimmy had been stationed there, and some of the NCOs remembered him. They must have liked him because they sure went out of their way to make life easy for me. The instructional courses were far from easy, so I was more than grateful for the time and patience the instructors took making sure that I did not goof off. I worked hard and got through with flying colors, and was now not only ready but a little impatient to get in on the action. But instead of being shipped out as expected, I was ordered to Dallas. Texas, for an interview with GI intelligence.

What the heck was all this about? I racked my brains for the reason behind this summoning, but although I conjured up many different reasons I did not come close to the real one.

The captain who was interviewing me looked like Edward G. Robinson, one of my favorite actors, and he even sounded a little like him. We were alone in his office. It was painted olive green. The only relief was a wall photograph of a cigar-smoking Captain Edward G. in flying gear, with a bunch of similarly attired guys standing in front of a twin-engine plane.

"Sit down, Mirena. First time in Dallas?" He didn't wait for my reply. He looked down at my file which lay open on his desk. "I see you speak Italian,"—he pronounced it *eyetalian*—"Is that correct, huh?"

"Yes, sir." I was tempted to go into my Edward G. Robinson impression, but I did not think the captain would appreciate it.

"You are a patriotic American, aren't you, Mirena?"

"Yes, sir."

"Your sympathies lie with the United States of America, not the enemy, right?"

"Yes, sir."

"Do you know who the enemies are, Mirena?"

"Japan and Germany, sir."

"Right—Japan, Germany, and Italy. You did know that Italy is our enemy, didn't you, Mirena?"

"Yes, sir." The captain stared at me. He had light blue eyes and he didn't blink. He closed my file, placed his elbows on his desk, and rested his chin on his fists. "Look, Mirena, let's cut the bullshit. I know you are a good loyal American, and we both know this war is no friggin' joke. Lots of American boys are getting killed, and it ain't gonna get better before it gets worse, you understand, huh?"

He leaned back in his chair, hand on his stomach. "Mussolini has betrayed the Italian people and it won't be long before they get wise to that friggin' fascist asshole. I sure would like to know what them Italians are gonna do, and when they are gonna do it. Sure, we have specially trained men out there, but we need more men, more information on what's going on, see. We need Italian-speaking Americans who love their country and want to see Italy out of the war. I think maybe you are that kind of American. I would like to train you and send you to Italy as one of our agents." He leaned forward and pointed an accusing finger at me. "I can't order you, Mirena. You have to volunteer, understand? I am going to give you twenty-four hours to think it over. You got the picture, huh?"

That night I turned the situation round and around in my mind. I wanted to do what was best for my country, but I couldn't relate to spying. Sure I knew it was necessary and that every power did it, but it was something I could not personally undertake.

The next morning I gave the captain my decision. He made no comment when I turned the offer down, other than, "Thank you, Mirena. That will be all."

Within three days I was sent to Norfolk, Virginia, and forty-eight hours later I was on board a liberty ship, en route to Europe—as a soldier, not as a spy.

By all the criteria I should not have liked Leicestershire, England. The weather in January 1944 was cold, wet, and misty, with only the occasional bright clear day. I'm told that it is like that every January, except sometimes it snows too!

The nearest town was Leicester, not exactly what you would call a big swinging city. The air base on which I was stationed had one or two drawbacks too. The main problem was that the base was downwind of a large herd of cows, and somedays you might think you were stationed next to one giant latrine. But, in spite of everything, I liked Leicester and I really dug merry old England.

The countryside, even in bleak winter, had a particular charm and beauty, but it was the people that got to me. They were so darn friendly. At first I thought they might be standoffish and set in their ways, but they were really easygoing. The relationship between the air force base and the townsfolk was great, except for one major difference of opinion.

The base commanding officer did not allow black American servicemen to take their off-duty time in town at the same time as white servicemen. Being an American, I understood the situation, although I did not like it. There were a lot of white guys at the base who would not take too kindly to the sight of black GIs drinking and dancing with white chicks. I must admit, I was a little surprised when I saw it—well, this was 1944. This situation would undoubtedly lead to heavy trouble, and the CO was rightly worried that things would get out of hand. The locals had never experienced racial problems; they could not understand the restriction and believed that the idea of segregation was a kick in the arse to democracy. They complained by letter and in person to the authorities.

It was a difficult situation. It was also a difficult time for me personally. I did not care a brass nickle about a guy's color or religion. I either took to a guy or I didn't. Back in South Philly I had known discrimination; in fact, as I grew up I always thought the Italians were the butt of prejudice. Every ethnic group had its own turf. The Poles and Slavs lived around the waterfront; the Irish congregated around 2nd Street and Tasker; 5th and 7th Street were virtually all Jewish; and the Italians dominated 9th to Broad Street. Every group had its gangs, and they fought against each other, but as the kids grew up it was no big thing to have pals from different racial or religious backgrounds. As far as I was concerned, I had Irish and Jewish pals, and although we never ran around together, I was friendly with a bunch of black kids that I knew from school. My mom had her own particular outlook: anyone who was not Italian was an Americano—she never would pronounce American—and everybody was entitled to be treated with respect. So I grew up never judging people by their color. In later life, a newspaperman asked me why I always seemed to be working with black fighters. I told him that if a boxer from Mars wanted me to handle him, as long as the guy could fight, I wouldn't care if he was green!

The immediate problem for me was that I had got to know, and had become friends with, a couple of guys in my unit who came from Georgia and were racists. How they could be nice guys in every other area perplexed me. I guess that they were just two young guys who unfortunately had been infected at an early age, with one of the most virulent diseases known to mankind— bigotry. I was glad when I was transferred to another base, because the frustration of knowing that I could not change anything was bringing me down.

My military bosses decided to ignore my aircraft maintenance training and transferred me to a clerical and organizational outfit. I didn't mind, if it meant that I could stay on this new base. I was stationed just outside the charming, sleepy old town of Newbury, famous for its racetrack and thoroughbred horses. The locals spoke with a strange, burring accent which I found difficult to understand—they did not understand us yanks much, either. It was a pretty place, very rustic and quiet. Boy, was it quiet! The town closed up at ten o'clock, except for Saturday nights, when the local dance-hall stayed open until eleven-thirty. There wasn't a heck of a lot to do in Newbury. The guys on the base called it "a cemetery with lights." Would you believe this, I liked it.

There were sixteen of us sharing the wooden hut we laughingly

called home. We were part of the 459 Service Squadron attached
to the 318 Air Force Group. Life in the hut was a lot of laughs. I
borrowed permanently a large regulation frying pan from the
kitchen, which I used for cooking my culinary masterpieces over
the pot-bellied stove that was stuck in the center of the hut for
heating purposes. I already had a reputation as a gourmet without
ever cooking a darn thing. Mom used to send me food parcels
from home containing salami, Italian peppers, and spicy cheese
which I passed out to the uninitiated. Can you believe some of
those guys had never tasted salami before!

I will not go into the exact method by which I secured the frying
pan—all I can tell you is that I had a buddy who worked in the
kitchen as an assistant cook. He had this big thing about cig-
arettes. He smoked like a chimney, and a gift of two cartons of
Chesterfields would make him turn somersaults. Do you get the
picture? I decided to cook the guys a real live "Mirena omelette."

Our base was surrounded by beautiful countryside, and countryside has farms, and farms have chickens, and—that's right—
chickens lay eggs. One short foraging expedition secured the eggs.
We didn't think the hens would miss them.

I cut up the peppers and salami, mixed them with the cheese
and eight freshly laid eggs, added salt and pepper, stirred until it
was all one gooey mess, then I poured the pungent mixture into
the gargantuan frying pan. The spicy aroma filled the hut, perhaps
the base, and the guys eagerly waited with watering mouths until
I served my masterpiece, known by all as "Mirena's Dago Special."
Need I add—it tasted sensational!

We had run out of the imported food and cooking a plain
omelette was no challenge. My buddy who liked Chesterfields had
come through with cheese, but how many cheese omelettes can
you take? One of the guys had an inspiration. "Let's get ourselves
some rabbits. We could have rabbit omelette." Not as off-beat as
you may think. We were in the country, and that is where rabbits
are!

We had seen them running through the grass, right outside our
hut. Next morning we were up before reveille. The sun was just
rising; the early morning air was crisp and fresh. We took up our
positions. Sixteen brave young servicemen with carbines loaded
and ready, waiting to decimate the indigenous rabbit population.
All for gastronomic gratification!

The rabbits were sighted. Fire! The air was filled with the sound
of firing guns. The bugler, about to sound reveille, nearly choked.

The base awoke seconds earlier than required. The sixteen crack-shots rushed into the field to gather their booty. They searched the field with growing disbelief. It was unimaginable—they could not find one rabbit, alive or dead. The sixteen marksmen had not hit one damn rabbit. No wonder we were in a service unit!

Under the direct scrutiny of Sergeant Goodrich, our unit handled all the accounts and records for the base. I did not know about the officers, but none of my unit, and that included Sergeant Good-rich, had taken any business administration training. It showed. The organization was slipshod and inefficient, and I thought I could improve on the running of things. I worked like a son of a gun, preparing new filing systems, thinking up new methods to clarify staff deployment, and defining areas of responsibilities. This off-duty work became a kind of obsession with me. Instead of going into Newbury with the guys for a night out, I would stay in the hut and work on my proposals for the reorganization of the 459 Service Group.

After a couple of months of hard work, my project was finished. I decided not to go straight to the CO, but to take my project to the guy who actually ran things, Sergeant Goodrich. He was im-pressed and began to implement most of my proposals immediately.

"Mirena, that's one hell of a good job you have done here. It's gonna get you your sergeant stripes—you can make book on it."

I felt elated. There was the enormous satisfaction from knowing I had done something worthwhile, and to make sergeant would be just terrific.

About this time, a PFC (private first class) by the name of Shelton was posted to my unit. On Sergeant Goodrich's orders I taught the newcomer all the programs I had devised. He caught on quickly. Shelton was a college graduate and had an air and personality that fitted in far better with officers than plain GIs, but he did a good job and caused no problems.

The postings of promotions were on the assembly hall board. I felt sick to my stomach. I was relieved that I was on my own. I would not have wanted any of the guys to have seen me, let alone speak to me. I quickly looked over the board again, then moved away in a state of shock. I couldn't believe it. I had not made sergeant, but Shelton had.

The next body-blow fell in a matter of hours. I was summoned to the major's office, where I was abruptly told that I was being immediately transferred from present duties and assigned to the Aircraft Supply Warehouse on clerical work.

It was like a nightmare, but I didn't wake up. Something stopped me from talking it over with my pals—maybe it was pride or embarrassment, but I couldn't do it. I pretended I didn't care, but I did, very much.

The next morning I did not get up at reveille. I was aware that I should, but I did not want to get up. I stayed in my bunk, missing meals, until the hospital orderlies came and delivered me to the base hospital, where I stayed as a patient for one week.

I had suffered a minor attack of depression, overwork, bad nerves—whatever. Let me assure you, I was not putting on any act to get out of duty, I was too much of a zombie to plan anything that cute. The week went by, and I felt better. Not happy, but I was able to cope. The first thing I wanted to do was confront Sergeant Goodrich, but he had been sent to France two days after I had been hospitalized. I wanted to know why he had double-crossed me. But it would keep; I knew we would meet up one day.

The postscript to this sad experience is that Sergeant Goodrich and I did meet again. It was 1971, in San Diego, and I was there with Muhammad Ali for the Ken Norton fight. Goodrich called me at my hotel and we arranged to meet for a drink. After the usual "How ya doing?" bit, I got right to it. "Tell me, J. J., why the hell did you pass me over and give the friggin' sergeant stripes to Shelton?"

"Hell, Angelo, it wasn't up to me. I got my arse kicked because I tried to interfere. The bastards sent me to France and Shelton took over the whole deal."

"I didn't know that you caught any flack. Why J. J.? What was it all about? It nearly broke my heart."

"It was the 'old boy network', Angie. The major and Shelton were old college buddies. You know the setup. What you don't know is that there were some discrepancies in the accounts, and you were gonna be the fall guy. But the brass didn't want any stink, and there was no proof against you, or anyone, come to that, so they booted you to the warehouse and sent me to France. The whole deal was smoothed over. What do you say about that?"

I thought about it, nothing to get ulcers about. "Let's have another drink, J. J. Say, would you like a couple of tickets for the fight?"

A few weeks after I left the hospital, I was in the company of another sergeant. This time the outcome was much more to my liking.

Sergeant James Mirena grabbed his kid brother and hugged him until he called out for breath. We had about an hour before we had to report to the air base; there was time for at least a couple of beers. Then we could grab a taxi—to hell with the expense—and still get to our destination on time.

I ordered, Jimmy insisted that he pay. I didn't argue, he was a sergeant and I was only a PFC. We sat down on one of the soft, red plush benches that covered the back wall of the hotel's bar.

We caught up on all the back news. My heart was full as I sat there looking and listening to my brother as he told me of his wartime experiences. He had qualified as an air gunner—the badge on his tunic testified to that—but he had been grounded because of air sickness. He was stationed near London, and his duties were now those of an air controller and radio operator. To wind up his news report, he told me that our photograph had appeared in the *Navy Yard Beacon*. The younger Mirena brothers had made the press—of course, it helped that we were the younger brothers of the well-known boxing manager, Chris Dundee!

I gave Jimmy my news. He loved the story about the sixteen marksmen trying to shoot rabbits. Over our second beers, which the PFC paid for, we tried to figure out how we had landed this cushy assignment. In answer to Jimmy's question I told him I had done a little boxing back in basic training, and I had a few bouts on the ship coming over, but I hadn't joined the boxing squad at Newbury. That last piece of information ruined one of his theories. For we were the official United States Air Force Tournament boxing corner men, or, as they say in England, "seconds," in the European Theater of Operations (ETO), and we wondered how the hell we had been chosen for this sensational duty.

We found out as soon as we reported to the gym on the air base. The sergeant in charge of arrangements for all ETO Tournaments was there waiting for us. Turning to the "brass" he said, "These two men are Chris Dundee's brothers, sir. Remember, I told you about Chris Dundee, the manager of the former Middleweight Champion of the World, Ken Overlin, who is now serving in the navy, sir."

"Yes, Sergeant, of course. Shame we couldn't have got him for the Air Corps." The "brass" beamed at Jimmy and me. "But we do have the Dundee boys, right?" Nobody bothered to correct him. The name Mirena would only have complicated things. "It will be a big help to our boxers to have experienced men like you with them." Jimmy and I smiled back at the "brass."

When we were in the locker room, changing for the corner work, Jimmy and I could not control our laughter. The "brass" thought we were "experienced men." All we knew about corner work had been picked up by watching at the Mason AC Gym in South Philly, and that was not one hell of a lot.

We got through the bouts. It was a case of the blind leading the blind. The boxers knew about as much as we did. The difference was they thought that we were experts; our brother's reputation had brainwashed them. If we had told our fighters to lead with their chins, they would have. I tried to imitate Jimmy, who, as cool as ever, looked as if he was the greatest corner man in the world, even as he nearly drowned the poor boxers with his over-enthusiastic sponge work.

That night in the bar of the Sergeants' Club—I was a special guest, so rank did not matter—Jimmy and I eventually found ourselves alone. We toasted our wonderful family and our famous brother, Chris Dundee, without whom we wouldn't have been standing, drinking in the Sergeants' Club, toasting his health!

Before we left in the morning Jimmy and I met at the PX to look for a gift to send back home to Mom. We looked, but we ended up sending a model aircraft to Carmen, Mary's son, who was seven years old, and Manny, Josephine's eleven-year-old son. Jimmy and I felt Mom would appreciate that. She would be more than satisfied with a letter that she could take out with her and show all her friends. "Letter from my boys."

When I was back on my home base at Newbury, the excitement and newness of the ETO boxing duty had completely changed my mental attitude. The transfer to the warehouse and the ignominy of being passed over for promotion no longer seemed important. I had no time to brood over bad memories; I was being sent all over Britain to different bases for the boxing tournaments. Jimmy and I worked together; it was like a dream come true for me. We would often meet in London at the Red Cross and have a night out together.

I began to spend my leaves in London, where I would pursue my favorite pastime—dancing. My regular haunt was the Covent Garden Palais de Dance. The ballroom had two big bands. One was led by an attractive lady clarinet player who played all the Artie Shaw arrangements, but best of all she played my favorite song, "Green Eyes." I think she used the Jimmy Dorsey arrangement, the one where the first chorus is kind of steady then there is a change of tempo and the second chorus comes in with a swinging beat. Boy! I sure enjoyed those times, jitterbugging, dancing up a storm. And I'll tell you, those English dames could really dance.

Unfortunately not all my time was spent on leave or attending boxing tournaments. I did have duties back on base in Newbury. I was one of the poor slobs who tried to keep tabs on aircraft inventories. With so much gear and equipment going in and out, it was not the easiest job in the world. Because of my continual absences, I wasn't expected to do or know a lot. But I could never work like that. If I was doing something, I wanted to give it my best shot. I kept a tight check on all inventories, and my records, in spite of my absences, were always up to date. Don't get me wrong, I was not a fanatic for work. If a chance came to sneak a night off, I took it, but if I had a job to do, I would try and do it well.

Orders came through, report to Ruislip for ETO boxing. Ruislip was within a stone's throw of London. There might be a chance that Jimmy and I could spend some time together. We had bought a couple of books on boxing at Foyle's, the famous London bookstore, and we were studying up on the sport, but I had other ideas than studying if we got any free time. You win some, and you lose some. It was straight to Ruislip, no free time.

The fights were good, not a lot of talent but heaps of enthusiasm, just like Jimmy and me. After the bouts we were just about to leave the auditorium when a well set up, nice-looking guy in Canadian uniform came over and introduced himself. His name was Eddie Borden and he was a stateside friend of Chris's, hence his coming over to say hello. He was an engaging kind of guy, nice and easy. You couldn't help but like him. We arranged to meet for a drink next time we were in London.

I met Eddie a couple of times. We had a few drinks and rapped about this and that. For me Eddie turned out to be a valuable contact. In 1947, Eddie had a conversation with my brother Chris in New York that was instrumental in changing my life. Eddie suggested to Chris that he use me in his business. "You couldn't do better than use your own flesh and blood. Angie is a nice kid, give him a chance, he'll do OK." Chris listened. But that was all in the future.

The New Year celebrations for 1945 were barely over, and I was having a ball in merry old England. The Allies seemed to be winning the war, and I was looking forward to a happy and successful 1945. In the third week of January my world fell apart.

I received the shocking news via the Red Cross. My mother was dead. On January 8 while shopping, she was hit by an automobile. She subsequently died in the hospital within hours. I was heartbroken. The Air Corps, under the auspices of the Red Cross, gave Jimmy and me a five-day furlough so that we could be together in our grief.

Irrationally, I blamed myself for not being with Mom. There had been no real reason for me to have joined the Air Corps. I could have stayed at home in South Philly and become an ensign in the Navy. I could have been there. I might have prevented it. If only. . . .

Somehow you learn to live with the sadness, and slowly the pain becomes bearable. The war went on, and I went on with it.

In February, Jimmy was posted to St. Quentin, in France. A month later I made staff sergeant. I was proud of myself, for I believed I had earned my stripes, but I was in no mood for celebrations. Two weeks after my promotion I too was flown out to France. I was stationed at Amiens, about forty or fifty miles to the west of St. Quentin. At least I was near Jimmy. The war went on.

Before I could decide if I liked being in Amiens or not, I was called to Paris for a major ETO boxing tournament. After the service contests Marcel Cerdan, the famous French middleweight, was boxing an exhibition match. In England I had watched the Heavyweight Champion of the World, Joe Louis, box an exhibition bout. Louis was an idol of mine, and to have actually met him was one of the highlights of my English tour of duty. Over the years I got to know Joe Louis and we became good friends. We shared a similar sense of humor and a common fault, an acute weakness for the dice table.

In the 1970's, Joe was working as host at Caesar's Palace in Las Vegas, and he was ideal for the job. He loved people and always found the time and the patience to sign autographs and pose for photographs with his many fans. But, unfortunately, Joe was in the right job in the wrong place. The gambling temptations were too much and over the years, Joe dropped a lot of money on the roulette wheel. I was a constant visitor to Caesar's, and I didn't fare too well either when it came to walking away winning.

On one particular night, I dropped a stack of money. As I sat at the table trying to control that particular feeling of panic you get when you've lost more than you can afford, one of the casino managers came over and placed a friendly arm on my shoulder.

"Hey Angie, your pal Joe Louis has lost a few big ones tonight; would you mind signing his marker? I've got his marker right here," he said, waving a piece of paper at me. I told him I have trouble enough with my own markers.

I didn't know whether to laugh or cry. The casino manager, like a lot of people, believed I was making millions with Muhammad and naturally thought I would be pleased to help out an old pal. If I had had the bread I would have, however with things being what they were, right there and then the idea was difficult, or more to the point—impossible.

"Tell Joe that I can't make it right now. I'm going to have a problem settling my own account. Just say that Angelo is having his usual run. He'll know what you mean. Yeah, and tell him that if he can give me a little time, I'll try and work something out for him. He'll understand," I told the manager.

Joe did understand. He'd watched one go down nearly every time I'd played. He'd always told me that craps and me just didn't get on together. From that time on he would always call me "the magician," and I asked him why. Joe smiled that sweet smile of his and said, "When you gamble you do one hell of a trick. You turn money into excrement."

It had been a hell of a thrill for me when I met the great Joe Louis for the first time. And now I was hoping I'd get a chance to meet the French champion, Marcel Cerdan.

Jimmy and I did our thing in the corners, then quickly found ourselves some space at the back of the crowded hall so that we could watch Cerdan. Marcel Cerdan had quite a reputation. In February 1944 he won the Inter-Allied middleweight championship, and before France had been invaded he was the national champion. He was a French-Algerian, so you can imagine the welcome he received from the Free French Forces in the auditorium.

After his exhibition bout, Jimmy and I had the pleasure of meeting and talking with this great fighter. Marcel and Jimmy conversed in French. My brother had picked up his French from a girlfriend he had met in St. Quentin. Not a bad way to learn a language! I sat and listened, understanding one word out of twenty; I found the French Champion immensely likeable. Three years later in the states, Marcel became World Champion by beating Tony Zale, only to lose his title in the following year to Jake LaMotta. Tragedy was to strike Marcel. On October 27, 1949, he died in an air crash over the Azores. I heard the news when I was working in New York, and although I hardly knew the man, I felt the loss. It was a sad day for boxing.

Being a staff sergeant is a hell of a lot different from being a dog-face GI. I had Authority with a capital A, and I loved it.

My main duties were organizational. I made certain that everything ran smoothly. I would check out that somebody else was checking out all that needed to be checked out. That's clout!

Although I am making light of it, checking the stores, cargo, and equipment for the guys who were doing the fighting and flying was a heck of a lot of responsibility. I tried to keep on top of the job, but sometimes, even the best of us goof off. At least I had an excuse; it started when I received the letter.

I re-read the letter from Rita. I crumpled it in my hand and threw it in the waste basket under my desk. There was no reason to read it again: a Dear John letter is a Dear John letter. Our engagement was off. It was all over. Rita had met someone else and was getting married. What could I do about it? Nothing! Her letter spelled it out: finis, kaput, the end!

I got through most of my duties for the day, but by late afternoon I felt like climbing a wall. I told my corporal to get me a fifth of whisky from the NCO Club—when you are a staff you can do that—and I sat in my office drinking while I tried to figure out exactly how I felt about the breakup. I came up with a bright idea, or should I say, the whisky came up with a bright idea. Talk it over with Jimmy. Problem! Jimmy was fifty miles down the road, and there were no cabs, trains or buses and I couldn't drive! Or could I? There was a jeep parked outside my office.

"Corporal," I shouted, "Where the hell are you?" He should still have been on duty.

"Yes, Sarge, what's the problem?" He was still on duty; good.

"Say, Corp, who belongs to that jeep out there?"

"I don't know, Sarge, let's take a look." I followed him out of the building.

"I don't recognize it. I guess it has to be from the pool, Sarge."

"Start it up, Corporal." He looked sideways at me but he did it. I got into the driver's seat. "Which way to St. Quentin?"

"Turn right at the base entrance and straight on, turn left when you hit Iussy."

I didn't like the word "hit." I smiled benignly at the Corp, "See you later, Corp." The jeep didn't move.

"How 'bout putting it in gear?" I figured out what he meant—I did know about it, I just hadn't done it before. I don't think the corporal knew at that stage that I couldn't drive; he just thought I was drunk, but when I pulled away in second gear in a series of jumps that would have done credit to a kangeroo, I suspect he had his doubts about my driving ability.

When I arrived at Jimmy's quarters, after an effortless fifty-mile drive in second gear, to say he was surprised to see me would be one hell of an understatement. "What are you doing here in that jeep? You can't drive." I grinned foolishly at him. "I know that, you know that, but this friggin' jeep don't know that."

We got drunk that night, and we sat talking about women in general and Rita in particular. It was very deep and profound, and neither of us could remember a word of it when we woke up in the morning.

I had to face the problem of driving back, and the problem of explaining the absence of both myself and the jeep. But first things first. I told Jimmy that I was OK once the jeep was going, but I couldn't reverse, so would he please point it in the right direction? So with a thick head I said so long to Jimmy and began the journey back to Amiens. Strangely enough I was no longer depressed over Rita.

Back at the base, no one seemed to notice that I or the jeep had been away, and if they did, nobody said anything. As I told you before, you gain a lot of clout with sergeant stripes!

There was talk of Germany collapsing, but right now Allied soldiers were still being killed. I felt that I would like to be a little closer to the actual fighting. Using a few connections, I arranged to go on a few combat flights. From an air base in Belgium I took off in a C47 cargo plane to drop para-packs to our forces at the front. We came in low and I pushed out the para-packs and watched them float down to our forces on the ground. As we approached, the ground forces waved, and I waved back wildly, feeling part of the team. It was a good feeling!

On my third flight, as we came in over our given position, I was about to push out the para-packs, but I became perturbed that our guys on the ground hadn't waved back at me. I edged forward to the cargo hold, trying to get a better look at the ground, when they opened up. Machine-gun bullets were flying through the air. I pulled back quickly as a bullet chipped away a piece of the still open unloading hatch. The skipper of our plane was no fool. He didn't wait to double check his position; he hightailed it back to base. Curiosity got the better of me, I quickly looked down to see who was doing the shooting. I recognized the uniforms—they were German. I got the hatch closed before you could say Adolf Hitler, and I thanked my lucky stars that I hadn't seen any artillery down there.

One positive result of my flight time was that it gave me points, which would help speed up my discharge from the army when the war ended.

It came around quicker than most of us guys thought. About eight weeks after my nerve-shattering flight over enemy lines, the Third Reich surrendered. On May 8, 1945, the war in Europe was over. Three months and two atom bombs later, Japan was taken out. It was all over.

I saw out my time in Erlangen, Germany, where I drank their wonderful beer and waited to go home. Early in 1946 I was shipped out. Staff Sergeant Angelo Mirena, who had not fired a shot in anger, landed in the USA, and became plain Angelo Mirena, known as Angelo Dundee.

CHAPTER SIX

BACK HOME

"In the fall of 1947, a conversation was taking place in New York, between a Canadian pal of mine, Eddie Borden, and my brother Chris, whom I hardly knew. The result of the conversation would change my life."

I was back in South Philly, once again working at the navy yard and living at home at 829 Morris Street. Things seemed the same, looked the same, but they were different. What was different, I suppose, was me.

To be fair to myself, there had been one momentous change that maybe had clouded my entire outlook on life. Mom was no longer living. I thought I was over the worst, but living at home, *her* home, reopened all the thinly covered mental scars, and it hurt. How could it be the same? Every day I was so aware that I would not find Mom in the kitchen, and every time I looked at the sad face of my father, my heart cried for both of us. I wondered if I would ever get over my grief.

When I first arrived back home it was early in 1946, but now I had been home over a year, and slowly but surely I became immune to the pain. As I said, life was the same, yet it wasn't!

I was back working on aircraft maintenance inspection, but I was uncomfortable about my job. Before I had left for the war, we had been working on prop-engine planes, but now all that had changed. This was the beginning of the age of the jet engine. It was now all advanced technology. I got by, I did what I had to do, but the work baffled me. I was out of my depth, and I'm the kind of a guy who likes to feel the ground beneath my feet. Technically, I knew how things worked, but I didn't know why! I read the blueprints, I checked the electric cables, receptacle to receptacle. It was painstaking, like working on a gigantic switchboard, and I had no overall picture of what was going on. The technological advances had left me behind and it was bringing me down. My pal and superior at the navy yard, A. J. Korch, tried to give me some advice. "Why don't you let me put you down for a course on electronics? With your past record and my recommendation, it'll be a cinch."

"Sure, and while we're at it, what about physics? Yea, and I guess I am going to need more than high school mathematics. You know, A. J., I think the boat just sailed without me."

A. J. was understanding, and told me to stick with it, and think about taking the course. I said that I'd let him know. Hell, I was thinking about it, but for my money it would be a waste of time. To learn all I wanted to know would take five years—that is, if I had started ten years ago! I would wait and see how things worked out, and in the meantime I was having a fun time, life was cool. Five years' study? No way!

I was back in the Rio football team, Monday was still darts night, and Tuesday through Saturday I became a "dancing fool." As I said, life was cool. A few of us guys would spend most weekends at Atlantic City, where we had one big ball. Our regular hangout was the Steel Pier, where we would dance to the big band sound, and try to score with the big bad broads.

In the summer months most of the neighborhood would rent, buy, beg, steal, or borrow apartments as near the sea as possible. My sister Mary had a small pad where all the family stayed at one time or another and it sure helped in the saving on hotel bills. There were so many people from South Philly vacationing in Atlantic City, the guys called it "South Philly on the Sea," or "SPOTS."

Eight of us arrived in two cars. It was the tail end of the summer of 1947, and we were the hard core of the Rio football team looking for one hell of a good time in Atlantic City. Al Piluso and I had arranged with my sister Mary to stay at the apartment on Florida Avenue, as long as we promised to keep the place clean and sleep on the floor of the lounge. The rest of the Rio boys had made similar arrangements with either friends or family. We were all going to meet up outside the Steel Pier; Al and I arrived early and we decided to take a walk along the Boardwalk. I hadn't taken ten strides when I saw two attractive girls walking directly at me. One I didn't know, the other was Rita Carlone.

After the introductions, Al and the other girl, whose name was Carol, seemed to have things to talk about. Rita and I took a couple of steps to the side so that we stood by ourselves. We had already gone through the polite enquiries, so we just stood and looked at each other, both hesitant to start the conversation. She was as pretty as ever and looked hardly a day older from the time I had last seen her, which was well over two years ago.

"Hey, I got to congratulate you on Jimmy's wedding to Louise. Do you remember how you and Louise used to dance? I thought you were going to pick her as your regular partner instead of me." She smiled, and her dark brown eyes held mine deliberately. She looked very desirable, but she was a married lady and I did not want to come on strong. To be honest, I didn't know how to play the scene. I said the first thing that came to mind.

"Yea, Jimmy and Louise got married. It was just a quiet wedding." I went silent, then I blurted out, "Did you know Mom died? Of course you knew, what am I thinking of. I read the card, you know, the condolences, the card your mother sent. Thank her for me, will you?" I was talking like a mentally retarded child.

Rita placed her hand on my arm. "You look great, Angie. The army must have agreed with you. I bet you broke a lot of hearts in Europe. Look, Angelo, I have to go, but I'm here in Atlantic City nearly every weekend staying with Carol. Why don't you give me a call, perhaps we could get together." She opened her handbag, took out a pen, and quickly scribbled down her telephone number on the inside of her matchbook that she had obviously picked up at "Sammy's Lounge."

I looked at the motif on the matchbook. "Is Sammy's a good joint? I hear its kinda fancy."

"No, it's a nice place. Maybe we could go together."

"What about er . . . Isn't your husband with you?" I had to ask, didn't I?

"He can't get away weekends." Rita did not expand on the subject. "Call me. We have a lot to catch up on."

I watched the two girls walk away. I held the matchbook in my hand thinking what to do. Al interrupted my thoughts. "She still looks great, Angie. Are you gonna see her?"

I didn't want to be second choice and I didn't like the idea of becoming heavily involved with a married woman. I made up my mind. It was all over and it should stay that way. "No, Al. She's a happily married lady." I crumpled the matches and let them drop to the ground. Atlantic City was no place to mope over memories. Al and I strolled over to the Steel Pier entrance to wait for the guys. I was going to have a ball—at least I was going to try.

So, life was OK. Sure, I had a problem at work, but I could handle it. I knew I was getting nowhere, but what the hell, there was nothing wrong in spending the rest of my life in South Philly, was there?

In the fall of 1947, a conversation was taking place in New York, between a Canadian pal of mine, Eddie Borden and my brother Chris, whom I hardly knew. The result of the conversation would change my life.

Chris phoned. After speaking to Pop, he asked to speak to me. Would I be interested in going to New York to work for him? I did not even have to think about it. "Sure, Chris, sounds good. When do you want me?"

CHAPTER SEVEN

NEW YORK, NEW YORK

"It was like that every day at the gym. There was always somebody there who was 'somebody.' I had met Doc Kearns, probably the most famous manager in the world. His list of fighters read like the Boxing Hall of Fame: Mickey Walker, Archie Moore, Joey Maxim, and the legendary Jack Dempsey. You never knew who would drop in at Stillman's."

I came from a big city, Philadelphia, and I had traveled around. I had been to Germany and France, and I knew my way around London in merry old England, but when I first arrived in New York, I was awed. Maybe it was the fact that I was going to stay and work there, but I do not think so. There was no doubt about it, Manhattan had its own brand of magic.

I wasn't going to live in some nice suburb on the outskirts of the city. No, sir! I was right in the heart of Manhattan, where all the action was. I was living in the center of the boxing world, practically opposite the world famous Madison Square Garden, known everywhere as the "Garden." Yea, when I think back, no wonder I was awed.

The train journey from Philly was no big deal, and I found my way to the Capitol Hotel without any problem. It would have been nice to spend a day or two getting a feel of the place before I got involved in my work—whatever that was going to be—but brother Chris believed in that old adage, "Waste not, want not."

Chris was paying me wages, so, on my very first night in the big city, I worked. I was the bucket boy in the corner of a boxer Chris managed, who was fighting at the Garden.

Boy, was I nervous! I was so scared I did not know whether the guy won or lost or what his name was. I concentrated so much on making certain that I didn't foul up, how could I remember details like names or who won or lost?

In between rounds, I would quickly put my bucket up into the ring, positioned so that the corner men could reach it easily, and that when the fighter spat out his water mouthwash, the fluid would go into the bucket and not onto the ring or onto anyone's feet.

I had done bucket work before when I was in the service, and at the Mason Hall AC gym in Philadelphia, but that night at the Garden was something else. The one-minute break between rounds seemed like ten seconds. Everything happened so fast. I was one step away from panic. That's nerves!

That night, after my New York debut, I didn't hang around. I was too exhausted both physically and mentally. I grabbed a sandwich and coffee from a deli and went back to the hotel, where I fell asleep listening to the radio.

Some people have a bedroom in a hotel, some people have an office in a hotel, but Chris had it all. The bedroom was his office, and that is where I lived and worked.

Room 711 in the Capitol Hotel, New York, was my new home. It was a small narrow room with a studio bed at one end and two desks, one sporting a typewriter, at the other end. It had a wash basin and a shower, which assured me that no matter what happened, at least I'd be clean. After I had made up my studio couch in the morning, the room looked like an office. At night, when I made up the couch into my bed, it still looked like an office! Details like that didn't bother me. I settled in very quickly and life took on a kind of offbeat routine.

On fight nights, I worked the corner. Each time it became a little easier and my nervousness disappeared. There was no more slipping away after the fights. I stayed on and went out with the boys. I say "boys," but I should say men. I was the youngest in the group. Most of the guys that I hung out with were sports writers or trainers and they were established in their profession. They had paid their dues and put their time in. I enjoyed their company, but when they talked boxing I kept my mouth shut and listened. I was learning.

It was past ten o'clock. I had made up the studio bed. I had shaved and showered hours earlier. As usual, I crossed the road and went to the cafeteria at the Garden and ordered a coffee, black, and an apple danish. Joe Chernoff, who owned a camera shop on 21st Street, had joined me. He was a big fight fan and knew Chris. Joe and I had got talking at the Friday night fights at the Garden, and we drifted into a kind of easy friendship—just for the record, we are friends to this day.

We were glancing over the sports section of the *New York Post*. "I see Louis has another exhibition fight coming up," Joe Chernoff observed.

"I bet Louis doesn't take a real fight the whole year," I said. I quickly looked through Al Buck's article. "There ain't nothing here about any forthcoming fight. Al has got nothing on it." I put the paper away. We were both disappointed. We were talking about the World Heavyweight Champion, Joe Louis, a fighter we worshipped, and as far as we were concerned exhibition bouts were for the birds.

"How many fighters is Chris handling now?" Joe asked as he finished his coffee.

"You know Chris, his left hand doesn't know what his right hand is doing." Joe nodded understandingly. I went on, "I guess about twelve, but I don't really know. He does so many different deals it changes week to week."

That was true. Chris had so many different arrangements with various fighters and managers that it took me a heck of a long time to understand it all—that is, if I ever did!

Joe had to get back to his shop. "OK, pal, I gotta go. I'll see you Friday at the Cranford fight." He got up to leave, but he changed his mind and leaned over the table and began to speak earnestly. "Say, Angie, did Billy pay you the ten yet?" I didn't know how to answer, I didn't want to make a big deal out of it. Billy was a young welterweight who hung around the gym.

"No," I said slowly, thinking of what to say. "I hear he's strapped right now. When he gets his next fight I am sure I'll get the ten back." Joe didn't believe it. I didn't believe it either.

"When I see the bum, I'll ask him. He had no right to put the bite on you. He knows you can't afford it, the lousy bum." I shrugged. What else could I do? Joe wasn't finished. "I feel bad, Angie. I introduced you to the louse. You know pal, you gotta learn to say 'no', OK?" Joe straightened up. "See you Friday."

He had meant well. I couldn't afford to loan money. Especially when nearly all the loans were never repaid. I had developed a bad habit. As the years rolled on I picked up another bad habit, called gambling, and I found them both very difficult to break.

So far, it had been a quiet morning. The phone had only rung three times. I had time to catch up on some of the typing. I took about a dozen five-by-eights from the photograph drawer in my desk. We had promotional photographs of all our fighters. It was one of my duties to type on the back of the photograph the fighter's record and statistics. It was pretty basic. I would send the photograph with a covering letter which gave the fighter's background—stuff like, "He is good to his mother and goes to church every Sunday"—and send them to sports writers in the cities where the fighters were scheduled to appear. It helped to remind the writers that our guy was on the card. Sometimes we even got a human interest story on our guy. When a fighter got a mention that was good publicity; publicity meant interest, and interest meant bigger gates; bigger gates meant bigger paydays for the fighter, and that meant more bread for the fighter's manager. It was something Chris latched on to early. I soaked up that knowledge. I still write to newspaper guys. Good habits, like bad habits, die hard.

At ten-thirty on the button Chris arrived at the office. Without smiling he said, "Hi, kid, any calls?" He walked over to the desk, flicking his hat onto the couch as he did so. "Gimme the mail. Where are my messages? I gotta make a call." I didn't bother to answer him, because he was already on the phone. I gave him the mail and the pad with his phone messages written on it. I went back to typing the backs of photographs.

I deduced by his uptight mood that he had lost playing pinochle during the train journey from his home on Long Beach to New York. Normally he arrived happy, because normally he won. I found out from friends that Chris was a very good player. That is how I learned most things about Chris—from friends.

Chris and I were of two different age groups. He never saw me grow up. He had already left home by the time I could talk. We didn't really know one another.

The fifteen-year difference in our ages made a difficult barrier to cross. To Chris, I was the kid brother he hadn't known, but now he was giving the kid a chance. To me, Chris was the brother that had sent me boxing gloves. He was the "manager of fighters." He was a somebody. But first and last, he was my brother, so I loved him. As I grew up, my pop would drum into me, "You love your brothers and your sisters. You love your family. You always show respect to your elders; you always show respect to your family."

These were some of the dictums my pop laid on me as I grew up. They became part of me, and they still are.

Chris was an elder brother, and that meant love and respect, but I still didn't really know him. It did not take me long to learn that he was hardworking and clever, but I guess the uppermost feeling I had for Chris at that time was one of admiration.

Chris had a home at Long Beach, Long Island—and that wasn't chopped liver. He had turned a nickel and dime business into a respected and successful operation, representing sometimes as many as twenty fighters. Everybody seemed to know him, even world champions would come over to Chris and give him a big hello. This was my Big Brother, making it in the big city. Not bad for an Italian kid who had left his home in South Philly when he was fifteen years old; a kid who had worked as a shoe-shine boy, a hawker on the railroads, and on a newspaper stand—not bad at all! Of course I felt admiration. Wouldn't you?

When I accepted the offer to work for Chris I didn't quit my old job, I took a leave of absence. I was too unsure of what the future would hold for me. Believe me, it had crossed my mind that I might have to return to Philly, and it was nice to know I had a safety net to fall into. At the back of my mind I was always aware that I hadn't been Chris's first choice for the job.

Chris had wanted brother Jimmy to come to New York, but Jimmy had only recently married Louise, and the job was too intangible and precarious for a married man. I found out later that it was Eddie Borden who had suggested me to Chris. I sure had been lucky to meet Eddie during the war years.

In the short time I had been in New York I had made up my mind about two things. I didn't want to go back to South Philly as a clerk, and I did want to do something that involved the fight game. I must admit that I did feel a growing confidence in my abilities. OK, I was only the bucket boy, but I did it well and I was gaining first-hand knowledge of what needed to be done when working the corner.

I got on well with the fighters, too. They could be highly sensitive and temperamental like nearly all highly trained artists and athletes. After training sessions at the gym or after the fights at the Garden, I would sit around and rap with them. No heavy stuff. Maybe re-live a fight, discussing what they should have done, or just everyday things with a few laughs thrown in.

As I left the Garden one night on my way to meet a few pals at the Ringside Bar, I was stopped by Chickie Ferrara, the trainer, who was also on his way to the Ringside Bar. "Hey, Angie, I've been watching you. You got a nice way with the kids. They like and respect you. Stay in the game, you gotta feeling for it. If you need any help, all you gotta do is ask."

I was a little embarrassed, but very flattered, because Chickie was one heck of a trainer. "Thanks," I said. "I sure appreciate it. Come on. I'll buy you a beer."

That night, as I lay on my studio couch, I thought about what Chickie had said. I am not going to tell you that his words steered me in any specific direction. At that time, the only direction I took was from Chris. Whatever he wanted me to do, I did. On the other hand, I could not tell you that those words did not influence me— I still remember them, don't I?

The day before the Cranford fight we had a busy morning. I gave Chris all his messages, and he must have been on the phone for at least an hour. Occasionally, in between calls, he would call out cryptic messages, for example, "Chicago, third week, March, Middleweight, Sunnyside, February 4th, headliner."

I wrote the information down, pleased that I knew what it meant. He was speaking to different promoters, as far south as Georgia, as far west as Chicago and as far north as Toronto, Canada. He would inquire about their forthcoming promotions. If their card wasn't filled, Chris would try and sell one of his own boxers to fight the local guy. If a fighter had dropped out through an injury sustained during training, or for something less heroic, like a cold, then Chris would offer one of his fighters as a substitute. If Chris didn't have a suitable substitute, he would ring up a bunch of managers until he found the right fighter. Naturally, Chris would work out a deal, so that he received a percentage from the manager's share.

The out of town managers always had time for Chris. He could arrange for their fighters to get a bout in New York, and maybe even the Garden, and that was clout. When he was working out a deal he could be charming or aggressive. He could sure negotiate; he had more moves than a chess board.

The phone session ended at around eleven forty-five, and then, as per usual, we were off to the gym to see our fighters work out. For me, going to the gym was the highlight of the day.

Stillman's Gym was to boxers like Harvard Law School is to lawyers. It was a place of training and learning. A school with any number of famous alumni. A university where you competed against your peers under the scrutiny and tutelage of astute and knowledgeable coaches. Attending the place didn't guarantee success, but it certainly helped.

As we climbed the well-worn stairs, the smell of sweat and

liniment oil filled my nostrils. The buzz of voices mingled with the sound of the thumping of a heavy punching bag. I could hear the staccato rap of a speed-bag being hit, and the monotonous whine that comes when a boxer is using a skipping-rope expertly.

To enter the gym, you had to pass Jack Curley, the doorman, but sometimes Lou Stillman, the boss, sat right by the entrance. There was an admission charge of fifty cents for spectators and a training fee of ten dollars a month for boxers. If you hadn't paid, you had a problem. Lou would scrutinize you as you came in with his hawk eyes. "You paid your dues?" he would snarl. If you hadn't, he would raise his voice to just short of shouting. "Out!" There was no second opinion.

Above his head was a bell which he would ring for attention as he announced who was sparring in what ring. "In ring one, we got Harold Green, middleweight. In ring two, we got Frank Alucci, heavyweight." His rasping voice would fill the gym. By his accent you could tell he was no Rhodes Scholar.

The gym was on two floors, neither of which, by any stretch of the imagination, could you call "a clean modern, health-oriented gymnasium." It was pretty old—one wise-guy told me that it was where George Washington used to work out!

The upper floor was used for "floor-work." It was where you worked on the punch-bags, or did skipping and bench exercises. The lower floor consisted of two rings, with fold-up chairs for spectators. The decor was early twentieth-century slum. The walls were stained yellow with dampness. The wall mirrors were tarnished, and the ceiling looked as if it had lived through an earthquake, there were so many cracks in it. I loved every square inch of it.

At the back of the lower floor, against the wall, were the pay phones. When they were all in working order, which was not often—there was a twenty percent casualty rate—five phones would be in constant use. Chris made for the phones, joining the other managers and promoters who, for the next hour or so, would use Stillman's wall of phones as their offices, stopping only to watch their particular boxer work out.

These telephones were used both for making and receiving calls. Frequently you would hear somebody's name being called to come to the phone. Some managers found out, the hard way, that it was not a wise thing to have business calls at Stillman's.

You see, when the phone rang for you, it could be answered by another manager who just happened to be standing by the phones. He would say that you were not there, after pretending that he had looked for you. He would then offer his own services and try to sell his own fighters. A lot of fighters would get bouts just because their managers had answered the phone first, and there were one or two nice little bouts between managers as a result.

I was standing by the number one ring watching the sparring session. The ring nearest Lou Stillman was the number one ring, and the one furthest away was the second or number two ring, where the lesser known boxers worked out. It was a mark of status to be able to use the number one ring.

Rocky Graziano was working out. Boy, was he good to watch, even in sparring! I watched him eat up three sparring partners in as many rounds.

Al Weill was sitting watching him, looking very pleased with what he saw. Al was big-time. He had manged Lou Ambers, the ex-lightweight champ. Al gave me a nod. I was flattered that he remembered me from the Garden. I saw a couple of other big-time operators that I had met. They smiled. It was like that every day at the gym. There was always somebody there who was "somebody." I had met Doc Kearns, probably the most famous manager in the world. His list of fighters read like the Boxing Hall of Fame: Mickey Walker, Archie Moore, Joey Maxim, and the legendary Jack Dempsey. You never knew who would drop in at Stillman's.

I moved around the perimeter of the ring, saying hi to familiar faces. The gym was crowded; a lot of reporters were in because of the Cranford fight. The place was buzzing. As usual, Moe Fleischer was in. Moe had steered Kid Chocolate to the championship and had taken Tom Heeney to an unsuccessful shot against Gene Tunney. He was a nice friendly guy, a real character, always good for a laugh. He was only a little man, and if some big guy was standing in front of him obscuring his view of the ring, Moe would hit the guy on the head with his shoe. The big guy would look up at the ceiling, with its peeling and splitting plaster. Moe would say,"The goddam ceiling is falling down, move over pal."

Lou Stillman rang the bell and announced that Jackie Cranford would be working out in ring number one. Jackie was one of Chris's fighters, and Ray Arcel was his trainer. I went over and stood by his corner watching the sparring. I listened to all Ray told Jackie. Listen, watch, and learn was my golden rule.

I went to Stillman's every day of the week, except for national or religious holidays when the gym was closed, and I kept to my golden rule. I watched great and not so great fighters in training, and I listened to all Ray and other trainers told me. I was learning.

It had been hectic. Besides the day-to-day work to take care of, there had been the weigh-in and the press conference. Chris had taken me with him to the Garden, not that I did much other than talk to some of the sports writers. I enjoyed it; I felt part of the action. The Jack Cranford–Gino Buonavino fight was creating a lot of attention; heavyweight fights always created interest. Maybe it was the continuing search for a "white hope."

I said to Ray Arcel after the weigh-in, "All these people, is it always like this?"

"Forget it, kid. This is nothing. Wait till you get a title fight, then you'll see something."

Of course he was right, but it would be a few years before I was involved in a championship fight, and by the time it did happen, promotion and hype would have grown beyond my imagination.

I never thought so many people could get into my bedroom— sorry, I mean office! At one time, during the afternoon, I reckoned there were at least twenty guys, talking, gesticulating, and shoving, in room 711. Some were directly or indirectly involved with the fight, like the trainer of Cranford, Ray Arcel, and Buonavino's entourage, and of course, the newspapermen, but everybody else was in the office for one reason only. They wanted tickets for the fight and, nine times out of ten, they wanted them for nothing.

Chris was very particular about giving away tickets. A few special people might be lucky, especially if they were doing current business with him, otherwise Chris gave it to them straight. "You wanna ticket? Go across to the Garden and buy one." If they offered to buy one, but pay Chris later, he would say, "What am I, a bookkeeper?" Chris was tough.

It was nearly five o'clock before the office cleared. I tidied the desk, found a couple of letters that needed answering, and ignored them—enough's enough. I was whacked and hungry, so I intended to grab a sandwich then catch a nap before I went to work at the Garden. I was just about to leave when the telephone rang. "Hi, Chris Dundee's office," I said wearily. "Hello. This is Jackie Cranford's cousin. I'd like three seats for the fight tonight. I'd prefer them at ringside." It was a female's voice. Her accent was pure "honeychile," southern drawl.

"Oh, you would prefer ringside," I said sarcastically. "Why, honey child, we're all out of ringside." My southern drawl wasn't so hot.

"Look here, I'm Jack Cranford's cousin, and I need the tickets for his Aunty Mildred, that's my mother, my sister Frances, and me."

"So, you're Jack's cousin. How come he didn't get you tickets?" I was so smart.

"Is Jackie there?" she asked, ice cold. Jack was asleep in his room, resting before the fight, and all his calls were being transferred to the office. He would be getting up at any time now, but I didn't want to be the one to wake him, just in case it was some broad trying to get to him. He was a good-looking son of a gun, big, blond, and the type a lot of chicks go for.

"No, Jackie ain't here. I'm here!" I was getting tired of it.

"Now listen here," she was angry. "I'm Helen Bolton from North Carolina, and Mr. Chris Dundee told me to call for tickets." Well, that was different, she knew Chris. I thought I should explain who I was.

"This is Angelo Dundee speaking . . . no, not Angela—Angelo . . . look, doll, there are no ringside seats . . . yea, AN-GE-LO. It's an Italian name. A well-known Italian name—OK? . . . there are *no* ringside seats . . . I don't expect you do get many Angelos in Salisbury, North Carolina."

She was putting me on. "OK, doll, I'll see to it that three seats are left for you at the box office in the name of . . ." I had forgotten her name.

"Bolton, Helen Bolton," and without giving me the chance to say anything else she went on. "I'll pick up the tickets at the box office. Thank you, Mr. Dundee. You have been so kind." She didn't mean it, I could tell by the way she slammed down the telephone receiver.

Most of the fight crowd had gone, but the Manhattan traffic was still heavy. I was lucky, I caught a cab outside the front of the Garden. I told the cabbie, "Toots Shor's, Broadway and 6th."

He turned to look at me. "I know where it is, pal." He must have had a bad night!

A whole bunch of us were meeting at Toots Shor's. I can't say it was to celebrate, because Jack had lost, but it is no use crying, is it? I figured there was no point hanging around the dressing room waiting for Jack to shower and dress.

The atmosphere there wasn't too good anyway, so I cut out,

knowing we would meet up later. I was at the bar when Chris and his wife Geraldine arrived with the Cranford party. They stood bunched together at the side of the room waiting for their table. The place was packed, and I had to push my way through the crowd to join them. A puffy-faced Jack Cranford was talking to a miserable-looking Ray Arcel; the other people I didn't know. Chris introduced me. There was the famous columnist, Quentin Reynolds, who was a big fight fan, and an out-of-town reporter, whose name I didn't catch. It may have been Al Fine, or Stein, or even Wine; I wasn't paying full attention, I was waiting to be introduced to the four attractive ladies who were standing behind Fine, or whatever his name was, talking amongst themselves. They were, Geri Marrott, who owned a boarding house, Mildred Bolton and her two daughters, Frances and Helen. At the introduction Helen looked me straight in the eyes. Her face was expressionless. She would have made a good poker player.

I had remembered her name instantly. I also remembered that the seats I had left for her had been lousy, right at the top in the very back row. I grinned, trying to be friendly. "How were the seats?" I asked.

"Great," she said deadpan. "I only had a minor nosebleed." The seats *had* been rather high up. I didn't know if she was mad at me or not. I gave her the once over; she looked sensational. She was wearing a large picture hat and high-heeled shoes with ankle straps. She looked as if she had just stepped out of a fashion magazine. The lady had class. There was no doubt about it, she was a good-looking gal. Her sister was pretty neat too, and let me tell you, so was the mother.

We stood around chatting. I found myself talking more to Frances than anyone else, who was more my type than Helen— she was shorter than I was. In my personal opinion, Helen was the better looker, but she was at least five eleven in her high heels and I, at five eight, was looking up to her—literally. Who needed a height complex!

Jack put his arms around his two cousins and tried to smile through swollen lips. "These two gals are real Georgia peaches. What d'you say?" I agreed with him.

"I thought you came from North Carolina?" I said to both the girls.

"No sir. We were born in Georgia, but we live in North Carolina," Frances informed me. No question about it, they were certainly not yankees!

"Helen is a great fight fan," Jack said. "She used to come to Washington to see me fight when I was in the navy. That's when I met Chris; he was living in Norfolk then." I had just learned another piece of information about my brother's life.

"If you want seats again, Helen, I promise you ringside." I smiled at her, she smiled back.

"What did you think of the fight tonight, Helen?" Jack asked her.

"You didn't fight tonight, you just got beaten," she answered. She certainly didn't pull her punches; maybe *she* should have fought Buonavino.

Toots came over, edging his way through the crowd, and told Chris that the table was ready. Toots was from Philly too. He always went out of his way to make us feel welcome. We became good friends.

At the table, waiting to order, Quentin Reynolds let it be known that he would like a drink. Mildred said that she had a bag-wrapped bottle in her handbag and would be delighted to give Mr. Reynolds a drink. True to her word, from her pouch handbag she produced a pint bottle of bourbon, wrapped in brown paper. After taking a snort, she passed it to Quentin, who toasted the fairer sex and took a swig.

I said to Jack, "Does she always carry a bottle with her?"

"Sure enough. If you want a drink in North Carolina, that's exactly what you do. It's against the law to buy drinks unless you're in a private club."

I shook my head in disbelief. "I ain't gonna visit North Carolina, that's for sure," I said.

"You never know," Jack said. He was right.

During the evening, it seemed that half of the male customers came over to our table on one pretext or another. And every one of those guys gave Frances and Helen the once over. I didn't blame them, they sure looked good. I had found out through conversation that Frances was only recently married and that Helen was still single and working in New York as a fashion model. By the attention she was getting from all the guys coming around, I didn't think she would remain single very long.

One newspaper guy that I had seen around a few times and hadn't liked too much was leaning over Helen a little longer than was necessary. I could see by her face that she was becoming embarrassed. I went over and heard enough to decide to break it up. I tapped him on the shoulder. "Hey, pal, I wanna word with you." He turned round. I could tell that he had had too much to drink. I put my hand over his shoulder and gently eased him away from the table. I spoke quietly to him, "Look, feller, that's Jack Cranford's cousin from out of town. She is a nice lady, so why don't you go to the bar and leave her alone." I looked into his bloodshot eyes.

"What the hell you . . ." I cut him off.

"Beat it," I said, as I applied pressure to the tendon on his shoulder, alongside his neck, until he winced. I propelled him in the direction of the bar. Fortunately, he went without any trouble. The last thing I wanted to do was get into a fight in Toots Shor's.

As I passed Helen, she smiled up at me. "Thanks," she said. I was now the one who leaned over her chair talking to her. We joked about my name, and I assured her once more that it was Angelo, not Angela.

She left before me. Two good-looking guys, reporters I think, took the four ladies on to a club for a few drinks. I sat at the half-empty table—Chris and his wife Gerri had left too—talking to the guys. "Nice ladies," Quentin remarked. "Yea," I agreed.

"Good looking dames," Quentin observed.

"Why didn't you take Helen's phone number?" Jack asked.

I smiled at him, "I did."

I had met a girl that I liked. I had her phone number, but it would be six months before I called her. Did I have so many other dates I couldn't fit her in? Was my social life so exciting that I forgot all about her? "No" to both questions. My time in New York meant only one thing to me—work. I was caught up in a way of life that embraced all that was important to me. Being involved in boxing was my hobby, my interest, my work, my play. There was little time for anything else. I would hang out with great trainers like Ray Arcel, Bill Gore, Chickie Ferrara, and Charlie Goldman. There were opportunities for me to talk to managers like Charlie Johnston, who looked after Sandy Sandler; Lou Viscusi, Willie Pep's manager; and Irving Cohen, manager of Rocky Graziano. There were so many good managers and trainers working in Manhattan that you must forgive me for not listing them all.

Madison Square Garden was holding championship fights: Rocky Graziano lost to Tony Zale there on June 10, and Sadler was going up against Pep in October. There were eight or nine other venues, including the esteemed St. Nicholas Arena, in or around the city. I tell you, New York was a good place to be for a fight fan. It was the heart of boxing.

In 1948 professional boxing was going through changes, many

badly needed. It wasn't just New York that had problems, it was a nationwide ailment. On February 20, in Illinois, a boxer by the name of Baroudi died after his bout. There was an outcry for pre-fight medical examinations. Another boxer, T. Harmon from Massachusetts, collapsed after excessive weight reduction. His license was revoked. In New York, Abe Greene was elected the first Commissioner by the NBA (National Boxing Association); Mr. Shepard was approved as Chief Boxing Inspector, and Mr. Eagan was confirmed as Athletic Commissioner. Boxing was getting organized, and positive action was being taken. It became mandatory for boxers to submit to a medical examination before a fight. It became a rule that a fighter must report any injuries before a bout. The famous middleweight Jake LaMotta was under investigation for not reporting an injury. Sixty-six boxers found unfit to fight had their licenses revoked—perhaps a boxer's life was saved because of that ruling.

There were inquiries and investigations into crime and monopolies in boxing. Newspaper headlines had screamed of bribery and corruption. Now something was being done about it. There was a strong faction that wanted to stop pro boxing on the grounds it was too violent. A boxer by the name of Dacona collapsed and died after his fight, which led to yet another outcry against the sport. It was a terrible tragedy, and the blame for the young man's death was laid at the feet of boxing. Later an autopsy report showed that the young boxer had a gland malfunction. The tragedy could have taken place while the boy was playing baseball, football, or ice hockey, but that never made the headlines. Boxing is a tough, body contact sport, but the two combatants only use their fists; out on the streets kids are using chains, baseball bats, and knives! I had read all about crooked fights and shadowy underworld figures corrupting boxing, but the people I worked with were fight people, not gangsters. Fixing fights never entered my head. I didn't even think about it until one night at the Whiteplains Country Center when I learned first hand that it really did go on. Well, in this particular case it didn't go on. Let me explain. I was working the corner for Bill Bossio, one of Chris's up and coming young fighters. Bill, a slick featherweight, had won a few fights around the New York area and was popular at the Country Center. The betting boys were making him a four-to-one favorite, but as I had never seen his opponent fight I just hoped Bill would win. I never paid any attention to the odds.

Charlie Goldman had warned me never to bet on any fight I was working, because if you bet on your own guy, your judgement could be influenced. Thinking about the money instead of the fight would cause you to lose the detached, analytical approach. You might exert too much pressure on the fighter by worrying too much about losing. Needless to say, if you had big bucks on the other fighter there would always be the temptation to ruin or damage your own guy's chances. I never had a bet on a fight in which I was involved. I don't regret it, even though I may have missed out on winning big money.

I stood at the back of the hall, watching the fight in progress. Our bout was next. Ray Arcel, the trainer and corner man for Bossio, didn't need me hanging around the overcrowded changing room, so I took the opportunity to catch the fight, soak up the atmosphere, and get acclimatized. It was an exciting fight. I was engrossed, and didn't notice the two guys who slid over and stood next to me. The round ended. I turned and looked at the two men. One was about forty and had black curly hair. I had seen him around. The other man was young, slim, and hard-looking. He smiled, leaned forward and spoke confidentially to me.

"What do you think of Bossio's chances?"

"Great. He'll probably stop the other guy," I said loudly to overcome the noisy buzz coming from the fight fans.

"Yeah. But if Bossio doesn't win, a hundred bucks on the other guy at four-to-one would net you four big ones," the slim guy said. He leaned in even closer and whispered in my ear. "I'll put the bet on for you. It'll cost you nothing. Listen Angelo, if you do us a little favor, I'll pay you your winnings right now."

I may have been naive, but I was no dummy. I knew a bribe when I heard one. Some of the guys that hung around Stillman's gym had told me that it went on. I just didn't think that anyone would ever be stupid enough to try and bribe me.

There was no way I was going to get involved with these two guys, but I wasn't looking for trouble either. I said easily, "Thanks, pal, but I don't bet. And believe me, my guy is going to win."

I started to move away, but the guy with the curly hair stood in my way.

"Listen kid," he said. "All you gotta do is drop something on the sponge in round four, and when you wipe his face just make sure he gets some water in his eyes." He smiled at me and continued, "You drop this," he held a jar of salve between his thumb and forefinger and stuck it right in front of my eyes. "And just for doing that little thing, you get this." He took a roll of bills from the inside pocket of his jacket and slowly peeled off four one-hundred dollar bills. He deliberately waved them at me.

The bell went for the next round, but I had lost all interest in watching the fight. I was steaming and had a problem controlling my voice. The anger must have shown when I said "I told you, I don't bet." I wanted to smash the creeps. I pushed the curly-headed bum and went to walk past.

"Hold it, punk. We ain't finished with you yet," he snarled.

"Yes, you are, " I said, throwing a short, hard left to his belly. He gasped for air and doubled up. I could easily have thrown a right and really hurt him, but common sense prevailed. There was no point in making a bad enemy. I stood there, staring hard at the slim guy. He was frozen, so I turned my back on him and walked back into the dressing room. I stayed there unobtrusively until it was time to enter the arena with Bossio and Ray Arcel. I stayed close to Ray, scanning the crowd, looking for the two guys. There was no sign of them.

Once I entered the ring I felt easier. And when the fight started, my concentration obliterated everything else from my mind except the job at hand. Bill Bossio won by a knockout in the third. I was elated, but when it was time to leave the Whiteplains Country Center, the elation had evaporated. It had been replaced by an acute attack of apprehension.

I left through the back door so close to Ray Arcel that we could have been mistaken for Siamese twins. Cautiously, I looked up and down the street, but there was no one hanging around. I got back to Manhattan without any problem.

Maybe they were only trying to find out whether or not I could be bought and were testing me. Who knows? I do know that I saw the curly-haired guy a couple of more times at the fights, but he never spoke to me. He would give me murderous looks. I was cautious when I left the arena, expecting him to be waiting outside, looking for revenge.

A few years went by before I spoke to him again. I was in Chicago, working with Carmen Basilio. Like our first meeting, I was standing at the back of the arena watching a fight. I had a little time left before I went to the dressing room to bandage Carmen's hands. But this time I was not alone. I was standing with one of the sports writers from the *Chicago Tribune*. "Curly Hair" walked by, recognized me, gave me a big smile and said, "Hi, Angie. How ya doin'?"

Do you know that guy?" the newspaperman asked me.

'No. Not really," I said. "Who is he?"

"Johnny Gold. A bad guy," the newspaperman answered. "He knifed a guy about a month ago. I'm surprised he's not inside."

I never said anything. I was too busy wondering if the friendly smile he had given me had sinister undertones. Fortunately I never did find out because I never saw the guy again. No one has ever tried to bribe me again.

A new phenomenon, television, had invaded the fight game. It would bring in much needed revenue, but it was also creating waves. Twentieth Century Sporting Club, Inc., an important promotional company, was in conflict with the Managers' Guild over television rights at the Garden and the St. Nicholas Arena. A boycott was put into operation, but after a short period the difference was settled. The Guild received fifty percent of telecast rights at the two venues. Things were sure changing in 1948. In New Jersey they ordered the seconds to dress neatly for television. Was nothing sacred!

It was an exciting time to be in New York, and I was finding my excitement at the Garden on fight nights and at Stillman's Gym every day. There was always something new to see, hear, or learn. Former Middleweight and Light-heavyweight Champion of the World, Dick Tiger, had a great trainer, Jimmy August, who was never too busy to give me advice. While he was in town he gave me some practicable instructions. "OK, Angie, now you've got it," Jimmy said as he watched me cut off the ends of the tapes with the scissors.

"How does it feel?" I asked the fighter who sat on the bench, bored with the whole thing.

"It's fine, Angelo. It feels good," he said as he opened and closed his hands. I slapped him on the back. "OK pal, now I'll take them off again." He smiled, and I began removing the hand wrappings.

For the last couple of days, Jimmy August had been showing me how to wrap a fighter's hands. In case you do not know, boxers have their hands wrapped in a gauze bandage before they put on their gloves. You may think anyone can wrap up hands, but to wrap a fighter's hands effectively and properly is a skill not to be underestimated. Over the years I altered and adjusted until I had my own individual technique, but I will always be in debt to Jimmy August for giving me his time and expertise.

Another fine trainer who was always helping me was Chickie Ferrara. He would explain to me the fundamentals of training and the finer methods of corner work. We worked together on some of

Chris's promotions so I had the chance to watch him and learn.

Bill Gore, who trained Willie Pep, was a marvel. He was so quick and sure. He would lean over the top rope and clean up Willie after every round, making him look as fresh and clean as possible. Bill believed that a fighter's appearance during a fight was psychologically important. I agreed with him. Coming out after a tough round looking fresh could demoralize the other fighter and also impress the judges. Ray Arcel went as far as wiping his fighter's gloves after each round, and he would never let his fighter start a round wet from the sponge. He would towel him off first. Another move of Ray's was to help his fighter from the stool physically. He would practically lift them off the stool. He explained that it made his fighter feel lighter at a time when his legs could be feeling like blocks of lead.

I was learning the tricks of the trade from the best in the business. There was another trainer who not only helped me, but gave me hours of laughs and good company. Charlie Goldman was sixty years young when I met him—a five-foot-one bundle of nervous energy. We used to go for coffee after the fights. Sometimes Chickie would join us, but mostly it would be just the two of us. He would take me to Jack Dempsey's, where we would sit and rap. Jack would often come over and join in the conversation and, naturally, the topic would be boxing.

Charlie had some unusual concepts. "If you get a good idea for your fighter, like a different move or somethin', tell your fighter in a way that will make him believe he really thought of it himself. You see, that way, he'll make the move naturally, without worrying about if he is doing it right. Plant the seeds, plant the seeds. You know what I'm saying?"

I thought he made a lot of sense, and later in my career I borrowed that advice when working with a boxer by the name of Cassius Clay. I planted seeds. Jack Dempsey didn't think it would have worked with him. He was probably right, because Dempsey was an innovator, he was an original. He changed the style of boxing, as did Muhammad Ali many years later. The difference was, Muhammad was receptive to new ideas.

Charlie Goldman liked the girls. I would bump into him all over town, and he would always have a different chick with him. They were all taller than Charlie, which was not too difficult, and they would always be introduced as "nieces." I figured he must have one hell of a large family.

Charlie dropped out of sight for a while. I missed his diminutive figure at Stillman's. When I did bump into him walking down Broadway with a very attractive young lady, I asked him where he had been hiding. He introduced me to Lilly, his niece, and explained what he had been doing. "I got this fighter that can punch like a mule. He's been fighting out in Brockton, Mass. He's had two fights there, two KO's, both in the first round."

"Sounds good," I said. "Why haven't I seen him at Stillman's?"

Charlie shrugged his shoulders, "Well, I'll tell you, Angie, the guy is a great puncher, but as for anything else he's a novice. I'm hiding the guy away until I can teach him. If I take him down to Stillman's, he'll get laughs. The smart asses down there might demoralize the kid, he looks so damn awful in training."

"What's the kid's name?" I asked.

"Rocco Frances Marchegiano—he's Irish!" Charlie laughed at his own joke. His niece laughed too. "He is fighting under the name of Rocky Marciano, I tell ya, Angie, this kid is gonna be a champ."

A few days later Charlie rang me and invited me to watch his boy workout. Rocky was short for a heavyweight, only five eleven, and on the scales he touched one hundred and eighty-four pounds—not too reassuring when he would be going in with guys over six feet three and weighing over two hundred pounds. In addition, he looked awkward and clumsy; he didn't look as if he would ever make it.

"What can you do with this kid? He looks like nothing," I told Charlie.

"Don't worry, Angie, I've seen this kid punch. What I'm trying to work on is to make Rocky stand shorter."

"Shorter?" I said. "He's short enough already."

Charlie laughed. "Sure! He'll be in a crouch, bobbing and weaving." Charlie demonstrated what he meant. "He'll make those suckers miss, he'll slip inside and unload. Those he don't catch on the chin, he'll wear down with body punches. I've got it figured. Rocky has the strength to do it. I've got him working on the heavy bag, punching upwards. That will build up more power in those body shots. Angie, I've a hunch this kid can do it."

I saw Rocky fight in Providence the following month. He stopped his opponent in three rounds. That was his fourth professional fight. Like Charlie, I had a hunch the kid could do it.

I don't want you to think that my life in New York was only work, and that I lived the life of a celibate monk. I did have a social life of sorts away from boxing. I had friends—of course they were fight fans. There was Joe Chernoff and Stanley Makow. Stanley lived out on Long Island and he would occasionally throw parties where I would meet girls. Most nights I would drop in at Dempsey's or Toots Shor's, or one of the bars where the sports writers hung out, and would invariably wind up at the Stage Door deli for a late night sandwich. I went to the movies and, some nights, I would drop into the Roseland ballroom. I wish I could tell you that I had a swinging time. There I was in New York. I was young and single—I was also broke! I was grateful that I could pay for my own expenses. Who could afford dates?

Nevertheless, I did have a nice lady who lived in the Capitol Hotel. Her boyfriend, an engineer, was overseas. She got lonely. She went out on a lot of dates but always came home alone—well, nearly always. When she felt lonely or didn't have a date, she would ring me. I was the substitute. It was handy, both of us living in the same hotel. I never had any expenses seeing her home! The only trouble was, she occasionally became lonely at anti-social times—I used to be very tired at work some mornings!

There were the odd dates with girls I had met either at Stanley's parties or at bars, but they were rare. I was very choosey. I didn't appreciate a pushover and I couldn't afford a steady. Girls were not high on my list of priorities.

Stanley Makow called me at the office one day and told me of a party he was throwing that Saturday at his place on Long Island. "It's going to be a nice party," he told me. "No spare guys or girls, just pairs, so bring a chick." I told him I would let him know.

I racked my brains, trying to think of a nice, good-looking girl to take to the party. I had a few days. Could I find one in that time? Was it that important anyway? Was it a slur on my manhood that I didn't have a girlfriend? What the hell!!

At lunch, at the cafeteria at the Garden, I was sitting with Joe Chernoff and a couple of other guys from the offices upstairs, and somebody mentioned Jack Cranford's name. I didn't hear the context, I didn't really care. Helen Bolton! Cranford's cousin. It was a long shot, but worth a try. I waited until six o'clock to call her, hoping that she would have arrived home from work. She had. The telephone conversation went fairly well. I got one or two laughs. I asked about Jack, I asked about her sister Frances, I asked about her mother; then I asked, "How 'bout a date on Saturday night?"

To my surprise and pleasure she said OK. We made arrange-

Mom and Pop.

The Rio boys hit the Boardwalk in Atlantic City—looking for action. *Left to right:* Andy, Angie, Nickie, Al, and Sam.

Brother Jimmy.

I'm in the Army now.

On leave—I've got muscles I haven't even used yet!

Left: "In the mood" in England.

Below: Stationed in Newbury, this is my office—and the big guy works for me.

Married to Helen. As we're both so gorgeous, let me tell you,
I'm the one on the left.

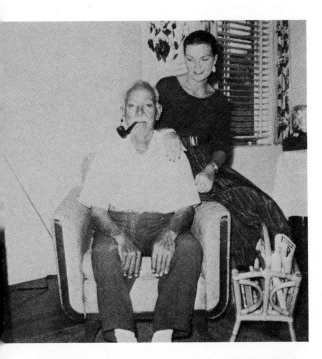

Pop stays with Helen and me in Miami—you can't see me because I'm taking the photograph.

Me and my son Jimmy. He's grown a bit since then.

Carmen Basilio, after beating
Sugar Ray Robinson at the
Yankee Stadium, New York,
in 1958. The guys holding
the champ are his managers
Joe Netro and John de John.

When the legendary Doc
Kearns talked, you listened.
That's Chris and me
on the left.

The promising newcomer's first visit to Las Vegas, with promoter Red Greb in the middle.

Renowned wrestler Gorgeous George, the master of hype.

Gorgeous Cassius learns quickly. He talks a lot, but he sure can sell tickets. Clay at the weigh-in with the menacing Sonny Liston. (Associated Press)

My great friend, "Little Big Man" Charlie Goldman, with his lion-hearted fighter Rocky Marciano. The guy in the middle is the famous referee Cy Gottfried.

The great Jack Dempsey takes time out to be friendly to the young Cassius Clay.

The Miami office. Dig the name-plates on the desk—that's in case we forgot who we were. (Time-Life)

ments, but I had one more thing to ask. "That's terrific," I said. "I'll see you Saturday. Er . . . listen, I er . . ." I was fumbling badly. I got hold of myself. "Look, Helen, you are a lovely doll, but you are tall. Would you wear flat-heeled shoes on Saturday, please?" There was a slight pause before she answered, "OK. See you Saturday." She replaced the receiver.

My favorite song was still "Green Eyes." I couldn't remember if I had ever noticed in the first place the color of Helen's eyes. I would check it out. I picked her up at her apartment on 82nd Street. Geri, the lady who owned the apartment, let me in. We remembered each other from the night of Toots Shor's, six months ago, but we didn't get into heavy talk because Helen came down the stairs almost immediately. "Great," I thought. I disliked ladies who kept you waiting. She looked sensational.

We caught the subway, then a train to Long Island. I kept the conversation light and got her smiling at one or two of my best jokes. She confessed to me, at a later date, that she never understood any of my jokes, she only smiled to be polite. Still, I didn't know that at the time. To me, we were getting on nice and easy. I discovered that her eyes were brown—you can't have everything!

I can't say that the party at Stanley's was an unqualified success. To start with, it was held in the basement which was a little damp. That in itself wasn't too bad, but I had a bad sinus problem, and I must confess it was rather embarrassing continually spitting into my handkerchief. What could I do? Use the floor?

There was dancing and drinking. It was a nice crowd, swell people, no loud mouths. Stanley was impressed with Helen. "How the hell did an ugly son of a gun like you meet a beautiful chick like Helen?" he asked me as Helen and I sat tucked away in a corner of the room.

"It's a gift, Stanley, I got charm," I said as I quickly brought my handkerchief into action once more. Helen saw the funny side of it.

"Yea," she said smiling, "charm is what you've got, but I think you need this." She reached into her handbag and handed me some tissues.

We danced to a few Sinatra and Dick Haymes records, and I fetched her a rum and coke a couple of times, to keep my whisky and sodas company. We talked. She casually mentioned the fact that I didn't have a car. "Who needs a car in New York?" I told her, and quickly explained that it was so much easier using the trains and subway, and that walking is good for you, and that I never had parking problems. I didn't bother to explain that I couldn't drive and didn't have the money to buy a car. I learned that she had left Georgia at the age of ten, and moved to Salisbury, North Carolina. At nineteen, her present age, she had decided to have a shot at modeling in the big city. Her mom had arranged for her to stay with Geri Marrott, she had found a job, and here she was for the last six months, a resident of New York.

I told her about my work, and I was delighted that she was so interested in the fight game. We talked about Jack Cranford. I told her I did remember that they really were cousins. We even got into the lousy seat she had at the fight, and the "Angelo, Angela" routine went down well too. We laughed a lot.

On the journey back to New York, we made a date for the following day. We would meet early and spend the day at the beach. Back in Manhattan, Helen caught a cab and went home. I wished I could have pre-paid the cab, but I didn't have the bread. I needed all I had for the following day.

The weather was on our side; it reached the low eighties at midday. We swam, we sunbathed, I tried not to stare too much at her gorgeous figure, but I did try to flex my muscles when I caught her looking at me. I soon forgot all about that—what you see is what you get! The day went pleasantly by and, bronzed by the sun, we went back to Manhattan to a cute little Italian restaurant where the food was good and the prices reasonable. I promised her that if she came to the fights on Friday night, her seat would not give her a nosebleed. She accepted.

After I had seen her home and received a gentle kiss on the cheek, I walked back to the Capitol Hotel thinking about the day. It had been great. OK, I was broke, but I would get through. I was looking forward to seeing her again.

The weeks rushed past, and Helen and I got into a kind of routine, seeing each other two or three nights a week. Every Friday night she came to the Garden. I had a regular seat for her. It was ringside, directly behind the corner where I was working. During the fights I would turn and look at her, and she always seemed to know when I was going to look because she would catch my eye and smile.

On September 18, after a lot of persuasion, I took Helen to South Philadelphia to meet my family. Now, let me explain this. I wasn't taking her to meet my family because we were committed.

We were not. We hadn't even mentioned "engaged," let alone marriage. I was making twenty-five to thirty dollars a week. I couldn't keep a cold, let alone a wife. The fact was, I wanted to go home, and I wanted Helen with me. I guess I wanted to show her off. As it worked out, she was the biggest thing to hit the neighborhood in a long time.

Dad had invited every known relative, and some unknown, to the house for a welcome home get-together, all in my honor. Except for phone calls, they had not seen or heard from me for nine months. It was like the return of the prodigal son.

Arriving home was wonderful bedlam. There was kissing, hugging, introductions, questions—ten conversations going on at once. When Italian families are in a party mood they are not the softest-spoken people in the world. The noise was awesome. Helen, looking lovely, was very charming and polite, perhaps a little shy—maybe she was in shock! When we sat down to eat, the volume of noise diminished to a happy background roar!

My sisters, Josephine and Mary, under Pop's expert direction, had prepared a mouth-watering feast—providing you like pasta. I most certainly did, but Helen, although she enjoyed it, had her figure to think about—she was a model after all—so she didn't consume the vast quantities that were necessary to placate an Italian chef—my pop! "Wassa matta, 'Ellen, you no like the food?" Pop's English was not yet up to Oxford standard.

Helen tactfully tried to explain. Jimmy, as smooth and cool as ever, came to her rescue. "Hey Pop, what are you trying to do? We got us a beautiful doll here. You wanna ruin her figure? Are you getting so old you don't appreciate a great shape?"

"I'm not a gettin' old, sonny. I see what a you mean. Let's have some more vino, that a don't ruin any figures." Pop poured the wine. "Salud," he toasted. The answering "Salud," from everyone at the table, nearly shattered my eardrums. Being home again with my family gave me a warm, satisfying feeling. Only one thing marred the pleasure. Mom was no longer there, and I missed her. I didn't say what I was thinking, because I knew it would upset Pop and spoil a happy and lovely evening.

Helen and I made our farewells early, not because we weren't having fun, but we wanted to leave with Louise and Jimmy, who were tired and wanted to go. As Mary was living with Dad, there was no room for Helen and me to stay the night. We were staying at Jimmy's place. There was really no room for us there either. We slept on the floor in the sitting-room. If Jimmy or Louise wanted to visit the bathroom during the night, they had to step over us. After the consumption of so much wine, their journey did become necessary.

Jimmy and Louise had met Helen in New York, and they had gotten on well together. This trip cemented their friendship. I was pleased, because I loved and respected my brother and his wife, and I wanted their approval. Not only did I want my family to like Helen, like most guys, I wanted to show off my girlfriend to my pals and win their approval. Now, as you know, South Philly was a predominantly Italian area. Most of my pals and their girlfriends were of Italian extraction. You can imagine the excitement I caused when I brought home a genuine Anglo-Saxon, long-legged, New York model. Jimmy made the understatement of the year when he said to Helen, "Angie's friends are looking forward to meeting you."

At the party my pals threw for me that night, Helen was the center of attention. If they were impressed by her looks, they were completely overwhelmed by the southern drawl. As at all Italian parties of that time, the guys gravitated to one room to talk "men's talk," and the gals were segregated in another room. Don't ask me why; it's an old custom. I have never figured it out. The local chicks were throwing a fusillade of questions at Helen, mainly about clothes, hairdos, and all that stuff. Helen loved it. That was when I joined the guys in the adjoining room and began to see the benefits of old customs!

Later in the evening, when we were de-segregated, Helen, at the girls' insistence, demonstrated how a model should walk. She placed a quarter in between the cheeks of her buttocks—fortunately she was wearing slacks—placed a hastily found small hardback book on her head, and sashayed around the room without dropping the quarter from its precarious position. She got a great hand from everyone. Then followed the hilarious sight of volunteers of both sexes trying to imitate Helen's walk. A lot of books were dropped, not to mention quarters. It became Helen's "party piece" every time she came to South Philly.

My next visit to Philly was at Christmas, but this time I went alone. Helen had gone home to North Carolina. I phoned her regularly, friendly calls. I told her I was looking forward to seeing her. I gave her an update on what I was doing—just friendly, nothing mushy. It would be late January 1949 when I saw her again. I was sorry that we couldn't have spent Christmas and the New Year together.

New York had settled down, back to work after recovering from the annual celebrations. The festivities had hardly made Chris miss a beat. He was back at work, in the office, on the phone—hustle, bustle. We continued, as if 1949 had not arrived. It was business as usual.

Chris was handling twelve fighters at the time, and he was arranging bouts for them in and out of the state of New York. He used various trainers to work with the fighters, and Chickie looked after five of them. Normally the trainer would go out of town with the fighter and work the corner. The better paid fighters would use two or even three corner men, but the less well-known fighters could only afford one guy in the corner, and that guy had to be able to do everything. Working around New York was a breeze, as Chris would always be there to handle the business side, but on the road it was a different ball game. You had to deal with the promoter, and make certain you picked up your correct purse without any last-minute invented deductions, although naughty tricks like that did not happen often. The corner man would check out the medication needed for cuts, bruises, and swellings; and make certain he had smelling salts, bandages, vaseline, and other requirements like scissors—how can you forget scissors, but you do! Gloves, shorts, robes, protectors, all part of the boxer's wardrobe, had to be at hand—some fighters would arrive with only a towel! Arranging the time schedule for the "pickup" was my job anyway, so when Chris told me I was going out on the road with the fighters I felt I could handle it. It would be my first time dealing with the business side, and my first time as a "boss" in the corner. I was excited about the whole deal. Sure, there was one heck of a lot I didn't know, but I believed it better to give it a try and fail, than not to try at all. Chris told me that I would make fifteen dollars for the night—it sounded good to me.

Chris supplied a car and driver, a guy by the name of Dick Vick. I would arrange the "meet" with the fighter, depending on where he lived and where we were going. Dick and I would pick the guy up and set off to the venue.

First time out I had no problems. It all went smoothly and our fighter won. It continued that way, running smoothly. Of course, our fighters didn't always win. I worked the corner two or three nights a week, and everyone seemed satisfied. It wasn't until I worked with Carmen Basilio, years later, that I realized how amateurish I must have been and how little I knew about my craft. Over the years I have discovered that you never know all about boxing, you are forever learning. Hopefully, you get better at it, that's all.

That first week I earned forty-five dollars from my out-of-town corner work, but when Friday came along Chris missed out giving me my wages. I didn't say anything, thinking he would pay me my wages later. Another week, then another week went by, and I still didn't say anything. After all, I was making more money than before, but I wondered what would happen if I stopped going out of town. I never mentioned my wages, and I never got them!

Helen and I took up where we left off. Working every day at the office, and three and sometimes four nights a week at the fights, cut down my free time, but I still saw Helen a couple of nights a week. She became the most attractive regular fixture at the Garden, sitting in her regular seat behind me. Some nights I would take her to a ball game, where I would overload her with dogs, beer, peanuts, and popcorn. She left most of it, but I could tell she liked being looked after, even if she wasn't too crazy about baseball. Sometimes we would catch a movie or simply go and eat. On Garden nights after I had finished work, we would go to Toots Shor's or the Château Madrid or some other up-market night-spot.

The only problem with going to those places was the cost. Helen knew that I was over-extending myself by taking her there, and sometimes when the check arrived I would ask her if I could borrow a ten or twenty to help pay the bill. She didn't keep a score of what I borrowed; neither did I. I only knew that if and when I made any real money I would make it up to her. I had confidence in myself, and felt that things would work out. I couldn't get worked up over a few bucks. When I saw my pals at the bar, be it Toots', the Château, Weber's, or the Ringside, I would be first in line to buy the drinks. I would sometimes pay with another five or ten borrowed from Helen. As I look back on those times I am fully aware that I must have been a hell of a date! I suppose that I should have spelled it out, and told Helen, if you come out with me, you go dutch. We virtually did anyway, but I did it my way— I paid until I was broke, and then I asked Helen to chip in. I have to admit, she was terrific. She was beautiful, she paid her way and she had faith in me, and never tried to talk me into getting a proper job. Helen was making good money, far more than I. She dressed well, she was intelligent; the only thing I couldn't figure out was why the heck she went out with me.

I would pick Helen up at work on 7th Avenue. Her boss, a tall, middle-aged success, who had hot pants for her, would barely nod to me. I was dying to kick him in the butt. I said to Helen, "Your boss is really crazy about me," the sarcasm dripping out of my mouth. "Don't he realize he's too old for you, not to mention too tall?"

"He thinks I'm crazy seeing you. He calls you "the little Italian." He says I should find myself a nice Jewish boy," she said, looking slightly down into my eyes. She was wearing those darn high heels again.

"Why Jewish? You're not Jewish," I said, smiling falsely as I thought how I'd like to kick that SOB in the butt.

"I know, honey, I'm not Catholic either." How could a nice Italian boy answer that? Helen and I never discussed race or religion. We had no hang-ups on that score. I guess it may be simplistic, but we judged people on how they acted, not what they were. We either liked them or we didn't.

We never discussed our relationship. If we talked about the future, we were talking about "tomorrow" or "next week." A big deal would be "next month." Helen would go home periodically, and I never questioned her as to whether she dated there. I didn't really want to know, but I suspected that she did. I must confess that I occasionally slipped a pretty companion into the Capitol Hotel. Heck! I wasn't in the position for a commitment, and I didn't think Helen wanted one either. Yet we wanted to be together. To sum it up, we were going steady, but not *steady* steady. I guess you know what I mean, and if you do, it's more than I did at the time.

CHAPTER EIGHT

GIVE MY REGARDS TO BROADWAY

"There was a new Heavyweight Champion too, Jersey Joe Walcott. Joe enjoyed his deserved success, but he was unaware that a guy by the name of Rocky Marciano, boxing out in Providence, Rhode Island, was relentlessly moving towards a confrontation."

I was going to North Adams, Massachusetts. I was looking after Bob Isler, a young, game fighter handled by the office. I asked Chris how much I would make on the night. I had bills to pay and needed money like a gal with a forty-eight bust needs a bra. Chris changed our financial setup once again.

"You're doing a lotta work with these fighters, why don't you take a piece of the action?"

A warning bell rang in my head. I tried to cover my apprehension and said easily, "Sounds interesting; what do you mean exactly?"

"Well, you are looking after some of the kids, like Bob, right?" I nodded my head. He continued persuasively, "I'll tell you what we will do. We'll do a deal on the kids you take out on the road. You take a third, the fighter two-thirds, and I'll take all expenses off the top. OK?" He began looking up a phone number from his desk directory. The matter was closed. Chris never had the time to get into a long, drawn-out discussion with me. If Chris thought it was OK, it was OK.

Lately, he seemed edgy and preoccupied as if he had a lot on his mind. Business wasn't as good as last year, and I guessed that was worrying him, although he hadn't said anything to me. Geraldine, his wife, had made an unusual remark the other night when Helen and I had baby sat for them. Gerri suggested, when she and Chris arrived back home late, that Helen and I stay the night. We decided, however, to call a cab—Helen had work in the morning and needed to go home to change.

"If you waited till the morning, you could catch the train and save money," Gerri said, shaking her head in disgust at our foolishness. "Money don't grow on trees, you know. Don't you know what's going on, Angelo? Don't you read the papers? Save your money—tomorrow we could all be looking for jobs."

"Gerri, leave the kid alone," Chris interfered. "It ain't tomorrow yet." He saw Helen and me to the waiting cab "Goodnight, kids. Thanks for babysitting; I appreciate it. I hope I'll see you at the Garden on Friday," he said to Helen. "I'll see you tomorrow, Angie. So far we still have our jobs, right?" He smiled and gently punched me on the shoulder. I felt like a million dollars. Chris had that effect on me.

Helen cuddled up to me in the back of the cab. "What did Gerri mean about not reading the newspapers?" she asked me.

"Oh, I guess she meant, hadn't I read about the rumor that Sunnyside was closing. One hall closing don't mean the end of boxing in New York. Though it's not like Gerri to worry," I reflected. "Let's forget it," I said, putting my arm around her shoulder and drawing her even closer. We smooched all the way back to New York.

The hall was about one third full, which, considering it was a large hall, made it look empty. Isler was going in against Saint Paul. On paper it looked a tough fight. Boy, was it ever! I don't think North Adams had ever seen such a brutal, bloody affair, which ended in a win for Bob Isler. I did my best to patch up Bob, but for the first time as a corner man I was painfully aware of my inexperience and inadequacies. The small crowd was ecstatic over the fight, but that was no consolation for me.

I collected the purse from the promoter, who was happy with the fight, but unhappy with the crowd attendance. In the dressing room I settled up with Bob. I deducted Chris's expenses, put his money in an envelope to give to him in the morning, and gave the other two-thirds of the money to Bob.

"Hey, Angie, you ain't taken your cut," Bob mumbled through cut and swollen lips. I looked at his bruised, scarred face, and my heart went out to him.

"Forget it, Bob. This one's on me." I turned away and busied myself packing my little black bag. Strangely enough, the drive back was a lot of fun. Dick Vick was a happy guy, although a little weird—he would never put on his dashboard lights, so on the trips at night the interior of the car would be in total darkness. He would tell us the latest jokes he had picked up from his Broadway pals, Bob cracked a few gags, and I told the stories I had heard at Stillman's. We had some laughs; the maulings and beatings of an hour ago were forgotten—that's the fight game!

When Joe Louis retired on May 1, 1949, he left a vacant championship. Chris had told me weeks before it was officially announced that it would be Ezzard Charles against Jersey Joe Walcott for the title, and he was right. Unfortunately, the fight was going to be held in Chicago, not New York. Chris was not happy. He was making arrangements to go to Cincinnati for the Lesvenich–Maxim, light-heavyweight championship fight. "Go round to the Forest, Angie, see Jack Kearns and give him this envelope and pick up my tickets. Can you believe what's going on? Cincinnati gets Joey Maxim against Gus Lesvenich, Detroit is getting Jake LaMotta against Marcel Cerdan, and Chicago the Charles–Walcott fight. New York is getting zilch."

I made my way to the Forest Hotel, where a lot of out-of-town fight people stayed. I'd run this kind of errand for Chris lots of times. I got to meet a lot of new people, and they got to know me. At first I was "Chris's kid brother," but eventually they discovered that my name was Angelo.

Joe (Doc) Kearns had just flown in from Cincinnati, where he had his fighter, Joey Maxim, preparing for the title shot. He was sitting in a bathrobe talking to a guy I thought I knew from the New York Boxing Commission. I gave Doc the envelope, and without bothering to open and check the contents, he handed me a similar-looking envelope. Reaching into the pocket of his bathrobe, he took out a roll of bills. He peeled off a twenty and gave it to me for my trouble—what trouble! I left feeling good. I shared the elevator with a sharp, well-dressed guy that I was sure I had seen before. I introduced myself.

"Hi, I'm Angelo Dundee. Don't I know you?"

"No," he said, "you don't, but I've heard of your brother Chris. I'm Frankie Carbo."

Frankie Carbo! Of course, I'd seen his picture in the Los Angeles papers. I have a great memory for faces. It was alleged that he was a "Mister Big" in organized crime. So that is where I had seen him before—in newspaper photographs! I smiled back at him, trying not to stare.

The elevator stopped, the door opened at the ground floor. He gave me a nod and walked out of the elevator. Unfortunately, he didn't walk out of my life. Our paths crossed again.

If Frankie Carbo was considered "infamous" by some, I did meet people who were definitely considered "famous"—Jack Klugman, star of *Quincy*, who went to school with my brother Jimmy back in South Philly; Eddie Fisher, who sometimes stayed at the Capitol Hotel, as did Nat King Cole. They were fight fans and always seemed to find the time to have a few words with me. They would give me a "Hello, Angie," like they were pleased to see me. I tell you, I felt good when someone famous acknowledged me and took time out to speak with me, especially if Helen was with me. It made me feel like somebody, not just Chris's kid brother.

Mildred, Helen's mother, came to New York for a few weeks' visit. She stayed with Helen at the apartment. It didn't take me long to see that they got on great together, more like sisters than mother and daughter. It was no hardship for Helen or me to take Mildred along on our dates. They were fun. The only problem was the usual one—money, or, to be more precise, the lack of it. After a fine meal, when the check came along, I would invariably find myself a little short of the cash to pay it. I would be as discreet as possible when borrowing a ten or twenty from Helen, but sometimes I would catch Mildred's eyes taking in the picture. Stupidly, I was even more eager than usual to buy my bar pals drinks. I guess I was just trying to show what a big man I was. Anyhow, it only resulted in another whispered request to Helen for another loan. We always had a good time, and nothing was ever said, but I was aware of the situation, and aware that Mildred was aware, too! The alternative, as I figured it, was not to go out at all, and that did not seem like a good idea.

I was making more money than when Helen and I had first dated, but I seemed to have less. Going away with the fighters, and being "boss" man, made me more vulnerable to be hit upon. One or two of the guys were married and always in need of a buck. I would get hit for tens or twenties, which were always going to be paid back after their next fight. After their next fight . . . there always seemed to be another next fight. Get the picture? My two pals, Joe Chernoff and Stanley Makow, kept telling me that I was crazy, and even Chris had a word with me. We were in the office settling up with a fighter. We were sorting out his expenses and paying what was left of his share. The guy took his money. "Angie," he said, "OK if I settle with you after the next fight? I gotta lot of problems at home right now." Chris looked at me.

"Sure, no problem," I said. After the fighter had left Chris pointed his finger in my direction and began laying in at me.

"What the hell you doing? You wanna end up broke? What are you, some kind of bank or something? If you wanna go into the loan business, I'll introduce you to some of the boys. You know these kids ain't going to pay you back. You ain't a charitable organization, are you?" I shrugged my shoulders. What could I say? But he wasn't finished with me yet. "Angelo, you gotta say no. Tell them you ain't got it and I'll tell you something for nothing— you ain't got it." Boy, was he right!

I knew he was right, but I couldn't get myself to worry seriously about money. I got by, but the continuing hassle was getting me down. I needed a break. It was Helen's birthday on May 18. She wanted to go home for the weekend, and she wanted me to go with her. I had never been to North Carolina; in fact I had once rashly promised myself that I never would go there, but what the hell, it might be fun. We decided we would leave on Saturday morning, after the Friday night fights.

Charlie Goldman called me on the Friday morning. He told me that Rocky had four straight KOs in a row, and none of them had lasted longer than five rounds. Rocky was still fighting out of Brockton, Massachusetts, and Charlie gave me an open invitation to come over to see Rocky fight. I wished them both luck and got back to the day's work. I wanted to clear my desk and have a worry-free weekend.

That night, after the fights, Helen went straight home. She wanted to pack, ready for the trip home. I had no such problem— I didn't have that much to pack.

Al Buck, of the *New York Post*, found me aimlessly hanging around the Garden. He suggested we go to Dempsey's for a drink. We settled in and talked about who we thought would be the next heavyweight champion—Charles or Walcott—and we both went for Jersey Joe. After our second round of whiskys, Jack Dempsey joined us at the bar, our usual hangout. I casually mentioned that I was going to North Carolina with Helen in the morning. Al said that it sounded like a cue for a song. Jack looked at me without speaking, then he started.

"Angie, I know you and Helen have been going out quite a spell now . . ." He hesitated. I was getting worried, and it showed. "Hey kid, don't get worried. What I want to say is that I got Helen's phone number from Gerri Marrott—she used to be quite a regular. I gave Helen a call and asked her over for supper. Hey, cut it out will you," he said, seeing my chin hit my chest. "This is all before she met you, you dummy. Would I try and cut in on a buddy?" The relief flooded all over me. "Anyway," Jack continued, "she came over, and would you believe this, she brought Geri along too. We had supper—the three of us—and that, brother, was that. I'm only telling you 'cause I want you to know what a great lady you got there. She's a nice kid; take care of her."

I beamed at him "You bet your life, Jack." North Carolina, here I come.

Salisbury, North Carolina, was a railroad town, maybe it still is—I haven't been there for years. I was a little apprehensive when I arrived, although Helen kept assuring me that I would have a good time. As usual, she was right.

Mildred greeted me like an old friend, and was delighted when I presented her with a five-pound cheesecake I had bought in New York. I didn't buy her the cake to get on her good side—I honestly enjoy giving people I like gifts. She introduced me to her husband, George, and I liked Helen's father immediately. To me, he typified the old covered-wagon settler. Straightforward and straight-talking, independent and capable. In many ways we were complete opposites. He was a tall, lean, sandy-haired Anglo-Saxon, and I was a short, stocky Italian. He was one of those lucky people who can turn their hands to practically anything. He could plant a broomstick, and it would grow. I got problems even changing a light bulb!

I took up his invitation to go blackberry-picking. Now I can get around Manhattan with no problem, and you can put me down in the middle of South Philly and I'll get by—but blackberry-picking! The Georgia boy went sure-footed across the untamed fields, over muddy creeks and small, sparkling rivers without putting a foot wrong. To cross one of the many meandering water obstacles, he grabbed a branch from an overhanging tree and swung himself across—the guy was Tarzan!

As for myself, how can I put it? I was Cheeta! Not that I could swing from tree to tree—I was Cheeta the Chump! Eventually we got back to the house with blackberries even! But before we did, I fell, or should I say slipped, down the muddy bank of a river and took an early shower. Fortunately, all that was bruised was my pride.

They say time flies when you are enjoying yourself, and that about sums up the weekend; it went by all too quickly. I liked Salisbury, North Carolina, and I forgave it for its anti-social drinking laws; I even got used to the idea of taking a bag-wrapped bottle of booze with me when I went out to eat. They called it brown-bagging.

It had been a much needed break for me. It cleaned my mind, and let me glimpse the kind of future I wanted. I knew that I wanted Helen to be a part of my life, but I was fully aware that I had nothing to offer her. I needed to make something of myself. I wanted to have my own fighters, to steer their careers and contribute something worthwhile. I had no conception then of how much chance, luck, and perseverance would play, not only in my life, but it seems to me, everyone's life.

I have a theory about luck. The harder people work for their goals, the luckier they seem to become.

The summer of 1949 arrived. On July 16 Jake LaMotta became the Middleweight Champion of the World. I knew Jake only slightly at that time. I didn't dream that he and I would be close friends a few years later. There was a new Heavyweight Champion too, Jersey Joe Walcott. Joe enjoyed his deserved success, but he was unaware that a guy by the name of Rocky Marciano, boxing out in Providence, Rhode Island, was relentlessly moving towards a confrontation.

The weather in New York was hot and humid, and Chris put the lack of business down to the weather. We both knew it wasn't the real reason, but hell, we had to put the blame somewhere.

I decided to go with Helen and visit her family for the weekend. Chris was spending the time at his home on Long Island, and I saw no point in staying in New York on my own. Besides, I missed Helen. Who needed another reason?

This time we didn't go to Salisbury, North Carolina; we went to a town I had never heard of—Macon, in the state of Georgia. We were booked into the Magnolia Court as Mildred's guests.

Mildred Bolton, besides being quite a looker, was a clever, hardworking lady. Although her home was in Salisbury, she worked three hundred miles away in Macon for her brother, Tena Cranford. Mildred ran his establishment, the Magnolia Court Motel and Grill, which owed a major part of its success to her fine management. She was completely involved in her job responsibilities and obviously enjoyed it, but the separation from her husband was tough to live with.

George would commute most weekends. It was difficult for both of them. I guess being away from each other put a strain on their marriage, but neither wanted to give up their jobs. Their marriage appeared strong enough to overcome the problem. (To date, they are still happily together—maybe absence does make the heart grow fonder!)

Mildred and George knew the value of money, so it was no surprise to me when Helen truthfully answered my question the way that she did. It was our first night in Macon, and we had enjoyed a fine meal on our own as Mildred was too busy to join us, and George was not arriving until much later. We were both in a warm, relaxed mood, and we decided to take a short stroll around the grounds of the hotel. The evening was dry and warm, and the fragrance of the night didn't clash with Helen's captivating perfume. The sky was alive with stars and the air was filled with the sound of crickets and the occasional croak of a frog. There was background music coming from the hotel. They were playing "Laura." The music suited the mood perfectly.

We stood still, holding hands, completely immersed in the breathtaking magic of the night. It was a romantic moment to cherish. I then asked Helen a question, and blew the whole thing!

I asked Helen what her parents thought about me. How dumb can you get? At a moment like that who turns to his girl and says, "Do your parents like me?" I'll tell you who—me! Well, if you ask a question, you normally get an answer. Helen answered me. "They like you fine, Angie. Daddy thinks you're a big laugh, he really likes you, and Mom thinks that you are er . . ." She hesitated.

"Yea? She thinks I am what?" We no longer held hands.

"Well, honey, she thinks you are a nice boy, and very good-looking, but she doesn't think you will ever have more than two cents to rub together." She turned and faced me. "Let's be honest, Angie, you spend it as fast as you get it. Every time we go out with Mom you buy drinks for everyone at the bar. Mom said to me when we were at Weber's Bar in New York, 'I swear Angelo can't know all those people at the bar.' "

"There were three or four reporter friends of mine at the bar that night. I don't usually do that," I protested.

She took my hand reassuringly, "She does like you, you know that, but I suppose she doesn't think that you will ever amount to anything."

I wanted to defend my case, but I wasn't too certain that I could, and for a second there I agreed with Mildred. But, what the hell! It was a beautiful night and Helen was a beautiful girl, so I did what I should have done in the first place before I opened my flabby mouth. I took her in my arms and kissed her. It didn't solve anything, but it sure made me feel good.

George had arrived, and all four of us spent Sunday at South Carolina's famous Myrtle Beach. Helen had bought me a pair of yellow bathing shorts which were rather daringly cut. So much so, that I got one or two funny looks from other sunbathers. The other guys on the beach were big, blond, Nordic types, wearing very conservative swim-shorts. Mildred suggested I get a top to my shorts to cover my hairy chest—those Nordic types don't have hairy chests—and I guess Mildred and Helen were worried that I was humiliating those guys with my masculinity. Well, that's my story!

Sun-tanned and full of resolve, I returned to New York, and all too quickly slipped back into my usual lifestyle. I was happy and I was still learning (in life, you are always learning), but as far as making money was concerned I hadn't moved even one rung up the ladder. I wanted to improve my situation, and not only to impress Mildred. I personally would have welcomed more bread and more control over my own life, but circumstances and my lack of positive action eroded my determination. It was all too easy letting Chris make the decisions, and the satisfaction I got from being boss-man in the corner suffocated my ambition. Sure, I wanted my own fighters. Yea, I wanted to call the shots, but it was easier just to carry on as I was, letting someone else take the final responsibility. I was having fun. I loved New York and I enjoyed being known in the swanky bars and clubs—even if I was only known as Chris's kid brother.

The months rolled by. The memories of the summer began to fade; soon people were wearing top coats, scarfs, and gloves, and another new year approached.

I spent the holidays in South Philly. Helen had gone to North Carolina to be with her parents. She was missed in Philadelphia, not only by me, but by my family and friends, too. During the fall, Helen and I had made a couple of quick trips to South Philly and had gone to parties at friends' houses. They were getting to know her better, and were disappointed that she wasn't with me for the Christmas holidays. I was disappointed too—next year for sure, I promised myself.

1950 began to slide by. On the surface everything seemed the same, but subtle changes were taking place. It wasn't until the spring of 1950 that the realization that things had changed came home to me.

Chris arrived at the office, as usual, around ten-thirty. I handed him the mail. "What's that?" I asked him, indicating a large buff-colored envelope displaying in large bold print the name of an insurance company. Chris stared at it, then began tapping his desk top with one of the pointed corners of the envelope.

"Why don't you open it? The repetitive tap was getting on my nerves.

"You know that Fort Hamilton and Sunnyside have dried up, don't you?"

He was talking about two halls that presented boxing. I had heard about their closing down, so I answered, "Sure, so?" I wondered what the envelope had to do with it.

"Look, kid," Chris didn't look happy and his voice was tired. "Things ain't going so good. That's another two venues gone, and there ain't hardly anything around here any more. You will be lucky if you work twice this week, and let me tell you, the out-of-town deals don't make me enough to pay the phone bill. Do you hear what I'm saying?"

I heard all right, and I didn't like what I heard.

"You see this?" He waved the envelope at my face. "This is my insurance course application. Yea, that's right." He went on to answer the question forming in my mind. "I'm gonna take an insurance course. I'm gonna sell insurance. I gotta make a living and I hear this is a good racket."

I could only stare at him. I didn't know what to say. What was he telling me? Were we going to close down? I knew one thing for sure, there was no way I was going to be an insurance salesman. No offense to that noble profession, but it wasn't for me, and I couldn't really see Chris doing it either. I would have to wait and see what happened. For the next few months the office remained open, and we managed to arrange bouts for our reduced stable of fighters. I worked enough to keep my head above water—just. Helen understood, and didn't worry about not going to the expensive joints; she had only known me broke, so I guess she hardly noticed the difference.

Right at the back of my mind was a feeling of anxiety; I tried to keep it submerged, but at lonely moments, and I had many, this feeling of impending doom would surface and I had a tough fight to keep it from taking over.

I had noticed that Chris and Gerri, and even Helen, at some unguarded moments, gave the impression of having worries. I guess it was the uncertainty of everything. I have found in life that very often the uncertainty of events is far worse than the actual realization. I wasn't as philosophical then as I am now, so I did the best I could and tried to bury my fears.

Chris was hustling and bustling as usual, yet he still found time to study his insurance course. Each day I wondered if Chris would say that he was closing the office, leaving me on my own. I had no plans for that eventuality. I do not think I really believed it would happen.

In the fall of 1950 the uncertainty was over. I knew what was going to happen.

I had been at Stillman's Gym, working with Bill Bossio, a good young featherweight that Chris handled. After the workout, Bill and I swapped a few stories and had a laugh. I liked the kid and hoped that he would do well. I gave him the arrangements for the following night's fight, and I made him write down the time of the pickup. That way, if he was late, he couldn't say that he had made a mistake over the time. Bill wasn't like that, but a few of the guys were. They had an answer for everything, so I began making them write down all the arrangements. Would you believe, some of those characters lost the paper.

I made my way to the Garden cafeteria to meet Joe Chernoff, and as I had no plans for the afternoon I thought Joe might have a bright idea on how to kill the rest of the day.

Chris was out of town. He had been talking to some guys from Miami over the telephone for the past four or five weeks, and he had gone south to the Sunshine State to follow up and check it out. I was hazy about the proposition, but I knew if there was a deal floating around, Chris would nail it down. I was hoping Chris could arrange for our fighters to get some action in Florida. Besides the business side of it, it would be nice to get a tan.

Joe was eating already. "Don't sit down," he said to me. "Chris is looking for you. He said for you to go straight to the office. He must have missed you at Stillman's."

The news dulled my appetite.

This is the way it went down. Chris was going to Miami. He was selling his home on Long Island, and he and Gerri would relocate on Miami Beach. He was going to promote fights on the Beach; there was a venue all set up.

I could keep the office—office, hell, it was my home. The rent was paid until the end of the month. If I wanted I could have Bill Bossio to manage, and if things worked out in Miami, and I wasn't doing anything special, I could come down and join him.

No sweat, no fuss. "Good luck, kid. I'll be in touch." That was about it!

How did I feel? The words "numb," "scared," "anxious," and "stupefied" come to mind. Hell, I didn't know how I felt. That's the way it was, that's the way it was going to be.

Underneath the pure funk, a tingle of excitement began to seep through. I had my own fighter, Bill Bossio. Heck, I was a manager. I would get by.

CHAPTER NINE

MIAMI

"The fight, that night, was something else! Mickey was working alone in Bob's corner and I was working alone in John's corner. . . . in the second round . . . Bob fell heavily against the ropes. The top rope fell off! . . . Mickey grabbed up (one) end . . . and yelled at me to do the same. . . . there we stood holding the rope until the bell rang. . . . We dropped the rope . . . and began our duties as corner men. As the bell rang . . . we removed the stools, rushed over to . . . the rope, and stood . . . holding (it). Mickey shouted over to me, 'Hey, Angie, tell your guy, if he is going to whack my guy again, do it in the middle of the ring.' "

In one way Helen was responsible for me coming to Miami in the first place. During the summer of 1951, when I was working on my own in New York, Helen, who was staying in Salisbury, went on a visit to her Aunt Nora and Uncle John who lived in Miami. While she was there she met up with Chris, who was promoting boxing on the Beach. He was doing OK, and he suggested to Helen that I could be of use if I decided to come down. Nothing definite, not an offer, but a suggestion. When she returned to New York, Helen pursued the subject.

We were having supper at the Stage Door Deli; Helen was telling me of the wonders of Miami Beach.

"You don't have to sell me on Miami," I said. "I loved it way back in '43. Did you fly down from South Carolina?" I asked.

"No, I drove. You know, it was so hot I couldn't put the top down." (She had a convertible.) "It sure was lovely, Angie. Can you imagine, if you were working down there you could go swimming practically every day." The waiter arrived with the sandwiches. "Do you want another beer, Angelo?" He knew me, I was a regular.

"Yea, bring another couple. Have you ever been to Miami Beach?" I asked him.

"Are you kidding? Me and the wife go every year. It's got more class than Atlantic City, and the weather's always good. I'll get the beers. Eat and enjoy."

Helen smiled and started to attack the corned beef sandwich. "I'll give Chris a ring," I said.

I had got used to working on my own, and I still enjoyed New York. I was working with lots of different fighters: Charlie Salas, a good middleweight; Alex Fimbres, a Mexican kid who looked like he was developing into a very good featherweight; and there was Bill Bossio, who was doing real well. Being out from under Chris's protective wing was good for me. I was getting work as a corner man. Although a lot of venues were drying up, I still found some work. I went further afield. There were a few promotions in Massachusetts at North Adam, Pitsfield, and West Springfield. Willie Pep's home town, Hartford, Connecticut, was putting on fights, and once or twice I had worked the Olympia in my home town of Philadelphia.

Those nights were great. My pals would come to the fights, and they would shout for the fighter in my corner whether they liked him or not. Naturally, on those trips I always got to see Pop. I think he was a little proud of me. I was getting by, but I could foresee that things would get harder as, slowly but surely, the promotions were drying up. Television, although helping boxing with one hand, was killing all forms of entertainment with the other hand. It was still a big novelty to sit home and watch TV, and once you had bought your set, you wanted your money's worth. People were staying home and living their lives through television.

Miami did sound attractive, but I wasn't certain yet if I wanted to leave New York. Helen spoke to me about Chris in August, and it wasn't until October that I finally made the move.

The autumn months in New York had been a lot of fun. I met and made new friends with whom I still have a strong and fond relationship. Mickey Davies was a young guy who lived only for the fight game. Managing a fighter now and then, involving himself in a promotion when he could, he made a living.

We had a crazy experience together that we will never forget. Mickey was working with a fighter by the name of Bob Garner. He was scheduled to fight in Charleston, West Virginia, against my guy, Johnny Haynes.

The weigh-in went just fine, but when Mickey and I and our two fighters decided to walk around and take in the sights we ran into a problem. Johnny Haynes was a black guy from Los Angeles, and the local populace didn't take too kindly to a black man, who was fighting the local hero, walking around the white part of town. As Mickey put it, "Let's get the hell out of here before the dumb bastards shoot the lot of us." We did just that. I thought, what else is going to go wrong? I found out.

The fight, that night, was something else! Mickey was working alone in Bob's corner and I was working alone in John's corner—we were both saving on expenses. The first round went about even, but in the second round Johnny caught Bob a good shot and Bob fell heavily against the ropes. The top rope fell off! There we were, with one quarter of the ring without a top rope. It obviously hadn't been secured properly. Mickey grabbed up the end of the rope nearest to him, and yelled at me to do the same. I rushed over, picked up the other end of the rope, and there we stood holding the rope until the bell rang for the end of the round. We dropped the rope and frantically got to our corners, placing the stools in the ring for the boxers to sit on, and began our duties as corner men. As the bell rang for the next round, we removed the stools, rushed over to our respective ends of the rope, and stood throughout the round holding the rope. Mickey shouted over to me, "Hey, Angie, tell your guy, if he is going to whack my guy again, do it in the middle of the ring."

Somehow we got through the fight. Mickey suggested that we go out and have a steak dinner, as we had worked our butts off. He didn't suggest that the winner pay, which was OK with me, as my guy had won.

Smoking cigars and feeling full and satisfied after our meal, we toasted ourselves with brandy and rapped about the fight game.

"I got a lousy deal on this fight," Mickey said

"So did I. Between you and me, after expenses, my share is fifteen bucks."

"Is that all? You're doing something wrong. I'm walking away with sixteen! This is great, we've made thirty-one bucks between us."

We laughed our heads off, and ordered two more brandies—doubles. After a few more night-caps, we eventually called for the check, which came to twenty-five dollars—and we left the waitress a six-dollar tip! Easy come, easy go! By the way, Mickey went on to become matchmaker at the Los Angeles Olympia. He was there over seventeen years.

Another character from that time with whom I still enjoy the bond of friendship is Gil Clancy. He was floating around New York during the late forties and early fifties, managing and training fighters. Gil had gained experience with the Catholic Youth Organization and was always looking for a good prospect. He and I teamed up to manage a good young lightweight with a lot of potential. Unfortunately, after a few months of club fights and our strict training regimen, the kid took his talent and potential and joined the army, leaving Gil and me out on a limb. Gil was philosophical about it. "What are you gonna do? The kid wanted a steady job, and nothing is more steady than working for Uncle Sam. We'll get together again, Angie, you see if I ain't right." It was true, we did get together again, but not for a while. It took nearly thirty years before we found ourselves working as a team again, doing color commentaries for CBS television on their boxing shows.

Miami looked very inviting, it held many attractions for me, but leaving New York was no easy move for me to take; it meant saying goodbye to all the warmth and camaraderie I had found there.

Helen's fashion season had finished for the year. She decided to go home to North Carolina permanently. I would travel down most weekends, and I would be on the phone every night we were apart—that was a habit I never lost—but her absence left a large void in my life.

I had spoken to Chris over the phone, too. In September he told me that if I came down he would find something for me. I would get seventy-five dollars a week. As it stood, I wasn't making enough to save a dime, so I prepared to kiss goodbye to New York. I needed some stake money, and I knew where to place my hands on it. During my spell in the service, I sent most of my pay home to Mom in South Philly. It had been for her personally, but she hadn't spent it. She had saved it for me. I made arrangements with the bank to withdraw the total sum of twelve hundred dollars. The office/home at the hotel was paid up. My business was such, that it took all of four hours to clear up everything! My only problem was what to do with my fighters.

Bill Bossio was taken over by Al Braverman. I was supposed to have retained a small percentage as I had worked Bill up to $5,000 for a fight at the Garden; Al told me he would send my money to Miami. That was in October, 1951; I'm still waiting for the check!!

Two of my fighters decided to take a chance and come to Miami with me. They figured even if things didn't work out too good, at least they would get a good suntan. They were Bill Neri, who was a lightweight, and Alex Fimbres, who was a featherweight fighting out of New York and living in Phoenix. They were nice kids and I hoped things would work out for them. I promised them nothing.

They knew the fight game was tough and precarious, and they knew me—they knew I would do my best for them.

I was in Miami staying in a hotel on 17th Street and Alton Road. It wasn't much of a place, but it was near the office, and it was an improvement on New York—at least I wasn't living in the office.

The four months I had been on Miami Beach had sailed effortlessly by, and as far as working for Chris again, it was as if I hadn't spent the ten months on my own in New York; it was just like old times. The notable differences were that there was no Stillman's—and that meant none of my pals were around—and the weather. Boy, how I loved the weather! Sure, I missed Manhattan, the hustle and bustle, the skyscrapers and the excitement, but I loved the clean, brightly painted buildings and the clear blue sky of Miami.

I had this love affair with Miami from the time I had first gone there in 1943 with the Air Corps. To be actually living there and earning a living should have made me feel great. But I didn't feel great, I was lonely. I missed Helen, that was about the size of it. I felt I could make a life for myself in Miami; even in the short span of time I had been there I had got the feeling that Miami was the place for me, and that really meant a place for Helen and me. Yea, I was thinking more about marriage than about my fighters.

After watching Alex Fimbres and Bill Neri work out at the Magic City Gym in Southwest Miami, I said to Jerry White, who owned the establishment, "Tell Chris I'll see him tomorrow morning. I've got a few things to take care of."

I had to sort out my personal life. I jumped a cab back to the hotel. As soon as I was in my room I hit the telephone. I would catch Helen at work; she could speak more freely there than at home. Since she had left New York, Helen had been working as chief of sales at a local shoe store. She was happy to be back in Salisbury, where she was the toast of the town. The local guys were falling all over her. I knew I had a lot of competition, but I didn't doubt that Helen and I had something special going.

The conversation was getting me nowhere. I wasn't in the mood for pleasantries, I wasn't interested in hearing about the shoe store, and I didn't want to talk about the weather in Miami. "Helen"—I interrupted her question as to whether or not I had seen her aunt and uncle.

"Helen!" She stopped talking. "Let's get married." Now that I wanted her to say something, she remained silent. "I can't live like this. It's not right. I miss you, Helen. Do you hear what I'm saying? I said, let's get married."

"I don't know, Angie. You know that Mom and Dad don't want me to marry you. I can't just leave home."

"Listen, Helen, I'm serious. I can't go on like this. I want you here with me."

"I don't see how I can leave Salisbury."

"What are you talking about? You gotta leave Salisbury. You're gonna wind up a country hick all your life unless you come down here."

"I don't know, Angelo."

"Either you come to Florida or let's forget it." There was a silence at the other end of the line. I thought I would change my tactics. "Helen, I have saved over eight hundred dollars. I am doing OK down here." The bit about the eight hundred dollars was not quite true; I hadn't saved any money, it was the balance left from the money Mom had kept from my Air Corps days.

"Look, Helen, you know how I feel about you. Hell! Why don't we get married?" There was another pause, then she answered me.

"All right, Angelo, I will see you the day after tomorrow. I'll telephone you when I reach Miami. 'Bye darling, I must get back to work."

So, I had proposed and I had been accepted. I was numb. Would she change her mind? After all, she had been engaged more than once before we met. That night I didn't sleep. Too many thoughts were running through my mind. In the morning, I rang her at work—everything was just fine. She would be in Miami tomorrow.

Families are a wonderful institution. It was a good thing that Helen had family living in Miami, because Dolores, Helen's cousin, met her at the railroad station. No one had told me when, or by what means of transport, my wife-to-be would arrive. I was at the gym instead of the station.

After Dolores had taken her home, Helen rang Gerri Dundee to ask her to pick me up at the gym—remember, I could not drive. Gerri barged into the gym and whispered to me, so that the whole gym could hear that Helen had arrived. I smiled sheepishly at the guys, grabbed Gerri's arm and left in a hurry.

Gerri was as excited as if she was getting married herself. I

calmed her down and told her that I was the one to be nervous
and to concentrate on her driving, otherwise there wouldn't be
any bridegroom.

Gerri got us to Dolores and her husband Fred's house in no
time flat. I was a nervous wreck, and made a mental note not to
use Gerri as a regular driver! Before we went into the house, Gerri
warned me not to mention anything about the wedding in front of
Dolores and Fred; Helen wished to keep it a secret for the time
being. I didn't understand what it was all about, but under the
circumstances, I said a quick hello to Dolores and Fred and
without too much embarrassment, got Helen and her two enormous suitcases the hell out of the house and into Gerri's car. Gerri
dropped us off at the Vanderbilt Hotel on Collins Avenue, a nice
hotel that unfortunately had seen better days.

Helen's room wasn't exactly small, but you had to open the
windows to stretch your arms! I had booked the room by telephone, and hadn't seen it. The hotel was near the office and I
thought it would be okay for a couple of nights, but I must admit,
the room was a real downer. I could see the disappointment on
Helen's face. "Don't worry, honey, you're not gonna be here long,"
I said, trying to console her.

Helen was tired, and we were both strung out. It was not a good
time or place to discuss our wedding plans. How did it go? As you
would expect, we had an argument. Helen cried, and I felt like a
heel. Slowly the mood changed, and it was fun making up.

Helen and I sat on the bed, drained after our argument. We had
become used to the tiny room, and I got a laugh when I suggested
that we hold the wedding reception there. I asked her why the
secrecy in front of Fred and Dolores? She gave me the story.

Her boss at the shoe store, and her parents, thought that Helen
was in Miami just for the weekend, and that her reason for being
here was that she was going to gently but firmly break off our
relationship. She told me how she had to sneak out her second
suitcase, because it would have looked strange taking two suitcases away for a weekend. I wondered how she sneaked it out; the
suitcases were nearly as big as me. As it was, they took up half the
space in the hotel room.

The bottom line was, Helen wanted to avoid any confrontation
with her parents. There was also another reason for her secrecy.
Although she hated to admit it, she wasn't really one hundred
percent certain that she was going to go through with the
marriage. She had been engaged before and backed away. Why

go through family arguments over something that may never happen? But she was here, the marriage was on, and if she wanted to keep it a secret from her family, that was all right by me.

It was fortunate that my own family knew about it, otherwise I would not have had a best man. Chris was chosen for that responsibility. I was glad that Chris was going to stand up with me. Having him there would maybe quiet a nagging worry that was bothering me, no matter how much I tried to ignore it.

Helen and I both believed in God, and we truly believed that in God's eyes all people, whatever their color, creed, or religion were equal. We were all his children. Yet, I was born and raised a Catholic, and I was marrying out of the Church, for Helen was a Methodist. Deep down inside of me was this nagging doubt: should I insist that Helen embrace my religion?

Chris had left home young and had learned early to make his own decisions. When he met the girl he loved, he married her; it made no difference to him that she happened to be Jewish. I agreed with his decision, and having him and his wife at my wedding would strengthen my resolve in my own course of action. From the moment we were married, as it turned out, my problem disappeared. Religions, like races, can live side by side.

"Do you feel all right, Angelo?" Doctor Kleinman asked me. I could not remember what had happened.

"Sure, I feel OK," I answered. But why the hell was I stretched out on the sofa? Oh no! I thought I knew. I didn't want to know! I looked beseechingly at the Doc, "I didn't, did I?"

"Look, Angelo, don't worry about it. This has happened to a lot of people."

"Yea! Well I gotta tell you, Doc, I do not think many cut men in the fight game faint when they see blood, especially their own."

Can you believe this? I actually passed out while having a blood test. The Doc had started to take a blood sample from my arm, I watched the action, and when I saw the blood—wham! While I was lying on the sofa, out to the world, Doc Kleinman grabbed his chance and took a blood sample from my ankle. How humiliating! But I was sure glad that he didn't wait for me to revive, because I have a feeling I would have whammed out again!

Getting married is not as easy as one might think. I do not mean the big things like blood tests, but little things like finding somewhere to live!

The day before we were married, we hired a car, and with Helen at the controls we went house-hunting. We knew we could not afford to buy a house, but we thought it sounded good, "house-hunting." It had a certain ring about it, and we liked the mental image it conjured up. Stalking through the long grass, guns at the ready, they hunted a big, dangerous, man-eating house! So, we went house-hunting, and wound up renting for seventy-five dollars per month, paid in advance, an efficiency apartment at 726 Jefferson Avenue on Miami Beach. Our new home consisted of a bathroom, a kitchen and one large room furnished with a table, two chairs and two studio couches at either end of the room. We decided without much discussion that we would pull the two couches together for our sleeping arrangements.

I bowed as I gave Helen the keys. "Here are the keys to your new home, madam."

"Thank you kindly, sir," Helen curtsied.

"Of course you realize that we are a two-way deal now, we both gotta pay. Half and half." I dare not repeat Helen's answer!

On Sunday, February 11, 1952, at twelve noon, Helen Bolton and Angelo Dundee became man and wife. We held the wedding ceremony at Chris's house. Judge Sapperstein officiated. I guess the wedding was unique; you had a Philadelphia-Italian-Catholic guy and a Southern Methodist gal being married by a Jewish New Yorker who lived in Miami!

That afternoon Chris and Gerri threw us a small party, and that evening Helen and I had our honeymoon in our new apartment. The following morning I was back in the office at work, promising myself that one day soon Helen and I would have a real honeymoon. It was a rash promise—it wasn't one day soon.

Two days after our wedding, Rocky Marciano fought Lee Savold in Philadelphia. He won by a knockout in the sixth round and moved a step nearer to a world title fight. On the same date, I left Miami Beach with my fighter, Alex Fimbres, for Havana, Cuba. It was to be the start of a period in my life that I called "The Cuban Connection."

CHAPTER TEN

CUBA—
I LEARN TO SAY
SI SI!

"It was arranged for Alex to fight in Havana on February 2. How did I know that I would be getting married three days before I had to leave for Cuba?"

Cuco Conde, the promoter of the fight, had arranged for a taxi to take us from the airport to the hotel. If you haven't driven in a Havana taxi, you haven't lived, and if you have, you're lucky to be living! Those old beat-up taxis look as if they can fall apart at any time, but they're tough. The cabbies, probably nice normal guys when they are not behind the wheel, are frustrated grand prix racing drivers with a death wish!

The roads added to the nightmare. There were no traffic lights. Whoever sounded his horn first, went first. God forbid there was a draw! Our cabbie was obviously a nut, he played "chicken" with articulated trucks. When we reached the Luna Hotel, Alex Fimbres, normally a fearless young man, leaped out of the taxi and kissed the sidewalk.

I first met Cuco in Miami when he came to the office trying to arrange fights for Cuban boxers on Chris's promotions. He dealt solely with Chris, but during the time Cuco spent watching the homegrown talent working out in the gym, we got a chance to talk together. We came up with the idea of using my fighters in Cuba. Cuco liked the look of one of my guys, Alex Fimbres, a Mexican kid who lived in Phoenix, Arizona, and who was in town for a bout. It was arranged for Alex to fight in Havana on February 2. How did I know that I would be getting married three days before I had to leave for Cuba?

I don't think I mentioned the trip to Helen before we married. It must have come out something like, "Hey, hon, I gotta go to Cuba tomorrow with Alex Fimbres. He's fighting in a couple of days and I gotta check it out. I'll be away about four days." Helen understood, this was how I made my living. Why didn't I take her with me? I didn't want my private life crossing over into my business life. Boxing was, and still is, a male-dominated sport. It is a rough, tough way of life, especially on the road when you haven't got the bucks to make it easier. No way did I want Helen hanging around third-rate hotels and eating in crummy restaurants. Not every place was like that, thank the Lord, but I did not want Helen to see the seamy side of the fight game. Sure, I loved the smelly, crumbling gyms that I had to use, where guys used language I hadn't heard even in the army. I was not offended, but I sure didn't want my wife there.

From the time I proposed to her, I decided to keep my private life separate from my work. I didn't want to be like Chris, who took business calls at home any time, day or night. When I went home after work I was going to try to be a full-time husband, and when the time came, a full-time pop, too. There was the office for phone calls! D'you know what I mean? Work was one thing, my family something else, something special.

When Cuco found out that I had only been married a few days, he was very understanding and tried to make my stay in Havana as pleasant as possible. He arranged for me to leave on the first available flight after the fight. The hotel was fine, nothing to write home about, but it was adequate, and the staff very friendly. The training facilities for Alex were good. He had no weight problems, so it would be a matter of keeping him sharp. He was fighting a tough cookie, Orlando Echevarria, a young kid with a string of wins behind him. Eventually Orlando would fight Joe "Old Bones" Brown for the world lightweight title. But Brown proved to be far too strong and experienced, and stopped Orlando in the first round.

I watched Orlando work out in the downtown Havana gym; he looked good and sharp. I told his trainer, Manolo Fernandez, that his boy looked in great condition. At least, I think I said something like that. I spoke only "gym Spanish."

Manolo invited Alex and me to join him and his brother Marzo for coffee and a sandwich after the training session was over. Alex had felt tired and had sensibly gone back to the hotel for a nap. I was tired too, but I liked the Fernandez brothers and I wanted to see as much of Havana as I could.

It was fun sitting outside with Manolo and Marzo at one of the many sidewalk cafes that sprout like mushrooms on the beautiful Prado boulevard drinking hot Cuban coffee. We had been sitting for an hour or so, when a harassed-looking Cuco joined us. "Angelo, I'm sorried. I got a call from Alex, he don't feel too good."

"He don't feel too good? What did he say?" Now, *I* was worried.

"He said he feels lousy and could I get hold of you." I didn't need to hear anymore. I hightailed it back to the hotel.

Alex looked awful. He gave me his symptoms. Throbbing head, aches and pains all over the body. I felt his forehead, he had a slight temperature. I did not have to have a degree in medicine to diagnose flu.

The hotel found me a doctor, who confirmed my suspicions. Alex had a mild flu virus. It meant he would have to spend at best two or three days in bed, which made things rather complicated because he was scheduled to fight in approximately forty-eight hours' time.

I let Cuco know straightaway, and he took the news well. He understood that there was nothing we could do about it—the fight was off. I jumped a cab—that's how desperate I was—and went to Cuco's office, where we sat trying to figure out if it was possible to put in another American fighter as a substitute. I called Chris, but he knew of no one that could make the weight and was in condition, but he did offer to give Orlando Echevarria a bout on his promotion the following week. Cuco liked the idea, and after making endless telephone calls he fixed a substitute bout between two Cuban welterweights for his promotion. Cuco sighed with relief, he had a bout to take the place of the Echevarria-Fimbres fight, and he also had a payday for Orlando Echevarria, who was going to fight in Miami on Chris's bill. The only guys behind the eight-ball were Alex and me. We hadn't even made coffee money, and I was afraid we were going to get stuck with the cost of the air tickets and hotel bills. Great!

I need not have worried. Cuco suggested that he and I fly to Miami in the morning to finalize the deal with Chris, and that the Fimbres expenses would be picked up by his office. Cuco need not have picked up the tab, he could have walked away from it—most promoters would have. I appreciated it. No doubt about it, Cuco Conde was a gentleman.

Next morning, after making all necessary arrangements for Alex's immediate welfare, I flew back to Miami with Cuco. Cuco sensed how I felt and he tried to make me feel at ease. "Don't worry so much, Angelo, there will be other times. When Alex is fit and well, I'll fix him another fight in Havana, maybe I'll get him in against Echevarria yet." He nudged me in the ribs with his elbow. "And don't get ulcers over the expenses. We'll do lots of business together. I'll make up the expenses, don't worry about it." Yea, Cuco was a great guy.

The next few days in Miami were hectic. There I was living in a new apartment with a brand new wife, who naturally wanted to see me occasionally! I was rushing around like a wild man, arriving home exhausted. And for what? I'll tell you for what. Zilch! I did not have any of my fighters with a bout, and for the last three weeks Chris had not paid me any wages. In New York, when that had happened I did not say anything, but this time I couldn't bite my tongue. The day before the Echevarria fight, Chris and I were in the office. I thought the time was right to bring up the subject of my wages.

"I wanna speak to you, Chris," I began.

"So speak. What d'you want, an appointment?" Chris looked up from whatever he was looking at on his desk.

"You haven't paid me for three weeks. That's over two hundred bucks I'm out."

"Angie, what are you worrying about? If you want to worry, worry about how bad business is. Do you know the expenses I've got?"

"Sure I do. I pay my share, don't I? And I type up all the expenses, don't I?"

"You only type the expenses you know about. I got expenses I don't tell you about. Better you don't know. Look, Angie, I'll take care of you. Don't worry so much. You got a few fighters now, and there's those two kids from New Orleans coming in the summer. You got an office." Chris waved his arms out, displaying what he meant. "You got a phone. Your boys fight on my promotions. Why do you want to bleed me?"

"Bleed you! Hey Chris, I pay expenses for the office and the phone. I work from eight in the morning until six at night, if I'm lucky. I work on all the promotions, the boxing, the wrestling, the goddam circus even, seven days a week. Sometimes I don't get home till midnight. What do you mean bleed you—for a lousy seventy-five dollars a week!"

"Don't get so excited, Angie. Don't I know that you work hard? You do a good job. Angelo, I know you don't want to take my money. Thank God you're making a dollar. Alex Fimbres is well now, he'll be fighting soon, you'll make a few bucks. Don't worry, it will work out, I'll take care of it." He smiled at me. "Listen, Angie, the Continental Restaurant wants twenty tickets for the fights tomorrow night. Will you take care of it?" Chris went back to whatever he was doing. Our conversation was over, it was back to business of the day.

"I'll take care of it," I said as I went back to my desk. I didn't quite know how the conversation had gone, but I didn't think I would see my seventy-five dollars a week again, or get the two hundred and twenty-five owed to me—and I sure was right.

Echevarria's fight against Johnny Gueverra on February 20 went as Cuco Conde predicted. Echevarria won comfortably. Cuco was pleased; Chris would be using more Cuban fighters for his promotion. Before he left for Havana, Cuco phoned me and told me that he had settled on a date for a Fimbres—Echevarria fight in Havana—April 19. This would give Alex time to get over his bout of flu and maybe get in a warm-up fight too. I was delighted with the news. I thought it would be a good fight and I would get another chance to visit Cuba.

It was reassuring to know that I had another fight in Havana, and I sure needed reassuring. The Fimbres fight was in April, this was only February, and I didn't have a lot going for me. My bankroll had shrunk a little, and I still had a couple of things that I had to buy. Helen and I decided that we needed a radio and a car. As far as the radio was concerned, there was no problem. I walked into a department store, saw a radio I liked and bought it there and then. That's class!

As for the car, well that was a little more complicated. I bought it from Harry Curley's girlfriend. Now Harry was no relation to Jack Curley, who worked the door at Stillman's. This Curley had been Doc Kearns's righthand man. Wanting a change of scene, he was trying his luck in Miami. His girlfriend was pressed for a few bucks, so she was unloading her Ford. Harry Curley told me that it was a good buy at the price, and it probably was, but it wasn't an automatic.

"It's stick shift," the girlfriend told me, as if that should double the price of the car. What did I know? I couldn't really drive anyway. I just hoped it would be easier to drive than the jeep I had used in France. Helen tried it out and liked it, and that was that. We had a car. Helen said that she would teach me to change gears in a couple of weeks. All I needed was a little coordination between hand and foot. Do you know, I never did drive that goddam car. The next car we bought was an automatic, and *I* drove it!

Helen and I loved our little apartment, especially with a radio to keep us company. We enjoyed being together and we understood each other's moods. She could tell that I was worried over the lack of bucks coming in, but she didn't press me about it, she suggested that we go fishing!

We took our rods and other necessary paraphernalia, and walked to the MacArthur Causeway, one of several magnificent causeways that join the Beach to Miami. There we would fish for snapper, grouper, and the occasional sea trout. It was good fun and it helped keep down our cost of living.

Once again, Alex and I landed at Havana airport. This time we were met by Manolo Fernandez, who drove us into town. I started to tell him what a crazy driver the cabbie had been on our last drive from the airport, but I quit very quickly when I realized that Manolo had the same disregard for life, the car, or property, that our previous driver had. A beaming Manolo let us out at the hotel. "Is not a long journey," he began in his fractured English. "It not take long time, I make quicker, but many crazy driver on the road." Alex and I could not think of anything to say.

This trip, I had decided to arrive in Havana the day before the fight—less chance of anything going wrong. As we had taken the same early flight from Miami, there was time for Alex and me to have a publicity call for the local media at the downtown gym. Cuco had arranged for an interview at a radio station. Alex, being Mexican, had no trouble with the Spanish interviewer, but I struggled with the language, and spoke a patois of Spanish and Italian. It went down well, and I got one or two laughs. Cuco went after as much promotion as possible. He knew its value. More and more I was realizing the importance of hype and publicity. The fight game needed it, and I intended to use it any chance I got. As the years went by, I learned just how powerful publicity and promotion can be.

The fight lived up to expectations. It was terrific. Echevarria and Fimbres went the full ten action-packed rounds, with Echevarria winning a close decision. Fimbres was disappointed, understandably, but the fight had been a real crowd pleaser, and Alex had won a lot of friends and admirers. Not everyone can be a winner, but we can all do with friends and admirers. They buy tickets to watch you fight, and that is the name of the game.

Alex and I had settled on a light supper and an early night, but Cuco had other plans for us. He took us to the Tropicana. I have since been to famous night clubs and supper clubs all over the world. But even after many happy visits to Las Vegas, seeing superstars in super shows, that first impression of the Tropicana will always stand out in my memory as the most glamorous night club of them all.

Only one thing spoiled the evening, although it didn't at the time: I began to get the taste for gambling. I was absolutely fascinated by the insidious charm of the casino. Blackjack, a basic card game, was my weakness. Obviously that first night I didn't lose a lot of money, for the simple reason I didn't have it to lose, but I played and I enjoyed it. It gave me a new excitement that I had never before experienced. I knew that if I returned to Havana I would be returning to the casino, but at the time I didn't think of it as a bad thing, just as something to look forward to.

Two days after I had returned to Miami, Manolo called me. The Fimbres fight had been so well liked, he wanted to arrange a return bout in Miami. Then, if Fimbres won, they would have a third, deciding bout back in Havana. That third bout would draw big crowds in Havana, and there would be a big payday for Alex and me. I told Manolo that I would talk it over with Chris and get back to him. Chris, who was in the office at the time, overheard the conversation and went for the idea. He had a promotion on May 7 that he could easily slot the Echevarria-Fimbres fight into. We did some homework on the figures, and eventually Chris was satisfied and gave me the go-ahead to get back to Manolo and confirm the bout.

Unfortunately Alex Fimbres never got into top gear. It sometimes happens in boxing, the fighter just cannot get going. Poor Alex was easily outpointed over eight rounds by Orlando, and blew the deciding bout. I was disappointed over the result and over the fact there would be no payday in Havana. Still, I had been around boxing long enough not to break my heart over a result. As far as Cuba was concerned, although no new arrangements were in the offing, I felt something would come along. I now had friends and connections in Cuba.

CHAPTER ELEVEN

THE GLADIATORS ARRIVE

"Two weeks later Charlie Goldman called me from New York. The little man seemed upset. 'Angie, I got some bad news for you. There's a story goin' around that the New York State Athletic Commission ain't going to give you a license.'

" 'What d'you mean? . . . [It's got] to be a mistake.'

" 'The story is that Carbo has been under surveil-lance and they had a bug under his table at Goldie Ahearn's. The whole night's friggin' conversation was taped, including yours.' "

1952 had to be an important year in my life, not only because that was the year in which I got married, but because so many things started for me. It was the year the Cuban connection began, which eventually led me to three great fighters who all became world champions: Luis Rodriguez, Jose Napoles, and Sugar Ramos; it was the year in which I first worked with the indestructible Carmen Basilio; and it was the year that brought two sixteen-year-old boys, Ralph Dupas and Willie Pastrano, destined to become world champions, to Miami, where they trained under my tutelage and guidance. Yea, I guess 1952 was a kind of important year, but then aren't they all?

Fresh out of school, a stocky Ralph Dupas and a skinny Willie Pastrano arrived at the Magic City Gym, in the southwest section of Miami, sometime in June. I had seen them fight in New Orleans, their hometown, and I had been impressed. They may have only been schoolboys but they boxed like seasoned pros. Dupas had a list of wins that was amazing for a kid so young. He had beaten Bill Neri, a good young fighter who had worked with me a few times, so I knew that the kid was a hell of a prospect. Yet it was the skinny Willie Pastrano who held a special fascination for me. He was one sweet boxer with a sensational left jab, but it was his warm, easygoing personality that I took to. I learned that Willie only took up boxing to lose weight. As a young kid he had been a fatso—I knew that feeling—and was too embarrassed to take off his shirt. His pal, Ralph, had talked him into taking up boxing, and that began taking the weight off. Now, he was a lean teenager who looked nothing like a fighter, but if you happened to be on the receiving end of his left jab, you knew that he was.

I worked with the two boys in the gym, teaching them and helping them. They were in great condition and they wanted to fight. Their manager, Whitey Esneault, wanted me to fix them some two-minute-round bouts. In New Orleans, Whitey could only get six-round fights of three minutes per round duration, but Florida had different rules. Our boxing commission allowed two-minute rounds, so I fixed the two sixteen-year-olds ten-round bouts, which was good for them, and they only boxed two minutes longer than they would have over six three-minute rounds.

Willie had six fights through July and August and won them all. Ralph did nearly as well: out of five fights he only lost one, to Jose Vasquez, whom he beat in a return bout in November. Not a bad start for my two protégés. I had grown to like the two kids, and I missed them when they returned home to New Orleans. Helen, too, had taken to the boys. I guess they brought out her maternal instincts. (Sure, we wanted children and we were trying, but nothing was clicking. Still, it was fun trying.)

After the boys had gone I got a call from New Orleans. It was Willie. "How ya doing, Mister Angelo?" He was always polite.

"I'm fine, Willie. What can I do for you?"

"Nothing really. I'm in Mister Whitey's office. He wants to talk to you. I thought I'd just say hi."

Whitey Esneault came on the phone. The story was short and sweet. Would I be interested in becoming co-manager for the boys? Naturally, I gave the affirmative. Whitey said that he would be in touch with the details of the contract. That night I took Helen to Jake LaMotta's club on Miami Beach to celebrate. We had a great night and, ignoring my insistences, Jake picked up the tab. Helen was pleased, because she knew that I would take her to the club again so that *I* could pick up a tab. I'm that kind of a guy!

In Miami the hurricane season is normally at its most dangerous in September, but I was praying that this September would not be ruined by a killer storm, because on September 22 Carmen Basilio was fighting on Chris's promotion, and I was working his corner.

I had met the craggy-faced fighter once before back in March

1950 in Brooklyn. I was working with Mike Koballa, who was going in with Basilio. Koballa was made a three-to-one underdog, but as so often happens in the fight game, the underdog won. Naturally I was pleased, we had got a result we didn't really expect, but I could tell that Basilio had enormous talent and should go to the top. I went round to his dressing room after the fight to pay my respects. Carmen was sitting on the table, legs dangling over the side, his rugged face puffed and bruised. He was partially dressed and was buttoning up his shirt as he answered the questions being fired at him by the local newspaperman. At the first lull in the conversation, I said, "Great fight, Carmen. I'm glad my guy won, but I'm sorry that you lost. You got a lot of talent."

One of Carmen's managers of that time put his arm around Carmen's shoulder and said, "Thanks, Angelo. It was one of those things."

Carmen managed a smile, "Yea, thanks, Angelo. Koballa sure surprised me. I'll take him next time."

The reporter put his two cents' worth in, "If I were you, Carmen, I'd forget it. You cut and bruise too easily. You ain't gonna make it. Why the hell don't you get out of the game?"

The reporter was a jerk! He was making me mad, and before Carmen's manager could answer, and before Carmen, whose jaw jutted out even more aggressively, could decide whether to take offense or not, I interfered. "What the hell are you talking about? What are you, some kind of expert or something? Carmen is a great fighter, and the only place he is goin' is up." To illustrate my point, I stuck my longest finger up under his nose. He could take it any way he wanted to. Fortunately the newspaper guy backed off and nobody else but me took offense at the jerk's remarks. I said my "goodbyes" and "good lucks," and left.

That was the last time I had seen Basilio, but now he was boxing in Miami, and I was in his corner. September 22 came around and Basilio, now with a big reputation, was fighting Baby Williams, a very useful fighter. Before the bout I wrapped Carmen's hands, which was very flattering, because for the last three years, since he had broken a hand in a fight, Carmen preferred to wrap his own hands. He gave me a shot at it and he liked the way I handled it. I felt good.

The fight was no walk-over for Carmen. Baby Williams gave him a lot of trouble and a couple of nasty cuts over the eyes. The knowledge and techniques I had learned during my years of apprenticeship in New York came to the rescue. I took care of the cuts without any fuss or undue trouble, but I was relieved when the bell sounded for the end of the fight and Basilio took the decision. The bout had been over eight rounds; I sure was glad it hadn't been fifteen.

When I was back home, having a nightcap with Helen, she asked me if anything had been said by Basilio or his managers about using me again. I didn't like telling her that nothing had been worked out. Other than thanking me for my work, nobody had said anything about any future plans. I wasn't too upset. I knew I had done a good job.

If my spirits had been sagging, which they were not, the news I received from New York on the following night would have lifted them. On September 23, Rocky Marciano won the World Heavyweight Championship by knocking out Jersey Joe Walcott in the thirteenth round. A few days later I called Charlie Goldman, the little man whose faith and guidance were so instrumental in Rocky's success. Charlie tried to give me a blow by blow description of the fight, but I had to cut him short—I was paying for the call! Which brings me to money. There just wasn't enough.

Sure, I was managing or co-managing a few fighters, but they were earning peanuts and I ended up with the empty shells. I made a few bucks from working as a corner man for whoever wanted me, and that was keeping my head above water. I was working seven days a week with Chris, doing a hundred different jobs, but I didn't get any wages for that. Being with Chris gave me a base from which to help my fighters and pick up work as a corner man.

Helen never complained. We both knew I could earn more money if I went back to the navy yard in South Philly, but that was out of the question. We both loved Miami and I loved what I was doing. I intended to stay in the fight game for good. I would have worked for Carmen Basilio for nothing; as it worked out, when John de John paid me my wages for the night, there wasn't a lot in it. Things were tough all over!

Still, Helen and I were happy. We had the same attitude as my family in South Philly: we weren't broke, we just didn't have any money!

I thought that there might be a chance of making a few extra dollars with Jimmy Cooper, a clever young featherweight. I arranged a bout with a good Cuban fighter, Puppy Garcia, in Havana on December 1. A good win for Jimmy would put us in with a chance of getting some good purses.

Unfortunately, Jimmy got stopped in five rounds, but the trip to

Havana wasn't a complete wash-out. I met a guy by the name of
Oscar Conill, a fight promoter, who seemed interested in using my
fighters in the New Year. I told him that I would look forward to
hearing from him. I was back in Miami in time to watch Jake
LaMotta fight in Coral Gables, a suburb of Miami. Jake wasn't in
shape and lost to Danny Nardico. After the fight, Jake and I
rapped; it was the beginning of a friendship that lasted through
some ups and some pretty heavy downs in our respective lives.

Helen and I spent Christmas with her folks in North Carolina.
Mildred and George had forgiven us months ago. They had come
down to Miami, where Mildred stayed with us and George stayed
with his in-laws, John and Nora. We would have loved the extra
guest, but the apartment was too small. Mildred was reassuring,
she told me not to worry, and that by this time next year we would
be in a larger home. As usual, she was right.

So a year of promise ended and I now dated my letters 1953.

I worked a couple of uneventful fights with Basilio. John de
John would call me, give me the details and I would be there.
Nothing long planned, a bout here and there. No complaints from
me, I was grateful for the work. There was no business from my
Cuban friends until we were well into 1953, so I had plenty of time
to work with Ralph Dupas and Willie Pastrano.

Willie was having a bad spell. He had lost a few fights in New
Orleans, but the promise was there, and heck, the kid was only just
seventeen. Dupas was having a good year. By November 1953 he
had won ten fights, drawn one, and lost one to Brian Kelly, whom
he beat in a return bout.

Most of Ralph's fights were in New Orleans, where he had built
up a solid reputation and got good purses. In my agreement with
Whitey Esneault, I received no share from fights held in New
Orleans. Sure, I could have used the money, but I was more
concerned about figuring out a way to get Ralph and Willie away
from the New Orleans club-fight scene and getting them greater
recognition.

In 1953 there were a lot of good, hungry fighters, and it took a
lot of time and a lot of luck to get out of the club-fighter category
and move into the big-time.

By today's instant television fame standards, Ralph would have
been on the verge of becoming a contender, even a contender
with a title shot in the not so distant future. In those days he was
making a living in New Orleans, but struggling to get a good purse
anywhere else.

To give you an idea of the kind of money that was being handed out in 1953, a fighter who was headlining a televised bout would pick up around $4,000; today that fee would be in the $25,000 range. I am not talking about championship fights, or big-name contenders. Their wages are always based on their drawing power. A big fight that includes closed circuit television rights can run into millions, and I mean millions. But, you've got to remember that in 1927 Gene Tunney received a record $990,445 for fighting Jack Dempsey, and do I have to tell you how the cost of living has gone up. In 1953, my fighters were picking up between $100 and $500. The biggest purse we had taken in Cuba was for $300, and the average was around $200. Out of that, the fighter took two-thirds after expenses, I took one-third. From my share I paid Chris for the office and telephone expenses! Don't ever believe that I was in the fight game for money!

It was April 1953, I was busy in the office I shared with Chris, working on the accounts of the last wrestling promotion, when the telephone rang. Chris answered. I carried on with my work, oblivious to the phone conversation that was going on. Chris hung up the receiver. "That was Oscar Conill. He said you'd met at the Cooper fight. He's got a promotion going. How much for Jimmy Cooper, April 19, Havana?"

"Jimmy is back home in Washington, but he's training. What do you think?" No harm in getting advice from the experienced elder brother. "Find out who he's fighting."

"Ask three hundred, take two-fifty. Oscar said that he'd find a good opponent. He'll let you know the guy's name if you can agree price. If Jimmy wins he'll put him in with Kid Anauhac. It'll be a good fight. I'll put the phone calls on expenses, you'd better get back to him."

"I'll call Jimmy, then I'll call Havana." I made the two phone calls; the fight was on. Another day, another dollar!

Jimmy won the first fight, then in May he beat Kid Anauhac. Naturally, Jimmy was feeling pleased with himself and was looking forward to his next fight, which hopefully would bring him nearer to his goal of fame and riches. First, he would have to beat a hot prospect or a contender, but even before that, I would have to arrange the bout, and that could be very tough too. If your fighter looked too promising, other fighters would try and pick easier game. Choosing the right opponent is a valuable, if not the most important part of a manager's responsibilities.

I went after a bout with Orlando Echevarria, but trying ain't getting. It was only after a lot of months and a lot of fights that Jimmy finally got into the ring with Orlando. Maybe Jimmy wished he hadn't; he was KO'd in one round. A lucky punch, a lapse of concentration—who knows? If the fight had gone on, Jimmy could have won it, he had the skills. It wasn't to be, and Jimmy's career never got off the ground. Not everyone can be a winner. That's just the way it is.

When I take a bout for my fighters, I do my homework, and check out the opponents before I sign on the dotted line. Over the years, if you watch the other fighters, you build up your own dossiers on them. You keep an eye on all the boxing results, you telephone pals and ask them what so and so is like, and can he punch or take a punch. A good manager should know the fighters to steer clear of, but eventually, if your guy is going to be champion, he has to face every challenger. You can pick your opponents, you can study them, you can define their weaknesses, but you can't guarantee the result; that is in the lap of the gods.

I accepted a bout for Jimmy Beecham, a middleweight who lived in Miami, to fight Bobby Boyd in Washington, D.C. It looked like a good fight on paper, an action fight that would win friends. I couldn't predict who would win the fight. How could I know? And how could I know that going to Washington would affect my life.

Beecham was tough. As a teenager he had gotten himself into some trouble with the law and had done a short stretch. He had straightened himself out, gone into boxing, and settled in Miami. I had my doubts about Jimmy beating Bobby Boyd. Boyd was a shade too experienced, I thought. I didn't relish the thought of going all the way to Washington and losing, plus the weather forecasts warned of low temperatures, with a chance of snow, and I did not own a topcoat. I did not have good vibes at all. So, why the hell did I decide to take the fight? Well, I didn't know how the weather would turn out. Washington isn't exactly the North Pole! As for the fight itself, anything can happen in boxing, I thought. Beecham had a good chance and thought he could stop Boyd. Besides, he wasn't exactly flush with money. Who was? I decided to take the fight and go to Washington. As it worked out, it was one of the worst decisions I ever made, and it had nothing to do with the result of the fight.

When I am working a corner I do not have anything on my mind except the fight and my fighter. My personal worries are shelved during the fight, and I only concentrate on the job at hand. Not once during the Beecham-Boyd fight did I think about the weather.

About two hours before the fight time, the sky over Washington darkened, and then, from the menacing grayness, the snow began to fall, and fall, and fall. I have nothing against snow. It looks pretty, and it can be fun, expecially at Christmas time. But the snow's timing was wrong. I wanted to catch a plane to Miami after the fight, and I was worried that flights out of Washington would be grounded. I wanted to go home, Helen would be waiting.

Do you want the good news or the bad news first? Here is the good news: Jimmy Beecham earned a draw. It would have been better news if he had won, but I wouldn't complain about a crowd-pleasing draw. Jimmy made a lot of friends, the crowd liked him. Now for the bad news: the flight to Miami was cancelled; I couldn't get home, I was snowed in.

Jimmy and I checked into a hotel. He was exhausted, and after ordering a sandwich and a glass of hot milk, he went to bed. I went to eat at a restaurant popular with the boxing fraternity, Goldie Ahearn's.

I sat in the warmth of the cab as I paid off the driver. I was wearing a suit meant for sunny Miami, not a snowstorm in Washington. I hurried into the welcoming heat and cordiality of Goldie's. It hadn't yet filled up, or perhaps the fight crowd had gone straight home because of the weather. I had eaten there a few times before when I had worked Washington from New York. The room was sometimes a little noisy, but the food was always good. Goldie Ahearn gave me a big hello and was surprised to find me alone. None of my pals from the press were in the restaurant. He showed me to a nice table at the back and told me he would join me for a drink later.

I hate eating alone; if I had known none of my pals were going to be there I would have stayed in the hotel and eaten in the room with Jimmy. I had a steak. Goldie joined me for a glass of red wine, but only stayed a minute. The place was getting busy. My spirits rose when a couple of the diners, as they passed my table, recognized me from the fight. They told me that they thought Jimmy had won the fight. I didn't tell them I thought he was lucky to get a draw.

I got the check and asked the waiter to get me a cab. I began to thread my way through the now crowded tables towards the entrance when a voice halted my progress. "Hi, Angie. How ya doin'?" I turned to see who had spoken. Directly to my left was a table seating three men. The one nearest me was looking up, smiling expectantly at me. I couldn't place the guy.

"Hi. Nice seeing you," I said with a false grin stuck on my face.

I was about to move on when one of the other guys said, "Frankie thought the other guy won the fight, but I thought Beecham sneaked it."

"Frankie thought"! I looked at the first guy again. He was still leaning back in his chair, smiling at me. I remembered. The elevator in the hotel in New York! Frankie Carbo, the alleged racketeer who had done a short stretch for fight fixing!

"Sit down, have a drink." Frankie said. His two companions moved their chairs and made room. I couldn't think of a reason to refuse. I tried explaining that I was waiting for my taxi.

"No problem. Tell the doorman that Angelo Dundee is at my table." One of Frankie's companions got up and went on the errand.

I drank a glass of red wine and we talked boxing. I stayed about five minutes, then went back to my hotel room, where I fell asleep as soon as my head hit the pillow. Red wine does that to me.

The next morning the snow had stopped. Jimmy and I flew out, back to Miami. The restaurant interlude went out of my mind, but not for long.

Two weeks later Charlie Goldman called me from New York. The little man seemed upset. "Angie, I got some bad news for you. There's a story goin' around that the New York State Athletic Commission ain't going to give you a license."

"What d'you mean? What's the story?" This sounded kind of crazy, it had to be a mistake.

"The story is that Carbo has been under surveillance and they had a bug under his table at Goldie Ahearn's. The whole night's friggin' conversation was taped, including yours, during the meeting."

"What friggin' meeting? I had a glass of wine with the guy. For chrissakes, I've only met the guy twice in my whole life. If they don't renew my license I can't work a fight in the State of New York. That means the Garden is out. If New York bans me, I'll be thought of as a crook! Charlie, what the hell is going on?"

"What can I tell you! The DA is investigating Carbo. This District Attorney ain't fooling around. He is fishing around everything. Bribes, syndicate infiltration, and the breaking of antitrusts and monopoly laws. There is a lotta crap going down. Look, Angie, all

I'm saying is you ain't looking too good. I thought I would give you the word."

"Thanks, Charlie, I appreciate it. I'll work something out. Jeese, I'm clean. Hey, give my best to Rocky. Take care, pal."

It was like somebody had hit me a good shot in the solar plexus. I felt sick. Sure, I knew guys who were in the rackets. Gee, I grew up with some in South Philly, but I kept my nose clean. For me, it was a "hello-goodbye, pal" relationship. Now I was in a jam for not saying goodbye quickly enough.

I burned up the telephone wires speaking to friends in New York. They advised me not to apply for the renewal of my manager-second license. I took the advice, but I also decided to go and see James Fuscass, lawyer to the Athletic Commission.

My meeting with Fuscass confirmed all that Charlie had told me. I was in bad shape, but at least there was no possibility of any legal action being taken against me. Jim listened to my side of the story with an open mind, and he believed me. He told me that the two police officers on the case, one a female, had informed him that my taped conversation was not incriminating. They felt that I was guilty by association. Jim and I felt that I was damned unlucky. Why the hell had it snowed that night!

Under the circumstances, James Fuscass advised me not to pursue the matter of license renewal at this time. The State Commission would be informed of my unwitting involvement in the investigation, and Fuscass assured me that my license would not be revoked. In the following year, when the Carbo investigation would have been resolved, I should apply as usual for its renewal, and it would be granted.

I thanked Jim warmly, and although I would not be able to ply my trade in the State of New York for one year, I felt relieved that the Commission would know that I was an innocent victim of circumstances.

Well, that is how it went down. The following year I applied for my license renewal and got it, but I sure wish that I had not taken the Boyd-Beecham fight in Washington.

Since I had first met Carbo in New York, way back in 1948, I had grown up and learned a lot more of what went on behind the scenes in boxing. You would have had to have been deaf, dumb, and blind not to have known that it was teeming with corruption. Ray Arcel, who had taught me the rudiments of working a corner, also instructed me on what was going on in the corridors of power.

"If you ever get a champion, Angelo, you'll have to play ball with Jim Norris of the IBC (International Boxing Club) or "Mr. Gray," (just one of the names given to Frankie Carbo, because of his gray hair. Carbo was also known as "The Wolf" or "The Uncle").

In 1953, Carbo and Norris had a vice-like grip around the neck of boxing and were strangling it to death. Norris and the IBC took over the Mike Jacob's empire in 1948, and from 1949 to 1953, all the thirteen heavyweight championship bouts were promoted under their auspices. Carbo had been involved in boxing since 1933. He had controlled fighters, mainly in the middle, welter, and lightweight division for many years. He had served time for fight fixing, and it was alleged that he was associated with organized crime.

Norris and Carbo were an unlikely duo. James D. Norris had come from a wealthy Chicago family. His father owned Stadia and hockey teams in the midwest. The young James D. inherited his father's business acumen. Perhaps because he came from the city that indulged Al Capone and Frank Nitti, Norris seemed to have a liking and respect for muscle. Maybe that's why he took to Carbo. There was no doubt that he liked Frankie. He even named his racehorse "Mr. Gray."

The IBC had Madison Square Garden and television deals. Carbo owned fighters, or the managers of the fighters. So if you were in boxing, somewhere along the line you had to do business with them. That is, if you wanted to stay in the business.

I was just a nobody. A new kid on the block. So I didn't have to deal with anyone but my brother Chris. He sheltered me, and warned me to be nice to everyone and keep my mouth shut. Chris could handle himself. He was his own man and he was liked and respected throughout the boxing game. As fortune would have it, he had been lucky or clever enough to have moved to Miami, keeping well out of any conflicts and power plays that were happening in New York, and to a lesser extent in Los Angeles.

Ray Arcel was not as fortunate. Attempting to run a Saturday night fight promotion for television without coming to terms with Frankie, he ended up getting his head smashed with a lead pipe. Ray knew who was responsible, but nothing was ever proven. Ray's television deal collapsed shortly after the incident.

During my stay in New York, I was in a position similar to a young actor landing his first small part in a Broadway play. The actor wouldn't know or care who the backers were. He'd just be glad to be working. That's how I felt. I called everyone "Mister," and went about doing my job.

After my brush with the New York licensing committee, I always made certain that if and when I met someone with alleged crime connections, it would be a very quick "hello-goodbye" relationship. I didn't even want to be in the same room.

The Carbo incident had taught me a lesson I'd never forget.

Helen and I had taken every test, and as far as the doctor was concerned there was no medical reason why we couldn't have children.

We were becoming a little paranoid about it. Why the hell couldn't I get Helen pregnant? At last, in February 1954, Helen went for a checkup and discovered that she was two months pregnant, and then proceeded to have a miserable seven months, feeling sick nearly every day.

Helen had been through a bad enough time without the added discomfort of a debilitating pregnancy. In October 1952, my pop, who was suffering with arthritis, came down to Miami for the sunshine. At first, Pop stayed with Gerri and Chris, but with Gerri out most of the time there was no one to look after him, so he moved in with Helen and me. The full responsibility of looking after Pop fell squarely on Helen's shoulders.

We only had a one-room apartment. I put one of the sofas at one end of the room for Pop to sleep on, hung a blanket up as a room divider and made up a bed for myself on the floor. Unfortunately the sofa only made up into a single bed, and I mean single. I tried it, but when Helen turned around I was knocked out of bed. The floor was safer, although a lot less fun.

It was no easy thing for Helen having a sick old man living in the same room as her and her husband. She never complained. As usual, I was out most of the time, and most weekends I would be away with a fighter. Sometimes Cuba, sometimes New Orleans—wherever it was, it meant Helen was on her own.

Murphy's Law says: if anything can go wrong, it will. So, the weekend Pop ran a high temperature, I was in Cuba, and Helen was on her own the whole weekend. Pop had a fever, it must have been a virus of some kind. His temperature was hitting 103 degrees, and he was having convulsions. Helen didn't want to move him, although she was prepared to call for an ambulance if his temperature didn't drop. She wrapped him in blankets and watched over him until the fever broke. She washed him, and gave him an alcohol rub, and nursed him like a baby.

When Pop was strong again he told me that Helen had saved his life. She probably did. Helen and Pop became very close, like father and daughter. I was proud of my Southern Methodist wife.

Sleeping alone on the floor was giving me a bad back and playing hell with my sex life. I decided enough was enough! We had to find a larger apartment. In late 1953 we moved into a one-bedroom apartment on 82nd Street, Miami Beach. We were moving up-town, to hell with the expense! Now, if someone stayed with us, Helen and I would have our own bed. Our guest could sleep in the living room on the sofa. From now on, the floor was for carpets! Although Helen and I didn't dwell on the subject, we wanted the extra space just in case we struck lucky and had a baby. Now, in August 1954, the baby was due at any time. We would need that extra space.

Helen was having a bad time, and thank goodness Mildred came down from North Carolina to look after her. I didn't know if I was coming or going.

Over the weekend, Helen and I discussed the baby: I wanted a boy; Helen, a girl. If it was a boy we would name him Jimmy, after my closest brother; if it was a girl she would be called Terri. But I told Helen, "Forget it, honey, this baby is going to be a boy. A girl wouldn't dare give you this much trouble."

Monday morning was hot and humid. I left for the office. I had to work on the details for the Tuesday night fight promotion, but it was hard to concentrate. Later in the day I got a call from Mildred. There was nothing to worry about, but she was taking Helen to the hospital. Jesus! It was starting.

When I visited the hospital that night, I didn't stay too long. Helen was in pain and I couldn't bear to watch her and not be able to do anything to help her. Mildred, seeing my discomfort, sent me home, telling me that there was nothing I could do, and the nurses didn't want me hanging around anyway. That night I lay in bed thinking the "what if" thoughts. You know, what if something happens to Helen, and what if the baby don't make it? I worried myself to sleep.

I need not have worried. On Tuesday, August 24, at the St. Francis Hospital, Helen gave birth to a healthy baby boy. We named him Jimmy Steven.

It was an unforgettable moment seeing my son cradled in my wife's loving arms. It gave me a sense of continuity, and I knew that my family would always come first. The pursuit of fame and wealth would always be second best as far as I was concerned. That was the way I felt then, and I still do.

Vickie and Jake LaMotta were Helen's first visitors. They arrived with enough flowers for the whole darn ward. Jake was a big spender type of guy.

Earlier in the year, Jake had a bout in Miami. He asked me if I would work with him. "Gee, Jake, I'd love to, but I gotta tell you, I have already committed to work in Billy Kilgore's corner."

"So, you're gonna be in my opponent's corner. What kind of crap is that?"

"Billy asked me last week. Hell, I didn't know you would ask me."

Jake smiled and put his arm around my shoulders, "Hey pal, I'm only kiddin'. If you're committed, you're committed. I understand." He thought for a moment. "How about gym work? You wanna work with me in the gym? Try and sharpen me up?"

"Sure, Jake. I'll do what I can. You sure need sharpening up. I'm gonna work your butt off, but we shoulda started months ago. Just one thing, Jake, on the night when I'm in Billy's corner I'll be rooting one hundred percent for my guy, understand?"

"Sure, Angie. We gotta deal."

Jake insisted that he pay me for my work, and I didn't argue. After all, you wouldn't make a suit for your friend for free if you were a tailor! It was the only time in my career that I got paid from both corners.

Jake lost that night, and as it worked out, it was his last fight as a professional boxer. He had a wonderful record of 106 bouts, out of which he only lost fifteen. His career spanned a period in which there was a wealth of great middleweights: Marcel Cerdan, Robert Villeman, Fritzie Zivic, and Sugar Ray Robinson. Jake fought them all; he was one hell of a fighter.

Helen and baby Jimmy were home. It was a strange and wonderful feeling to come home and find them both there. The first thing I did when I came in was to kiss Helen, then I would go and look at the invariably sleeping Jimmy. Gee, I never realized babies were so cute and tiny.

Helen was still very weak. Although she took care of Jimmy, who was not four weeks old, it was Mildred who ran the apartment.

One evening when I happened to be at home at a reasonable hour and had time to watch television, Mildred brought me over a freshly made cup of coffee. "Can we have a talk, Angelo?"

"Why sure, any time." I turned down the television sound, which was already practically inaudible because Helen and Jimmy were both sleeping.

"I can't stay here indefinitely, Angelo. I have to get back and I want to take Helen and Jimmy with me so that I can really look after them. I can't stand the weather here in September, it's so humid. It isn't good for Helen either. She can't get out and walk around in this heat."

"What does Helen say about it?"

"I haven't mentioned it yet. I thought I'd talk it over with you first. That's another thing, you are hardly ever here. Most every week you're flying out to Cuba. How will Helen manage if you're not here and I am not here, in her present state?"

Mildred was right. There was no point in putting things off. Mildred and I spoke to Helen the next morning and they arranged to leave the following day.

It was a sad experience watching them drive off, but I knew it was a sensible move and it would only be for a short while. In the meantime, it was going to be business as usual—I had a wife and son to keep now!

I fixed Willie Pastrano three fights in Miami. He won them all. In fact, he went through 1954 without a defeat. Ralph Dupas had one setback when he lost to Paddy Demarco in New Orleans, but he won all his other seven fights during the year.

Ralph was a quiet kid, maybe a little introverted. It was amazing how he could soak up all the attention and glamour from being a star in the ring, and be so quiet and unassuming away from it. He was a great little fighter. When I hear the expression "fast hands," I always think of Ralph. Boy, was he fast! Ralph went from lightweight to welterweight, fighting the best of both divisions until he eventually made his mark as a junior middleweight. Ralph had to wait a long time before he got his due recognition.

Ralph was boxing most of the time in New Orleans, and he never came with me to Cuba. Clarence Hinnant, a light-heavyweight, took a few trips with me to Havana and was one of the fighters who were helping me build a reputation in Cuba as a manager-trainer.

Clarence had three fights in Havana, winning all of them, but he never became a champion. He was a good fighter, who, like a lot of professional boxers, never made the headlines or the big money. They were first-class athletes and a credit to their sport, as was the quiet man from Syracuse, Carmen Basilio. Every time I worked with Carmen, my belief that one day he would be champion was reinforced. He was fearless, completely dedicated and a better boxer than many people, who should have known better, realized. Being in his corner was always a worrying experience, because Carmen cut easily. In early 1954, I had to prove my worth as a corner man.

It was the Basilio-Langlois fight in Syracuse. Norm Rothschild was the promoter. We had met before and he was the kind of guy who had time for people. He spoke to me before the fight. "Do you have your black bag with you, Angie? I think you might need it tonight. Langlois is going to give Basilio a tough time tonight." Boy, was he right!

Carmen's eye was badly lacerated. The skin of the eyelid was split, it looked real bad. I used the styptic ointment, that my fighters had affectionately nicknamed "the Dundee ointment." I also applied thymol iodine and alum. I pressed a solution of chloride 1-1000 into the wound and carefully pushed the loose skin upwards until it was immersed into the ointment. I secured it with a thick layer of vaseline. The repair would hold until the wound was struck again. In between each round I worked on the cut and kept my fingers crossed that Langlois would get discouraged and go for another target area, like Carmen's jaw—Carmen's jaw was like granite!

Basilio got through the bout and took the decision, but after the fight we had to take him to the hospital, where his wounds were attended to. There was no argument that Basilio cut easily, but not once during the years that I worked with him was a fight stopped because of cuts.

It had to happen—I felt it. I didn't know when or where, but I just believed that I would be involved in a world championship fight. 1954 was over, and I wondered how long it would be before I realized my dream.

I analyzed my chances. I knew it was too early in the careers of Willie Pastrano and Ralph Dupas, although Ralph was stringing together a lot of wins. Unfortunately for my bank account, his fights were nearly all in New Orleans. I didn't really care about receiving no percentage from those fights, but it was making it difficult for Whitey Esneault to turn down the attractive purses local promoters were paying, and let Ralph take less money to fight out of town and build up his reputation nationwide.

Would Jimmy Beecham be my first fighter in a title shot? I

didn't think so. He wasn't ready. The other young, talented fighters with whom I was involved just were not good enough. It would have to be a fighter that I didn't manage. One I only worked with. One fighter stood head and shoulders above the rest. In early 1955, Joe Netro called to tell me that Carmen Basilio was getting a shot against Tony DeMarco for the world welterweight title. The bout was scheduled for June 10, in Carmen's home town of Syracuse. Did I want to work the corner? Is the Pope Catholic!

I arrived in Syracuse ten days before the fight so that I could be on hand for the final stages of Carmen's training. Although nothing specific had been said, and I was only paid to work the corner as a second, my duties had widened. I guess it began when I unconsciously started giving instructions and advice during a fight. John de John and Joe Netro, who was the tactician, were nearly always in the corner with me, but they let me control it and they never curbed my natural enthusiasm to say what I thought was best for Carmen. The instructions I gave seemed to work, and Joe Netro obviously agreed with what I said. More important, Basilio agreed with what I said.

Carmen had a mind of his own. He was a man who knew what he wanted and was capable of getting it. He was meticulous in his preparation. I had never before or since known a fighter who was so self-contained. He would arrive at a fight with all that was required for a boxer. Bandages, tapes, cotton gauze pads, towels, vaseline, iodine, and even a pair of scissors. Many of the guys I have worked with arrived at a venue armed only with confidence, and even that you couldn't guarantee.

I was flattered that Carmen had enough faith in me to let me control his corner in a championship bout. Need I tell you I was on cloud nine? This was one hell of a thrill for me. Since my days in New York I had wanted to be involved in a world title shot, and hell, this was it. Sure, I was excited, but I knew that I could handle the job.

I liked and admired Carmen. He was as tough as any man could wish to be. Because he cut and bruised easily, his skill at boxing was often overlooked. He could slip punches and hook with both hands. By any standards, Basilio must rank with the greatest.

His opponent, the reigning world champion Tony DeMarco, had not been defeated since 1952. That gives you an idea of how good he was. He had won the title from Johnny Saxton, who had in turn taken it from the legendary Kid Gavilan. It was a time of tough, talented fighters. To become a champion you had to beat awesome opposition.

Both DeMarco and Basilio were only five feet five and a half inches tall, and would come in weighing around 147 pounds. They were two lethal packets of dynamite.

I soaked up the atmosphere. This was for the world title—I had made it. I looked around at the packed auditorium. It was a magnificent sight and the excitement charged through me, making my heart beat faster and electrifying every nerve in my body. The bell sounded for the beginning of the fight. From that moment on it became just another fight. To me, there was no such thing as an unimportant bout. This one just happened to be a championship bout. All my concentration was on my fighter and the fight in progress, and brother, I wanna tell you, it was one hell of a fight.

The end came in the twelfth round. Carmen, bloodied and cut, proved too strong for DeMarco, who finally fell to one of Carmen's unique right uppercuts. It was all over. Carmen Basilio was the new Welterweight Champion of the World.

1956 had only just begun. I received an invitation from the Chicago Sports Writers and Broadcasters Association to attend their annual award ceremony on February 14.

On the given date, wearing my first tuxedo and black bow tie, I attended the ceremony. I watched the after-dinner proceedings with growing excitement. The supremely talented Sugar Ray Robinson had been voted Fighter of the Year. Chuck Speiser, a college graduate, whose prematurely receding hairline belied his youth, was Rookie of the Year. The Man of the Year award went to Julius Helfand, the New York boxing commissioner. The award for the Boxing Trainer of the Year went to—you've guessed it— Angelo Dundee.

After the ceremony, flushed with happiness and emotion, I spoke with Dave Condon of the *Chicago Daily News*. Dave was flattering. "Congratulations, Angie. You deserve an award after the way you took care of Basilio in the Langlois and DeMarco fights. You sure did a number on those cuts. I'd have taken odds that the ref would have stopped the Langlois fight. You did a great job."

"Hey thanks, Dave. That's what I'm paid for."

As we stood rapping, the boxing commissioner of New York stopped by. "Congratulations, Angelo, well done."

"Congratulations to you, sir. Things have sure changed for me since 1953 when I last had dealings with the New York Commission." I smiled and winked at him. He winked back; he knew I was referring to the Carbo episode.

"That's right, Angelo, now you're famous. Isn't that right, Dave?"

"Why sure—Dundee the famous trainer. Next it's gonna be Dundee the famous manager." Helfand and Condon nodded affirmatively, their faces split into beaming smiles.

I knew that I hadn't been Basilio's first-string trainer, but it was my work with him that gave me the spotlight. I also knew that these knowledgeable sports writers and broadcasters were aware of the work I had done in training Johnny Holman, Willie Pastrano, and Jimmy Beecham. I gratefully accepted their recognition. But I knew that I was not famous.

"Hey, guys, I'm not famous. You're putting me on." I grinned sheepishly.

"Okay, so you're not famous yet. You will be," Dave Condon said confidently. Julius Helfand smiled in agreement.

I felt that my life was going into another phase. It was a strange feeling.

On April 27, 1956, Rocky Marciano retired as the undefeated Heavyweight Champion of the World. It was the end of an era in boxing. I felt Rocky's retirement was an omen. It was the end of an era for me too.

CHAPTER TWELVE

THE BRITISH CONNECTION

"Jack Hart, the referee, came over to our corner as I finished attending to [Willie's] eye. . . .

" 'Remove the Vaseline so that I can see the cut,' Jack requested unreasonably.

" 'What are you talking about? If I remove the Vaseline I may open the cut again.'

" 'I want to examine the cut.'

" 'Well, examine, but I ain't removing the Vaseline.'

"Jack Hart's mouth became a thin unyielding line. He signalled the timekeeper. The fight was stopped. Pastrano had lost."

They loved Willie Pastrano in England. We had arrived on October 15, which gave us one week to acclimatize and grab as much publicity as we could. The pre-fight promotion was lukewarm, but after they had seen Willie fight, the press went overboard. One paper said, "It took an American to show us how to box the British way."

Willie fought a six-foot-three Welshman with a big reputation and following. When I first met Dick Richardson, I thought he might be too big and too strong for Willie, but I remembered what Willie had done to the six-foot-six Johnny Holman, so I knew we were in with a good chance.

I asked the promoter, Jack Solomons, if I could see some film of Richardson, and he obliged. After viewing the action, I felt sure that Willie would be too fast for the mammoth Welshman. I was right. Willie was superb. He boxed in the classic British style, upright and using a lightning left-hand jab, but we had added a little American know-how. Willie could slip punches and hit and run better than the Commandos. Willie boxed masterfully for the ten rounds and won the fight without any argument.

I watched and listened to Willie giving interviews after the fight. He was confident and relaxed, and so different from the first time I took him and Ralph Dupas for an interview. The interviewer had

begun by asking some questions about my two young fighters. So
far so good. He then addressed a question to them. "Tell me,
Ralph, Willie, do you like being here in Miami?" They both nodded
their heads. That was it. Problem was, it was on radio!

Now Willie was turning into a sophisticated young man who
could charm both in and out of the ring. London fight fans fell
under his spell.

To be back again in England was like going down memory lane.
It hadn't changed too much since the wartime days of my last
visit. The Stagedoor Canteen in Piccadilly had gone, but the
Covent Garden Palais de Dance was still there, although I didn't
have the guts to go dancing.

I remembered what some of the British Tommys said about the
American servicemen stationed in Britain during the war: "There
is only three things wrong with the yanks. They're overpaid,
they're oversexed, and they're over here!" I don't know about the
overpaid bit, but the other two observations fitted Willie perfectly.

We were staying at the Piccadilly Hotel, right in the heart of
London's West End. It was a nice hotel with a charming and
friendly staff. Willie found some of the staff very friendly. One
morning he told me he didn't feel like coming down for breakfast,
so I went alone. When I returned I found him in the sack with the
chambermaid. He just laughed and said, "I fancied eating in bed."

Because of the big impression Willie made on the fight fans, we
postponed our departure for two days to negotiate future bouts in
England. Jack Solomons, the jovial Tsar of British boxing, invited
me to lunch to discuss plans. He met me at the hotel, and together
we walked the short distance to the restaurant he had chosen. I
expected a grand exclusive joint, for Jack was no piker, he smoked
cigars the size of the Empire State Building, but we stopped
outside a small deli. "I know you have good corned beef in New
York, but you haven't lived until you have tasted the stuff here at
the Nosh Bar. By the way, here in England we don't call it corned
beef, we call it salt beef. Corned beef is something entirely
different." He took my arm and led me in.

We had a plate of Scottish smoked salmon to start, followed by
corned beef on rye. The portions were smaller than stateside, but
I've got to tell you, it was sensational. Over a tea with lemon we
discussed business. Considering that I had a South Philly accent
and Jack spoke English with a cockney accent, we understood
each other pretty good. "Quite a boxer, your Willie Pastrano. I've
never heard a crowd applaud a fighter for making the other fellow

miss." Jack wasn't kidding. Halfway through the fight, every time the elegant Willie made the huge Richardson miss, the crowd broke into applause.

"Who do you have in mind for Willie next?"

"From what I've heard about Pastrano, what about the chorus line from the London Palladium." Jack laughed at his flip line, and nearly choked on his cigar.

"That'll be fine for one night, but what about the rest of the week?" I said, straight-faced.

Eventually we got round to talking business. It was agreed that Willie would fight Brian London, a tough British boxer who came from a fighting family. His father, Jack London, had been a British champion. We set the date for February 1958. (Later in his career, Brian London went in against Muhammad Ali, but perhaps the occasion overwhelmed him, for he never showed his true capabilities. He went out in round three.)

I left England with a feeling of optimism. I had called Helen, and everything was under control back home. Jimmy was three years old and now he had a baby sister to keep him company. In April, Helen had made another trip to St. Francis Hospital. This time I was there to drive her to the hospital. After a ten-day stay, she left with an adorable baby girl who had been born on April 16, 1957. We named her Terri.

I thought to myself that if Willie beat all the British heavyweights, it would put him in line for a world title shot. If he won! Well, that's what dreams are made of. As it stood at present, the British trip would pay off the cost of the air conditioning that I had installed in my Miami home.

The success of the trip to London, plus the fact that I knew I had a contract for another fight over there, instilled in me a little more confidence, and it showed in my relationship with Chris. I was still doing all the dogsbody jobs, but there was a slight change in Chris's attitude towards me. Chris began including my name when he referred to the fighters. Everyone at the 5th Street Gym, which Chris had leased since 1952, used to assume all the fighters working out of the gym were part of the Chris Dundee organization. Now, they were beginning to realize that Angelo Dundee had something to say. By the time I left for England again in 1958, the guys at the gym knew that I was more than just a gofer for Chris. They realized that Dupas, Beecham, Hinnant, Cooper, and Pastrano were my guys. Dupas and Pastrano were on the verge of the big-time. They had to give me credit for that.

Willie Pastrano had taken a house in Miami. He and his wife would visit with Helen and me, and naturally Helen thought Willie charming. Having Willie on hand made it easier to keep him in shape, ready for his fight with Brian London scheduled for February 25, 1958. The time came round quickly enough.

London in February was cold and damp, but the press reception warmed us up. Jack Solomons and I were on the same wavelength. We both believed in promotion and publicity, and we both had a natural affinity with the members of the Fifth Estate. I made friends with a bunch of the British newspapermen. Over the years, on subsequent visits to England, I renewed my friendship with some good reporters who knew the fight game; men like Peter Wilson, Ken Jones, Reg Gutteridge, Desmond Hackett, and George Whiting. I guess one good pro recognizes another, and that holds true on both sides of the Atlantic.

Willie trained once again at the Thomas A'Beckett Gym. A strange kind of setup—it was situated over a pub. I made certain Willie left straight after training! The gym had a good atmosphere and I met some good guys there. There were twins by the name of Cooper. Nice kids, and one in particular had a big talent. I couldn't know then that I would be involved in a controversial fight with him within a few years. Henry Cooper was the kid's name, and in 1963 he was to give my guy, known at the time as Cassius Clay, a very nasty scare and a very hard left hook. Cooper's manager, Jim Wicks, was a wily old fox who knew the fight game, and he and I got on well together. Jim had a love of boxing and great respect for his fighters. We both knew that no two fighters were the same and you had to treat and train each one differently.

I was enjoying my brief stay in London. I made time for myself to get out and see the city and meet a lot of people.

The night before the fight, Jack Solomons called me at the hotel. "Tell me, Angelo," Jack sounded a little perturbed. "Have you been socializing with a fellow by the name of Albert Dimes?"

"Yes, a nice guy. He's a *paisano.*" In case Jack didn't know what I meant, I explained. "He's Italian, well, English-Italian, and he is introducing me to London's Italian community."

"Well, Angelo, do me a favor. Stay away from him. He's a boss of the underworld, and he's a very naughty boy."

Naughty boy! I love the English understatement. After my experience with Frankie Carbo in Washington I was going to be careful. I stayed away from Albert, although he seemed such a nice guy, and such a big fight fan.

The night of the fight arrived. On February 25, Willie Pastrano outboxed Brian London to chalk up his second win in England. Not surprisingly, we were offered another bout. Did we want Joe Bygraves? I called the States and spoke to Whitey Esneault. Willie's co-manager wanted to take the fight if the money was right, and Whitey also had some good news for me. We had an offer for Ralph Dupas to go in against Joe Brown for the lightweight title on May 7 in Houston. What did I think? Joe Brown was about thirty-two years old. I knew he was good, I had seen him when he won the all services lightweight championship. But thirty-two! "Let's go for it," I said.

I got the bread we wanted for Willie against Bygraves, and I also agreed to give Brian London a return fight in the fall. Then from out of leftfield we had another fight offered, and we agreed for Pastrano to fight Franco Cavicchi in Bologna, Italy, on June 15. We had been busy little boys!

Before I left London, I was approached by another big wheel in British boxing, Harry Levene. He offered me a bout for Pastrano against the nice young kid I had met at the Thomas A' Beckett Gym—Henry Cooper, the more talented of the twins. I would have liked that fight, but I told Harry that I would have to talk it over with Solomons, as he had been the guy responsible for bringing us over. It seemed the right thing to do, and I felt I owed it to Jack. I am glad that I played it that way, because unknown to me, there was a power struggle going on in British boxing between Levene and Solomons. I didn't take the fight, I played straight with Jack, but it didn't lose me any points with the Levene organization either. As time went on, I had fighters on many of Levene's promotions.

Sadly, Jack Solomons has passed away, and Harry Levene is no longer as active in boxing as he used to be, which is a pity. They were good for boxing. They had the initiative and flair to bring the world's best boxers to Britain. Nowadays Britain has new boxing promoters: Frank Warren, an enterprising young man, and the experienced Mickey Duff and Mike Barrett, to name but three. Yea, Britain has a lot of good promoters, trainers, and fighters— you notice I didn't mention heavyweights!

It was time to get back to the States. Once I knew the business was finished and there was nothing to keep me, I got that overwhelming urge to get home to Helen and my kids. It was always that way. While I had things to take care of and my mind was occupied, I could cope with being away, but once it was over, I had to go.

Armed with a doll for Terri, a British Bobby's toy hat for Jimmy, and a bracelet for Helen, I boarded the plane for the States. Willie Pastrano accompanied me, but I didn't see much of him on the plane. He spent the time trying to get a not too pretty and slightly overweight stewardess to make it with him in the toilet. I don't know if he succeeded, I fell asleep.

It seemed that no sooner had I arrived home than I was off again. March flew by, and before I knew it we were in the middle of April. Time to return to London for the Joe Bygraves fight.

Helen, God bless her, understood that I had to go. I wanted to be home at nights, play with the kids, take my wife out to dinner, but it was a case of necessity. I had to earn a living, and to do that I had to travel. If Helen had asked me to give it all up and get a nine to five job I don't know what I would have done. Fortunately she never asked.

During the time I was home, we hired a babysitter and got out a few nights, but whether we went out or stayed in, we enjoyed being together. Helen and I discussed my summer schedule; I was going to do more flying than a Pan-Am pilot. April in London, May in Houston, June in Bologna; and that didn't include all the trips I would be making if Carmen Basilio wanted me—and he would. Then there were the bouts I was working on in the Caribbean and Cuba. It was a physical impossibility to make all the bouts with my fighters. I couldn't make a trip to Paris with Ralph Dupas. I had to turn down corner work for other fighters if they clashed with my fighters' bouts. I believed my guys needed me in their corner, and I tried to be there, but it wasn't always possible.

Whitey Esneault, my partner in Dupas and Pastrano, was not a strong man. He was to lose a leg because of an obscure disease, which made travel virtually impossible for him. I began to keep my eyes open for someone I could trust to go on the trips with my fighters. I used different people at different times, but I never found the ideal person. The real problem was that I was needed in the corner, and I couldn't find another me.

Helen saw no point in staying alone in the house during Miami's hot and humid summer, so we decided that she and the children would accept Mildred's standing invitation and spend the summer in North Carolina. Mildred had a nice home with acres and acres of land. It was ideal for the kids, and Helen would have Mildred and her old friends to keep her company. I would commute when I was back in Miami. Helen and I still believed it would get easier as I grew more successful. We were naive.

Willie and I arrived in London for the third time. I had heard about April in Paris, but I settled for April in London. So it rained, who cared? England was becoming a home away from home. I have never experienced a situation like this one: we were treated like the local boy, and the Britisher, Joe Bygraves, like the stranger.

I couldn't wait to get to the venue, which was at Leicester. I attended the weigh-in, and checked the ring as I usually did, then I cut out. I hired a taxi and drove to the old USAF base where I had been first stationed when I arrived in England during the war. It was still there, deserted and kind of forlorn-looking. Memories, not all good, came flooding back. I asked the taxi driver if the base was used for anything. In that unique Leicestershire accent he answered, "Not a lot. It's a good place at night for courting couples. On a Saturday night, after the pubs close, there is nearly as much action in the back of the cars as there was during the war." What could I say? It brought me out of my reverie. I thought of Willie!

April 21, and another win for Willie Pastrano, elegantly executed. Joe Bygraves worked hard, but was outpointed over the ten rounds. There was no time for celebrations, I had to get back home. Ralph Dupas was going for the World Lightweight Championship in Houston on May 7.

There wasn't much time and I was whacked out from the traveling. I spent a couple of days with Helen and the children, checked in with Chris, and began overseeing Ralph's training. I didn't like what I saw, and blamed myself because I should have anticipated it. Ralph had been fighting as a lightweight, very successfully too, but he had put on muscle in the last couple of years, and now at twenty-two, making the weight of 135 pounds wasn't easy. Whitey should have made Ralph shed the extra weight earlier. With just over two weeks to fight night, I was worried that taking the pounds off now would weaken him.

Joe "Old Bones" Brown wasn't a champion for nothing. He was clever, experienced, and strong. I knew we were in for a tough fight. When we arrived in Houston, I arranged as many personal appearances for Ralph as possible. The hotel in which we were staying was holding an Elk convention. I called the organizer and asked him if he would like his fellow conventioners to meet Ralph Dupas, challenger for the world lightweight title. He was as excited as a schoolboy on his first date and arranged for us to make an appearance the following night before dinner. Maybe it helped sell a few more tickets, maybe not, but the name of the game was sell the fight and sell the fighter, and if you don't try you don't get.

Ralph gave it a good shot, but I could tell by round five that he was getting tired. I was reluctant to stop the fight—after all, this was for a world title—but in round eight I knew that I wasn't going to allow Ralph to start round nine. The referee saved me the trouble. He stepped in between Brown and Dupas, who was against the ropes, and stopped the fight.

Ralph was heartbroken. Though I did all I could to snap him out of his misery, he believed that all his years of building up to a title shot were wasted. "Nothing is ever wasted if you learn from it," I told him, but I don't think he was listening. It wasn't easy making Ralph understand that his world hadn't collapsed. I told him that it isn't the act of a fighter to go to pieces because he loses a fight. So it was for the title! So what! Had the world stopped turning? What you gonna do, curl up and die? We would try again. He could do it. He had the talent, the heart, and the determination. Right? What we would do next time is fight at a more natural weight. We would see how things went as a welterweight Right!

I left Ralph Dupas feeling down but not destroyed. He would get over it in a couple of days. My next date was with Pastrano, who was feeling on top of the world. He was in condition, not so much from gym work, but because he had fought in February and April and he hadn't laid off long enough to do much damage.

As usual Willie clowned around, but I kept after him and made him do his training sessions. After three weeks' work in the 5th Street Gym, we were ready to leave for Italy and meet Franco Cavicchi.

Bologna is known for its cuisine; Willie and I were like two kids in a candy store. It was rough keeping Willie away from the restaurants. It was just as tough keeping myself away. I told Willie, "You are sharp at your present weight, if you put weight on before the fight, you're gonna slow up. When you have beaten Cavicchi, after the fight, you and I will put on the feeding bag, and you can eat the restaurant out of food."

Willie won the fight on points, which ain't too easy to do in Bologna against an Italian fighter. Maybe being of Italian extraction helped. I'll tell you, winning a fight on points against the local hero is never an easy job.

That night we ate and drank, and it was a case of pure gluttony. I foolishly mixed my drinks, a thing I should never do. When I got back to the hotel I didn't feel too good. Willie and I were sharing a room and when I went up to the room to use the bathroom, Willie stayed in the lounge drinking with some admirers.

I was sick. I vomited. I lay on my bed for a spell, then vomited again, head bent over the toilet bowl, wishing I was dead. The smell was nauseating. I lay back on my bed with the lights out, hoping I would sleep. I heard the door quietly open and Willie whispering in Italian to his companion, "It's OK. My friend is fast asleep. Just come in for a little while, I gotta get my arms around you." I heard them enter the room. "Momma Mia!" It was a female voice. "That smell! It's revolting. I can't stay here. It's horrible."

I heard the sounds of someone leaving the room and Willie's voice protesting. The door closed and Willie's sigh filled the air. I just pretended to be asleep, and although I still felt ill, I fell asleep with a smile on my face. And it was arrivedercci to Bologna.

I sure was busy. It was a hectic summer but I revelled in the work. Time was found for weekend visits to North Carolina, where I recharged my batteries both mentally and physically. Being with Helen and the kids was all the tonic I needed. I was lucky to have a mother and father-in-law to whom I could relate, and who understood the peculiarities and demanding requirements of the fight game. Mildred and George gave my children the opportunity to play in green fields and grow up appreciating the beauty of the countryside.

Another warm and enjoyable weekend in North Carolina came to an end. It was always difficult saying goodbye, but once I was on my way back to Miami, my thoughts honed in on the immediate job in hand. This time, in September 1958, my thoughts were on the return fight between Brian London and Willie Pastrano. Willie had beaten London comfortably last time, which gave us a psychological advantage. But London was strong and had something to prove in front of his own countrymen. Still, Willie should dance home a winner. Would I ever learn that anything can happen in a fight?

The Pastrano-London fight was held in London on September 30. I had Willie ahead on points, but somehow he had suffered a nasty cut over his left eye. Maybe it was a clash of heads, perhaps a blow, it may have been a butt, who knows? I didn't. London had no chance to win the fight by staying away and trying to out-jab Willie, so he bored in, quite rightly so. It was obvious to me that Willie had a fight on his hands, but cut or not, I had him winning.

Before the fifth round began, I cleaned up the blood on Willie's face and around the cut eye. With a gauze swab I applied a coagulant ointment and then carefully covered the cut area with a thick layer of Vaseline. Jack Hart, the referee, came over to our corner as I finished attending to the eye, and asked to look at the cut. The bleeding had stopped, and all that anyone could see was the layer of Vaseline.

"Remove the Vaseline so that I can see the cut," Jack requested unreasonably.

"What are you talking about? If I remove the Vaseline I may open the cut again."

"I want to examine the cut."

"Well, examine, but I ain't removing the Vaseline."

Jack Hart's mouth became a thin unyielding line. He signalled the timekeeper. The fight was stopped. Pastrano had lost.

Sure, there were arguments after the fight. The press took sides. It was a good newspaper story! American fight manager questions English referee's decision. It was controversial, but no big deal. It died a natural death and no enemies were made. Jack Hart later refereed another bout where I had a fighter, Gomeo Brennen, fighting for a British Commonwealth title. It was a very close fight and the decision could have gone either way, but Jack Hart awarded the fight to my guy. I like to think that Jack leaned towards my fighter to make up for that bad decision in the Pastrano fight. I'd like to think that, but I don't really believe it.

If you are wondering how I, an American, was involved in a fight for a British Commonwealth title, let me explain. Gomeo Brennen was from Bimini, a tiny island off the coast of Florida. At the time, Bimini was part of the British Commonwealth, now it is part of the Independent Bahamas. Later in his career, Brennen and I had a falling-out. He was one of the few boxers that walked out on me. He charged that I gyped him out of some money. In fact, he walked away owing *me* money. I took his records, cash receipts, and check receipts to be examined, and was completely exonerated of any malpractice, but I lost the fighter and lost the money I had personally loaned him. As they say, you win some and you lose some!

It wasn't until 1959 that Willie and I returned to England. This time it was to meet Joe Erskine. I didn't know too much about Joe, but I was told that he was a nice boxer without a big punch. It promised to be a good fight. Joe Erskine had a big following in his

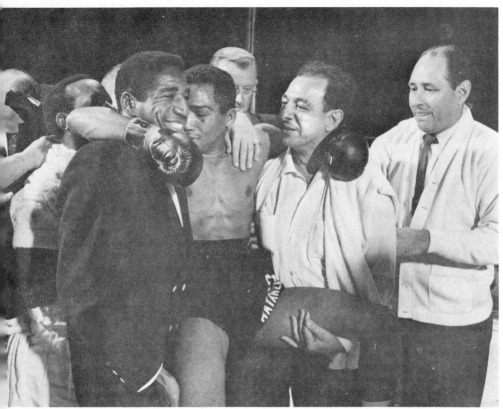

ugar Ramos wins the world title. A laughing Luis Rodriguez, who had won his
le earlier that same night, helps me hold up the champ. (Sports Illustrated)

he tragic blow that ended the fight—and also Davey Moore's life. (Sports Illustrated)

Me and the four brothers—Jimmy, Frank, Chris, and Joe. (Bill Mark)

Helen with Muhammad's mother, Odessa, out collecting snapshots for the album.

Professor Dundee and his magic box of tricks. (R. Stiggins)

Waiting for the decision. Emile Griffith seems to know he has lost his title; Luis Rodriguez's poker face gives away nothing. (Sports Illustrated)

The Angelo Dundee hand-wrapping special. It ain't as easy as it looks! *Above:* With Muhammad Ali. (Keystone) *Below:* With Willie Pastrano. (Sports and General)

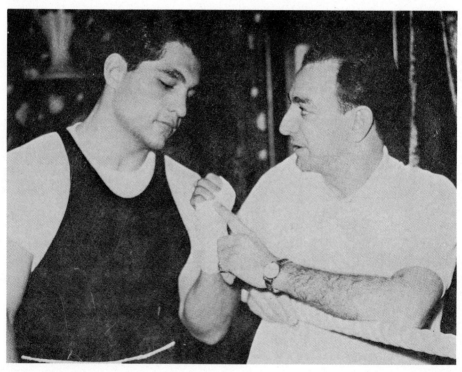

Joe Louis with my son, Jimmy, on the left, and Gary Glick, son of the Miami Beach Boxing Commissioner, on the right. (Miami Beach Sun)

With Jimmy Ellis after his loss to Joe Frazier in Melbourne, Australia, 1975.

Sharing bread with José Napoles in Paris,
before the Monzon fight.(Associated Press)

Tying the gloves and last-minute advice before a training session.

These photographs show the controversial punch that did it! *Top:* Liston jabs. *Center:* Liston, up on his toes, is reaching for the elusive Ali, who throws a long right hook over Liston's left jab. *Bottom:* The blow has landed. Liston is flat-footed, his shoulders have slumped, he is about to crumble. Ali wins with a first-round knockout! (Manny Spiro)

"Hey I don't wanna fight Joe Bugner; he's too big!" That's the famous promoter Don King on the left—the Ali-Bugner fight at Kuala Lumpur, 1980.

Either I'm making notes on the fighters, or I'm doing my laundry list!

native Wales, and his fans would travel to London to see their guy whip the yank.

Willie was confident. The cut that he received in September 1958 was just a memory; after all, this was February 1959. A different year, a different ball game. Willie was now twenty-three years old and had seven years' solid experience behind him. We couldn't worry too much about how good his opponent might be, Willie had to beat them all if he was going to be a champion. Floyd Patterson was World Heavyweight Champion, and there was talk of a title defense against Ingemar Johansson, the Swedish blond bomber who was the European champion. Johansson had stopped Erskine in thirteen rounds the previous year. Willie had to beat Erskine if I was going to get on the phone to Cus D'Amato, Patterson's manager, to ask for a shot at the title.

On February 24, on a cold, damp night in London, Willie Pastrano lost a ten-round contest against Joe Erskine.

No excuses. No cop-outs. Erskine was brilliant and the better man on the night. I was surprised at his skill. If he had only been a bigger man, and if he could have developed a heavier punch, he would have been a world beater. As it was, he beat Pastrano and a lot of other good fighters.

Willie and I left England knowing we had to re-think our plans for the future. I thought about how tough it was going to be for Erskine, because of his stature and weight, and the thought crossed my mind that perhaps a lighter and faster Pastrano might find the championship that had eluded him so long. The thought stuck, and in the near future I would act on it.

CHAPTER THIRTEEN

STILL IN
THE GAME

"I turned to a clean page in my notepad and began writing out a list of my confirmed bouts and the names of all the boxers that I either managed or co-managed. I was involved with fifteen fighters . . . only four or five of those boxers were world champion material. I listed Pastrano, Dupas, and Luis Rodriguez."

Back in the States after the Erskine fight, psychologically Willie was low, and even talked of quitting the ring. He was living with his wife and children in Miami. On the Sunday, I invited them over. The kids would play together, they got along well, and it would give us grownups a chance to talk. I didn't think I would bring up the subject of his quitting. I would pretend I hadn't taken it seriously. "Hey, Willie, I've got a new welterweight coming to the gym tomorrow. A kid by the name of Luis Rodriguez. He was the Cuban champion. I've seen him fight, and I tell you, he's something else."

"Yea? I'll come down and watch him. Maybe I'll do a little sparring. Give the guys a laugh. I had better brush up on my Spanish. Si Señor?"

It seemed Willie's threat of retiring was just that—a threat. He had made it before and he would probably make it again. When he lost a fight he could become very depressed. It was my job to lift him mentally. If ever he wanted to quit for logical or personal reasons I would be one hundred percent with him. I arranged a fight for him in July in Louisville. I never talked quitting to my fighters, I only talked winning.

Ernesto Coralles, Luis Rodriguez's manager, was waiting for me at the 5th Street Gym. He was talking with Rodriguez's trainer,

Luis Sarria, and Chris, who had arranged for a couple of sparring partners to work with Rodriguez.

The Cuban champion went to change, giving Chris and me a moment together. "If you do a deal with Corrales," said Chris, "I'll put the kid on a few promotions here in Miami. You gotta put him in at a give-away price to me; after all, Cuban fighters are gonna be a dime a dozen. That jerk Castro is ruining everything."

We watched Rodriguez work. I had seen him in real live action, so I knew what he had, but he looked good just sparring around. Willie arrived looking like a goddam film star. Everything stopped while he did his impersonations of other fighters. He got his usual laughs, and as usual he created a fun atmosphere.

Corralles and I sat on two hard wooden chairs that were part of a row of spectator seats. We came to an agreement. We would co-manage Luis Rodriguez.

That evening I stayed in the office after Chris left. I wanted to think. So much had happened since the Basilio championship fight. I wanted to get my head straight. Where was I going? I was working and traveling like a man possessed. I had so many things to take care of.

I looked at the notepad on my desk. It was covered with doodles. I didn't know I was doing it—doodling I mean. I couldn't read my own notes.

I deciphered from my notes that I had to take home photographs of the wrestlers for Terri and Jimmy. I took the kids to the weekly wrestling promotions and they were crazy about it. I examined the page for further information. At the top was a phone number, not yet covered by my contagious doodles. It was Joe Netro's office number. I had to call him—something about Basilio.

Since the welterweight title fight in 1955 I had been a regular member of the Basilio team. I occasionally missed out working his corner if I was needed by Willie, Ralph or any other fighter in whom I had a percentage, but that had been rare.

Carmen's explosive career was turning him into a boxing legend. In September 1957, Carmen beat Sugar Ray Robinson, who was already a legend, for the middleweight championship. Carmen then relinquished his welterweight title. He was having trouble keeping his weight under 147 pounds. He was more comfortable, but to my mind not as effective, at the middleweight limit of 160 pounds.

In a return bout in 1958, which was a vendetta fight, Sugar Ray

Robinson won back the title in Chicago on a split decision. American boxing was going through a power struggle, and a third and deciding bout with Robinson was lost in the political shuffle between the rival factions. It might have been one hell of a fight!

Against my advice Carmen's managers had agreed to the bout against Gene Fullmer. The fight was tentatively set for August, only six months away. I had already been asked to work the corner, and naturally I wanted to be with Carmen. But, I asked myself, was I spreading myself too thin?

I turned to a clean page in my notepad and began writing out a list of my confirmed bouts and the names of all the boxers that I either managed or co-managed. I was involved with fifteen fighters. In my personal and private opinion, only four or five of those boxers were world champion material. I listed Pastrano, Dupas, and Luis Rodriguez. The other possibilities were two Cuban fighters that I had recently become involved with: Douglas Vaillant, a very young 135-pound fighter and Florentino Fernandez, a junior welterweight at 140 pounds. Both these boxers were still very young and had only fought in Cuba, but I thought that they had big potential. Cuco Conde had recently called and asked if I was interested in another Cuban fighter. I always find it hard to say no, so I hedged the questions and told him that we would talk about it when I next came to Havana—God willing and Castro permitting!

OK, this is how it was going down: I was a reasonably successful manager, with some pretty good fighters; I was also a top-class second and trainer who was part of the Basilio team—and that was something to be proud of. Yet, I still felt that I was nowhere. It wasn't that I was nowhere. It wasn't that I was unhappy. It was just that I knew I hadn't really established myself, achieved anything. There were so many goals that I had yet to reach.

I had one hell of a lot of commitments. I had to start arranging bouts for Rodriguez. I'd speak to Chris about that tomorrow. Dupas was fighting next month in Jamaica against their champion. I'd have to check his training and his weight. Willie was going to Louisville in July to fight Johnson. I'd have to fix him some warm-up fights now.

The list went on, but I was tired and everything would keep until morning. I left the office, not forgetting to take the photographs of the wrestlers home for the kids.

Ralph Dupas and I flew to Kingston, Jamaica, for the fight against Gerald Gray, the Jamaican champion. We were made very welcome, even after we beat their champion. Friendly people. I was approached by Gray's manager who wanted to know if I would be interested in representing the Jamaican champion. I became Gerald Gray's co-manager—I told you that I find it hard to say no!

The few days in Jamaica had been a pleasant break. The island looked lovely—that is, what little I saw of it, because I was in the hustle and bustle of Kingston. The marriage between the black Jamaicans and the British was fascinating, and I loved their sing-song way of speaking. Their accent kind of reminded me of Joe Erskine's. He was Welsh, so I suppose it was just one of those things.

As beautiful as Jamaica was, I was glad to be back in Miami. I guess it is true to say that no matter how wonderful the places were that I visited, I was always pleased when I arrived back in Miami, and it still holds true today.

Back in the office, it was business as usual. I arranged with Chris to have Rodriguez fight in Miami in June. I would have just enough time to work with Rodriguez before I took Pastrano to Louisville for the fight against Alonzo Johnson. Hell, this was only March. I was always living in the future. Still, sitting on my butt wouldn't change anything. It was time to go to the gym anyway. I drove home, picked up Jimmy, and took him with me to the gym to watch the guys work out. I knew I had a wrestling fan for a son; maybe he would like boxing too!

The summer arrived, as I knew it would. It hadn't let me down so far! June in Miami is one of the better months. The weather has not yet reached the uncomfortable temperatures. June can float by in the low eighties, which ain't bad at all. In early July Helen and the children would leave for the more pleasant weather of North Carolina. Until then they would stay in Miami and enjoy the delightful June.

Jimmy, and occasionally Terri, would accompany me to the 5th Street Gym and watch the fighters work out. For at least a little while we were all together as a family. It sure made life easier when my fighters had bouts in Miami.

On June 17, Rodriguez had his first fight in the States at the Convention Hall on Miami Beach. The Cuban champion had no walkover fight. It was typical Chris philosophy: get them cheap and make them work. Well, he didn't pay Luis a lot of bread and he sure made him work. His opponent was Virgil Atkins, who was an ex-world champion, circa 1958. The fight went the full distance of ten rounds. Fortunately for me, Luis took the decision. It wouldn't have looked good to have my Cuban champion, whom I had praised to the high heavens, lose his first fight in America. For the record, Luis fought two more fights on the Beach during 1959, and won both of them against top-class opponents. He was on his way.

Willie Pastrano and I were on our way too. We were off to Louisville, Kentucky. I had left a day earlier than I had originally arranged. I thought maybe an extra day away from the temptations of Miami, and an extra workout in the Louisville gym, would do Willie some good.

I sympathized with him. It was depressing to have made such an impact in Britain and then watch it erode. His defeats by Brian London and Joe Erskine had taken away a lot of his confidence and his will to fight. I had tried to arrange a few fights between March and June, but nothing came along that was acceptable. Maybe Willie would not make a champion, in fact many people thought so, but I had no intention of giving up on him.

When I got Willie into the gym in Louisville, he seemed to cheer up. Bill King made a big fuss of us and reminded Willie that the last time he had come to Louisville there had been a horse race named in his honor, "The Willie Pastrano Classic." Willie laughed and said, "I'm entitled to have a horse race named after me—I'm a stud ain't I?"

Willie went through the motions of training. I watched him shadow-box. How good this guy could be, I thought to myself.

"Excuse me, Mister Dundee. Remember me?" A voice interrupted my concentration. I looked up at the handsome brown face.

"Why sure. How you doin'?" For the moment, I couldn't remember his first name. I knew his second name was Clay. He was the amateur I had met on my last trip in 1957. We stood by the ring and watched Willie. The bell sounded, signalling the end of three minutes. Willie wiped the sweat from his eyes with the towel I handed him.

"Hi, Mr. Pastrano. You're looking good," Clay said.

"Hi, Cassius." Willie had remembered the kid's name. "How you doin'? You still boxing?"

"Why sure. I'm gonna be in that Olympics next year. I'll be in that there Rome and I'll bring home a gold medal."

Willie and I smiled. "I sure hope you do, Cassius," I said, pleased I could use his first name now.

"Do you mind if I spar a round with Mister Pastrano?"

Willie answered before I did. "Sure, kid. Are you changed?"

Cassius nodded and began to remove his tracksuit pants.

I don't normally like amateurs working out with pros. The inexperienced kids could sometimes be clumsy and accidently hurt my guys, or what was even worse, the amateur would try and make it a fight and win a reputation by decking a pro. If that was attempted the professional could lose his temper and hurt the kid. I do not believe in gym wars. If you are a professional, when you fight you get paid for it. Everything else is training.

Clay climbed through the ropes. He towered at least three and a half inches over Willie. "Take it easy, guys. Make it graceful," I shouted out to both of them.

It was three minutes of pure pleasure for me. Not only for me: one by one the other guys in the gym stopped what they were doing and watched the two stylists box in the ring. Bill King placed an arm round my shoulder and said, "Ain't this something? That's what I think they mean when they talk of the noble art of self-defense."

The time-bell sounded, and the two guys in the ring laughed at each other as we all gave them a round of applause. Clay left the ring and sat down to watch Willie do another round of shadow-boxing. Willie went into his impersonation act. After all, he had a captive audience. He shouted out the name of the fighter, then imitated his style—Kid Gavilan, Floyd Patterson, Gene Fullmer. He closed his exhibition by shouting out the name Cassius Clay, and then giving an excellent impression of Cassius's individual style. Clay laughed louder than anyone.

The following day Cassius was again at the gym. We talked, and I liked the guy, but I didn't encourage any more sparring sessions.

Bill King, Willie, and I were having a light lunch after the training session. Tomorrow, no gym work. Just the weigh-in and the fight. During coffee Bill King brought up the subject of Cassius Clay. "What do you think of our local amateur champion, Angie?"

"Nice kid. Very talented. Made Willie work out for a change." I winked at Willie.

"Made me look good," Willie grinned at us. "Nice boxer, gotta lot of good moves. Don't you think, Angie?"

"Oh sure, the kid's a very talented amateur. He should do very well at the Olympics. He's big, strong, and fast. But he bounces around too much, takes the steam out of his punches. Hell of a nice kid."

Bill King nodded in agreement, then said, "If he can make the

Olympic team, that's one thing. If he can take a gold medal from those Russians and other so-called amateurs, that's something else—then he's gotta be good." We left it at that.

Willie lost against Alonzo Johnson on July 24, and we returned feeling down. I had just over a month before the Basilio-Fullmer fight for the NBA middleweight championship, and I wanted to get Willie into action quickly so that he would not lose confidence. We got lucky.

Basilio had a barn-storming win over Fullmer, and was once again a champion, and four days later, on August 30 in Knoxville, Willie KO'd Tom Davis in four rounds. He was still in the game, and if you are in the game there is always a chance of winning—right?

CHAPTER FOURTEEN

I GET THE GREATEST

"Cassius had made his prediction: 'Moore will go in four.' I helped Cassius with the 'poems,' but with rhymes like Moore and four who wants to take credit?"

It was September. The Olympics were over and Helen and I had watched the competition on television. Naturally my main interest had been in the boxing, and when Cassius Marcellus Clay won the gold medal for the light-heavyweight division I was overjoyed, like millions of other Americans, and kind of proud. Business activities pushed the event out of my mind until about a week later, when I read in one of the boxing magazines that Cassius Clay, the Olympic gold medal winner from Louisville, was turning professional under the direction of Dick Saddler and Archie Moore.

I didn't quite understand the setup, as Moore was still actively fighting. Dick, who I knew was a good trainer, was training Moore. Maybe Dick and Archie had a piece of Cassius Clay. I hoped the kid would do well, and then forgot all about it.

I had things on my mind. Tony Padron, a new fighter I was involved with, was going against Cuco Conde's fighter, José Napoles, and I was trying to get Rodriguez in against Emile Griffith. OK, I was very glad that Clay had won a gold medal, I wished him luck as a professional but I had other things to worry about.

I was in the office trying to get things sorted into some form of disorder that I could at least understand, when the phone went for about the hundredth time—and it was still not lunchtime! Chris was in the Convention arena with some television people from New York, creating more problems by giving them assurances that he could never keep—a typical day in the life of a fight promoter.

"Hello, this is Angelo Dundee," I said into the telephone.

"Hi, Angelo, this is Bill Faversham. I'm calling from Louisville. We met in the gym there. Cassius Clay introduced us." I couldn't remember.

"Oh sure," I said, lying through my teeth. "What's new?"

Faversham went into this story about how a group of Louisville businessmen had got together to back Clay in his career as a professional boxer. I said the appropriate things to keep the guy happy and give him a chance to breathe.

The story went on. The Louisville syndicate had made arrangements for Clay to train with Dick Saddler, who was currently working with light-heavyweight champion Archie Moore, but Cassius wasn't hitting it off with Moore, and he, Bill Faversham, had brought up my name as trainer. Clay liked the idea, and so did the rest of the syndicate. Bill Faversham headed the syndicate, and he wanted to know if I was interested and how I would handle the situation, so that he could report to the other members. I didn't take too much time to think of an answer, I knew I wasn't going to say no, but I didn't want to commit myself immediately. One must play hard to get.

"Well, Bill, thanks for thinking of me. I gotta tell you, Dick Saddler is a friend of mine and a damn good trainer, so I don't wanna step on any toes. From what I gathered, Cassius is in training for his first pro fight. I don't like to come in half-cocked. Let things stay as they are until after the fight. Then we can talk. I'll say this, Bill, if I work with Cassius, as good as we all think he is, I'm gonna take it nice and slow, nice and easy. A lotta people who should know better forget that there is a big difference between amateurs and professionals."

"It sounds good to me, Angelo. Cassius fights on October 29 here in Louisville. I'll be in touch after the fight and we can talk terms. By the way, Angelo, Bill King sends his regards. Take care."

So that's the way it stood. I must be honest—at the time it was no big deal. I told you, I had things on my mind and things to do. If Faversham got back to me, great. If not—what the hell.

I got back to Miami from Havana on October 16. José Napoles had beaten Padron, which really didn't surprise me. I'd seen Napoles before and I knew he could be a handful. My Cuban friends, Cuco Conde and Higinio Ruiz, who managed Florintino Fernandez, were kind of unsettled by the Castro take-over, but they still didn't believe that he would interfere with professional boxing. For my part, what did I know? Cuco asked me if I wanted to go to the Tropicana . . . you know that I find it difficult to say no! I left the Tropicana with a thick head and a thinner wallet.

As we got nearer to October 29, I got more interested in the Clay fight. If Faversham did get back to me and gave me a definite offer to train Clay, I wasn't too sure I wanted to take it. I knew I was spreading myself kind of thin. My fighters were pretty active, and to my mind they needed me in their corner. Luis Rodriguez had won another couple of fights earlier in the year in Los Angeles, and Ralph Dupas had made a couple of victorious trips to Australia—without me, I hasten to add—and was on a winning streak as a welterweight. My local fighters were getting some action, and my Cuban pals were offering me co-managership deals with some very good Cuban fighters. The only downers so far in the year of 1960 was Carmen Basilio going in again against Gene Fullmer and getting stopped in round twelve. That was in June. Carmen was thirty years old, Fullmer was four years younger, nearly three inches taller, and a natural middleweight. I hadn't wanted the fight, but I didn't have control.

The other downer took place in Glasgow, Scotland, in September. Wilfred Raleigh Pastrano, Willie Pastrano to you, lost a ten-round decision to Chic Calderwood. I guess I must take some of the blame for that defeat, although I thought he won the fight.

When we arrived in Glasgow I thought it would be a good promotional bit if Willie and I went to a local church. As Willie hated flying, it seemed a nice gesture to go to church and give thanks for arriving safely. The local press liked the thought and gave it a lot of coverage. A photograph of Willie with a Catholic priest got a lot of space. How was I to know that at that particular time there was a lot of friction between Catholics and Protestants, and that the majority of fight fans and officials, not to mention Chic Calderwood, were Protestant?

No way would I say that Willie being a Catholic had any bearing on the decision. But I thought we won!

I didn't want to push or interfere, but I thought I should see the Clay fight. I rang Bill King and let him talk me into coming up to Louisville. Bill was one of the syndicate backing Cassius. He was excited about the fight, and seemed excited too that I was going to be involved.

"Nothing fixed yet, Bill," I told him.

"Oh, we'll get together. The kid likes you. Hey, do you remember how he carried Luis Rodriguez's bag at the Atkins fight? That Clay is something else."

Bill was talking about the Rodriguez-Atkins fight that had taken place in Louisville in June. Clay had been at the gym as usual, and was on cloud nine for making the Olympic team. There was no doubt in his mind that he was going to bring home a gold medal, then turn pro and become champion of the world. Luis Rodriguez loved him, and although Luis' English wasn't too hot, he and Cassius spent the morning in the gym gagging with each other. That night Cassius was in the entrance hall when we arrived for the bout.

"I'll carry your bag, Mr. Cuban Champion," Cassius said, taking the bag from Luis.

"That's nice, Mr. Gold Medal," Luis answered.

"Save me buying a ticket," laughed Cassius as he strolled into the hall.

Now the clowning was over. It was time to see what Clay could produce in the ring. Everyone wanted to see the local hero in action. It was only a six-round contest, but after only ever fighting three rounds in his amateur career, it was an enormous step. I didn't know anything about Cassius's opponent, a kid by the name of Tunney Hunsaker, who is famous today because he was Clay's first professional opponent.

The fight went the six rounds. How was Clay? No one could deny Clay's natural ability, but his style gave a lot of hardened fight men the jitters. I listened to the comments, which were the same sort of remarks I would be hearing for quite a while.

"He's off balance when he punches." "He drops his guard, he'll get nailed." "If I wanna dancer, I'll go to Roseland." "He's got no punch." "That dancing might be OK for the amateurs, but no way can he get away with it for over six rounds."

I listened. There were truths in the opinions, but they were trying to compare Clay with other fighters. They were thinking how to change his style. I never went that route. To me, each and every fighter was different. I never tried to change them, just improve on their individual skills and get rid of bad habits. And a bad habit was only one that didn't work.

I was in the office when Bill Faversham called. The syndicate wanted me to take over as trainer, starting immediately. I suggested we might as well wait until after Christmas. That was turned down. Cassius wanted to start work right away. Before I asked what kind of deal they were offering, Bill said, "We'll pay you $125 per week every training week and for the week of the fight, or you can have a piece of the action. Say ten percent off the top. What do you say?"

"Well, Bill, we've got a deal one way or another. Send the kid down here to Miami and we'll start work. As for the financial arrangement, I'll let you know which deal I want in a couple of days. OK?"

"OK. Looking forward to working with you." Faversham hung up.

I met Cassius Clay at the station when he moved down to Miami, and took him to his chosen one-room apartment in the cheapest part of town. He didn't have to stay in such a joint, there were expenses to cover his accommodation, but he had a pal sharing his room and Cassius really didn't mind where he stayed. I don't think he even noticed. He was in Miami to train, to fight, to win, and to become a champion. Where he slept was incidental as long as it didn't interfere with his objectives. I asked him about the neighborhood. Was it too rough, I asked him. "No problem," he answered. He had made friends, the people were just fine. I realized that there was a lot to learn about this young man. When I arrived at the gym he was always there, ready to go. When our training session was over he was the last to leave. There was always an extra minute on the speed-bag, or the heavy bag.

Willie caught on fast. "Is this guy for real?" Willie was gagging, but there was respect and affection behind the remark. Don't get me wrong, it wasn't a heavy scene at the gym, in fact there were times when I thought I was working with the Keystone Cops, especially when Willie, Luis, and Cassius were there together. There was a lot of ribbing about who would make world champion first. On the surface you might have thought they were kidding, but I never thought so.

I had to go to Havana early in December to work with Sugar Ramos, the fighter Cuco Conde wanted me to co-manage, and on December 17 Luis Rodriguez was going in against Emile Griffith in New York. Griffith was managed by my old pal from New York days, Gil Clancy. Way back in 1949–50, Gil had said that one day we would work together; he never said we would be friendly rivals. I was looking forward to New York.

While I was away, there was no need to worry if Clay was training. Getting Cassius to train was no problem, stopping him was another thing! If only I could engender the same dedication in Willie. Maybe hanging around Cassius would do him some good. Becoming a champion seemed to be eluding Willie, and I was worried that disillusionment would set in. Boxers are highly trained athletes, tuned up to a degree not known in other sports. They ply their trade alone, and there is nowhere to hide. It is a marriage of top physical conditioning with unrelenting bravery. In my years in the fight game I have found that the professional boxers who successfully carve out a name for themselves are highly sensitive and complicated people. It is no wonder that boxing champions react in so many different ways to the pressures that fame and wealth bring. If you take the endurance of a tennis player, the courage of a racing driver, the sensibility of an actor, the continued discipline of a long distance runner, and mix those ingredients, you are on the way to knowing what it takes to be a professional boxer.

Not for the first time or the last, I disagreed with the fight decision. I thought Luis Rodriguez beat Emile Griffith on December 17, 1960, in New York. Gil Clancy, Griffith's manager, would have none of it. We were pals, but we didn't have to agree. I told Gil, "Luis will beat him next time, I'm gonna give the judges glasses so that they can see what's going on." It would be two years before we got another shot at Griffith. Gil was no fool.

I was back in the gym on the 19th. Cassius would have his second pro fight on December 27. We worked up to the 23rd. He was in good shape. I sent him home for Christmas. I had no worries that he would over-indulge himself. He was back in the gym on the 26th. I had flown down from North Carolina, where I was spending Christmas with the family. The fight was one that I could have done without. But it was a bout, and that's what the kid needed—bouts. I was kind of anxious to see how it went. Had he learned?

His controversial style hadn't changed, but I noticed the modifications. He knocked out Herb Siler in four rounds. Bill Faversham was delighted, and he thanked me. "Don't thank me," I said. "I didn't knock out Siler, Cassius did." But I was pleased.

Before I left for North Carolina to join my family, I confirmed with Chris that Clay would fight again on January 17 in Miami. Once I was surrounded by my family I relaxed, but I couldn't help talking about this new fighter I was training, to Helen and to anyone else who would listen. I must have bored everyone with my stories of how I had first met Cassius and how things had worked out, me ending up as his trainer. Mildred wanted to know if he was any good. I told her that with his dedication and natural talent he couldn't miss. I had them laughing when I told them about the phone conversation I had with Dick Saddler. When Dick learned that I was taking over as trainer, he called me.

"So you're working with Clay? Good luck, Angie, you're gonna need it."

"Yea? What's the story, didn't you get on with the kid?"

"Oh, sure. He's some character. He came with Archie and me to Texas. Cassius and me went by train. At every hick stop, deep in the heart of red-neck country, he would stick his big black head out of the window and shout "I'm the greatest." I thought we were gonna get lynched. He's some joker."

I laughed and said, "He sure is, but I hear he didn't make a hit with Archie. What was the problem, too many 'stars' "? I had gathered from Bill Faversham that Archie Moore and Cassius had a clash of personalities.

Dick Saddler explained, "Yea, I guess you could say that. One day Archie gave Cassius a broom and told him to sweep up the room. Clay didn't like that. He said to Archie, 'I didn't do that for my Ma,' and handed Archie back the broom. He can be a difficult kid. If you are gonna train that kid permanently, you deserve seven purple hearts." Helen liked that story. Many times in the coming years she would ask if I was earning my purple hearts.

I hoped to return to Miami feeling fit and relaxed so that I could tear into 1961, but I didn't. I was playing football with Jimmy and Frances' two sons, Ronnie, aged twelve, and Bobby, aged nine, when I tried to demonstrate how the great running backs of the famous Rio football team of South Philadelphia used to sprint and change pace. I slipped, fell heavily, and somehow broke a couple of ribs. Helen and her sister Frances were watching and nearly collapsed laughing. When they saw I was really hurt, they were all concerned, but as they helped me into the house, I'm sure they were hiding secret smiles!

This would be the last family gathering in Salisbury, North Carolina. Mildred sold the house and had a beautiful home built in Macon, Georgia. She was a bright lady and saw the profit potential in land development; her mini-mansion in Macon proved that. When success came to me, Mildred talked me into investing in property. We became partners in a few long-term projects. She knew that, left to my own devices, I would either spend my money or make bad loans with it. She was probably right. And I tell you, it's a nice feeling to know that you have something of value behind you, especially when you've spent so much time living on tomorrow's money.

We had a beautiful farewell supper. I toasted Mildred and George and wished them luck and happiness in their new home. The next morning I said my goodbyes. Helen and the children were spending the rest of the holidays with George and Mildred, Frances, her husband Danny, and their three children. I arrived back in Miami, my chest wrapped in a bandage and feeling sorry for myself.

So I had the blues, but when I got to the office I found Chris on cloud nine. As usual he was on the phone. He waved for me to sit down and shut up. I lit up a full-sized cigar, a habit I had picked up in Havana, and tried to ignore my aching chest as I attempted to make myself comfortable on my hard-backed chair. Chris eventually hung up and smiled broadly at me. "I got the Patterson-Johansson title fight. It's gonna be here in March. It's gotta be a sell-out. We're in for a busy time, Angie. We could make a lotta bread with this one." What was the "we" bit? I wasn't even involved with the hot-dog concession! Still, I knew what he meant and it was great news. Floyd Patterson, the former World Heavyweight Champion, was fighting Ingemar Johansson for the third time. Patterson had lost his title to Johansson, and this coming fight would be the decider. It should be a great fight and would certainly pack the hall.

Floyd Patterson intrigued me. He had a fine record both as an amateur (he was the Olympic middleweight champion in the 1952 games) and as a professional, knocking out Archie Moore in five rounds back in 1956. He had a strange style, known as the "peekaboo" style. He held his gloves high, hiding his face, and peeped out over his gloves. I had watched him fight Joey Maxim a few years earlier, and I hadn't been too impressed. Joey beat him over eight rounds and never got a return. I didn't blame Cus D'Amato, Floyd's manager, for not chasing after a re-match. To my mind, Floyd was a puffed up light-heavyweight. As Chris told me about the Patterson-Johansson bout, I couldn't help thinking that if the big, young Clay, six feet two and a half inches tall and over 190 pounds was as good as I thought he was, he would have no trouble with the six-foot, 182-pound Patterson.

"How do you think Clay would do against Patterson?" I couldn't resist asking Chris.

"You crazy or something? Patterson was a champion, Clay is just a kid. No contest." Maybe Chris was right then. In four years time *I* was right.

For me, 1961 went by like a seesaw—all ups and downs. Cassius Clay won his next two fights by knockouts. In June, we went to Las Vegas, where Cassius outpointed Duke Sabedong over ten rounds. That was an important step. Our work was bearing fruit. We had proved that Clay had the stamina and conditioning to last ten rounds. Clay and I were getting on just fine, and I was becoming more impressed after every fight.

Luis Rodriguez was having an up-and-down year, as was Ralph Dupas; and for Carmen Basilio it was the moment of truth. He had another chance to regain the middleweight title. The middle-weight division was in a state of confusion. In 1959 the National Boxing Association stripped Sugar Ray Robinson of his title for not defending it within the six-month limitation. The NBA considered the first fight in 1959 between Basilio and Fullmer, which Fullmer won, as a title fight, but the New York State Commission didn't agree. The two sides became polarized, and a chasm formed in boxing which still hasn't been resolved today. In 1961, I had two fighters competing against two different opponents, for the World Middleweight Championship! Carmen Basilio fought Paul Pender in April for the New York State Commission version of the title, and in August I had Florentino Fernandez, one of my Cuban imports, fighting Gene Fullmer for the NBA version.

Unfortunately, Fernandez narrowly lost the fifteen-round bout on points, and missed his chance of becoming a champion; and Carmen, on a cool April night in Boston, fought his heart out— only to lose on points and fail to regain his title. Three days later, on April 25, 1961, the magnificent, lion-hearted battler retired from professional boxing. Carmen Basilio was a credit to the fight game, an honorable man, and my friend to this day.

Although I had great friendship and affection for my fighters, I never believed in letting my business life cross over into my private life. When I went home I left one world and entered another. The camaraderie I had with fighters was something I will always cherish, but it was never permitted to swamp my private or social activities. I believed in the old adage, "familiarity breeds contempt." I tried to make sure that it did not happen to me and my fighters. They had their lives to live outside of boxing, and so did I. It seems to have worked out OK. That doesn't mean to say we never communicated outside boxing. The Rodriguez family would occassionally come over to the house, and Luis's children would play with Jimmy and Terri while us grown-ups would rap—about boxing, naturally! And, many times Willie Pastrano would visit us with his wife Faye and their children—it became five kids eventually—but Willie was different, he was living only a couple of blocks away and he practically grew up with us. He was like family.

Young Cassius Clay was away from his folks, whom he adored. We thought he might enjoy a home-cooked meal, so Helen and I invited him over for dinner. I've got to tell you, he was some likeable guy. He called Helen "Mrs. Dundee" and was as big a hit with her as he was with Terri and Jimmy. When the kids went to bed, exhausted after playing with Cassius, we had a chance to talk.

We both had unfulfilled dreams. Mine were mainly centered around my wife and my children. Cassius, unmarried at that time, wanted things for his family, too. A beautiful house for his mom was top of his list. For himself, what he wanted more than any other material thing was a brand new red Cadillac.

I have known so many fighters who only wanted to take, and give back as little as possible. When you are subsidizing a boxer, you leave yourself open to all sorts of extravagant behavior. They can spend your money with a skill and dedication that you would love to see in their work. Clay was different. He had this inborn sense of what was fair. He would eat at the famous Chef restaurant and keep the bills to show me. That first year, I do not think I ever gave him more than five dollars for a meal. He would run to the 5th Street Gym, and run back to the modest apartment room he shared with Allan Harmon, his Jamaican friend, who sometimes sparred with him and Willie and who also had boxing aspirations. Cassius never once complained about his living conditions, or anything else that I can remember. All he wanted to do was fight and improve, then fight again.

It was a pleasure having him in my home, and I think Cassius enjoyed the evening as much as Helen and I did.

The next morning Helen was in the garden, I was long gone to the office, when she heard our neighbors talking loud enough to make certain that she could hear. They were saying the Dundees had a nigger back for supper! The Dundees had actually let a black man enter their house and entertained him! What can you say to junk like that? I was upset when Helen told me, but I had been through that scene in the army. Some poor souls are stricken with the disease called bigotry. Please God, one day they will be cured.

With Cassius fighting in Miami or Louisville, I was home a little more than usual. For example, I was home on March 13, an unlucky night for Ingemar Johansson, because Floyd Patterson knocked him out and became the first man to regain the World Heavyweight Championship. I watched Patterson carefully; I had a hunch we would be adversaries in the not so distant future.

I was also home when four-year-old Terri badly cut her big toe falling from her tricycle. Hearing her cries, I rushed into the garden. I saw her ripped toe and her blood spurting from the wound. I thought I was going to faint. As it was, I was sick and Helen had to drive Terri to the hospital, while I was stretched out on the sofa, on the verge of passing out. Once again the famous cut man had been KO'd by the sight of blood!

Terri was four years and three months old when that incident happened. She was born under the sign of Aries, and the astrologists say the Aries woman is supposed to be self-motivating. Well, that's my girl. She graduated from high school, excelled at college, and made a career for herself as a speech therapist for the mentally retarded. Some lady, my daughter.

My birthday is on August 30, which makes me a Virgo. I checked out some other Virgo personalities, famous ones, of course. Peter Sellers, Maurice Chevalier, Lyndon Johnson, D. H. Lawrence, Robert Benchley, Leonard Bernstein. So I figured it out, I should have been a comic, singing president, who writes with humor and conducts symphony ochestras. Where did I go wrong!

I was home too for my fortieth birthday, for which Helen had arranged a small family celebration. I had just come back from Dallas with Luis Rodriguez, who had unaccountably lost to Curtis Cokes, and the news that Willie had only earned a draw with Lennart Risberg in Sweden didn't put me in birthday party mood. But once I was surrounded by my family, I could cut off all thoughts of my vocation and just saturate myself in the pure enjoyment of my loved ones.

Except for the money problems, there wasn't too much to worry about. To be perfectly frank, I had bought a new De Soto, making us a two-car family, and I had over-extended myself. Please don't tell me that I should have been doing well. Sure, I was earning money, but that don't mean nothing if you are spending more money! I wasn't losing hardly anything gambling on the ball games, and I was breaking about even at the Havana casinos. So where was the money going?

We lived well, and I had two children and a wife who wanted for nothing. What the hell, they were worth everything. Anyway, I didn't believe they were the cause of my lack of funds. I hated to admit it, even to myself, but I was back in the money-lending business. The difference between my operation and the bona fide money-lenders was that I didn't charge any interest on my money, and I hardly ever got it back! The fighters would try and hit Chris first for an advance on their purses, but Chris would tell them straight: "No way. Go and see Angelo. He's the softest touch in boxing." I guess he was right!

My other nagging worry was Willie. He had retired again. He had become involved with a couple of guys and they had opened a "Health Spa" at the Americana Hotel on Miami Beach. The Swedish bout was Willie's only fight in 1961. I understood his disenchantment with boxing: he should have been a champion, but it had escaped him. I would never try to talk him back into fighting, but I still hated to see him give up on his life-long ambition, and I believed the championship could yet happen for him. As I was always telling him, "You never know in boxing." I guess that you could say, "You never know in life." Cuba proved that.

By the end of 1961 the Cuba I had known no longer existed. I had continued my visits since the Castro take-over. I had even met the guy. When Sugar Ramos won the Cuban featherweight championship in Havana on February 27, 1960, Castro had been there and I had been introduced. If I had known what he was going to do I would have said to him, "Look, pal, with all the other problems you've got, why the hell do you wanna stop pro boxing and gambling? What harm are we doing?" Well, I wouldn't have said that exactly, but if he had asked me, then maybe I would have said something like that!

In twenty-four hours it would be Christmas. 1962 was looming ahead. Helen and I sat in our comfortable lounge, the children were in bed. I got up from the sofa and looked at the photograph of my mother and father. Tears came to my eyes. Now, both my parents were gone. My Pop had passed away earlier in the year, aged eighty-one. Helen must have sensed what I was feeling. She came over and put her arms around me. "I miss him, too," she said, her eyes full of sadness. "We have each other, and two wonderful children." I swallowed hard, holding back the emotion I felt. Helen was right. It wasn't a bad thought with which to start our Christmas festivities and face the New Year.

"How many fights has he had so far, nine or ten? I'm gonna leave the back a little longer, it's fashionable." Mike Composto was cutting my hair and talking about Cassius Clay.

I thought that I'd give him a free hand with the haircut and answer his question. "I'll leave it to you, Mike. Cassius has had ten fights, ten wins."

Mike continued: "Sonny Banks is a banger. He's tough opposition. Television coverage. Madison Square Garden. The kid is doing OK. Did you see the ball game on television? The game stank. Moe Fleischer came in yesterday for a haircut. He said as he didn't have a full head of hair I should charge him half price." Mike went on talking as only barbers can. They never care whether you answer or not, they just rap away. Mike was my regular barber and we had become pals. It goes without saying, he was a big fight fan.

One of his remarks stuck in my mind. The bit about Sonny Banks being a big banger. Banks could punch, no doubt about that. He would be Cassius's toughest opponent to date.

I believed Clay would win, naturally, otherwise I wouldn't have taken the fight, but it is no good trying to pre-guess a result. We would find out in a few weeks' time, on February 10. I sat in the chair as Mike snipped at my hair, thinking about New York and this opportunity for Cassius to make a name for himself. He knew the power of media exposure. We had discussed it many times and he knew how strongly I felt about it. If there had been a doubt in his mind about the necessity of publicity and promotion, it was put to rest when we had gone to Las Vegas last June for the Sabedong fight. The boxing promotion had been very badly attended, the hall was only a quarter full. The promoter, Red Greb, took his knocks philosophically but while we were eating, after the bouts, he voiced his opinion. "No doubt about it, guys, being an amateur champ don't sell tickets. You gotta have a big name bout top of the card. Too many other attractions around, not to mention television. If you want to pack them in, Cassius, you gotta have a name."

Of course Red was right. I knew that. Although Cassius had done good business at his fights in Louisville, that didn't mean anything. He was a hometown boy making good; Las Vegas was a long way from Louisville. "Stick around tomorrow night," said Red. "I'll show you what I'm talking about. We got wrestling on and Gorgeous George is headlining. This you gotta see." We took Red's advice and stayed over.

The place was packed, and when Gorgeous George, in his

glittering robe, made his entrance into the ring, the crowd went crazy. Cassius was completely bowled over by the theatrical and outrageous George, and when they met in the dressing room after the bout, Cassius found it hard to believe that the astute and intelligent guy he was talking to was the same character he had watched in the ring.

"You see, Cassius, without my Gorgeous George image I would be just another wrestler. It's my gimmick, I suppose without it this place would have been empty tonight—right, Red?" Red agreed, Cassius and I looked at each other, we agreed too. "Of course, you must have the talent to carry it off," George continued, smiling, "and a very thick skin. You sure get some abuse in this game. Not everyone loves me, but they all know my name." George can never have dreamed of the effect his words were having, and that the young, polite black man sitting listening to him would one day become the most famous human being in the whole darn world. But then, who did?

The sound of Mike's voice cut through my thoughts. "OK, Angie, we're all through. How d'you like it?" Mike placed a mirror behind my neck so that I could see the styling reflected in the large mirror facing me. The haircut was fine.

"Say, Mike, have you heard of Gorgeous George?" I asked.

"Oh sure, the kooky wrestler. Sure." When I asked Mike to name another wrestler, he was stumped. He thought for a moment. "Who knows wrestlers?" I guess George had been right.

I got back to the office, where I had a lot of things to take care of. The last three months had been hectic. At the end of 1961, Luis Rodriguez had met Curtis Cokes in a return bout and reversed the last decision by winning the ten-round contest. After that result, I was hustling to get a title bout at Emile Griffith, but I was having problems.

Teddy Brenner, the matchmaker at the Madison Square Garden, didn't like Rodriguez's style of fighting. Can you imagine! It would have been laughable, except for the fact that the Garden controlled the Saturday night television fights, and that meant two things: big bucks and big exposure. Well, that's how things go sometimes. Luis was unfortunate. First the late Benny Paret, when champion had sidestepped him, and now we couldn't get Griffith for one reason or another. I decided to get Luis as many fights as he could manage. If he kept winning they would have to give him a shot at the title. Thank the Lord, Luis wasn't of the same temperament as Willie, otherwise he might have decided to go into business too.

I've got to admit the Willie Pastrano situation was bugging me. He shouldn't have given up. He had been in there with a chance, and it could have still happened for him.

As we moved towards the Clay-Banks fight in February 1962, I was keeping an eye on Willie's business venture. Believe me, I wished him luck, but I didn't like the guys he was hanging out with and I had my doubts about the success of the venture. Willie was too straight a guy to try and give me a snow job. He called me in early February and confessed to me that business was for the birds and could I get him some fights? I told him to start training, and I would be talking to him after the Clay fight. I had an idea for him that might work out to be a good deal.

When I tell you I was chasing my butt, you had better believe it. 1962 was going to be a busy year. I had started off with a 2,000-plus-mile flight to Los Angeles. I was working with Sugar Ramos, now based in Mexico City. He fought and beat Eddie Garcia, knocking the guy out in nine rounds. A good start to the year, I thought, and agreed with Cuco that Ramos was world champion potential. That was January, now it was February. Time to go to New York for Cassius Clay's bout with big puncher Sonny Banks.

The New York press went for Cassius like a drowning man goes for a lifebelt. I knew a lot of the press guys, old friends like Al Buck, Jimmy Cannon, Bob Waters, and Red Smith. I stayed in the background and watched Cassius turn on the charm. Love him or hate him, he had charisma, and those hard-boiled masters of their craft could spot it. I knew there and then that if Cassius could deliver the goods in the ring, the press would turn him into boxing's biggest attraction. What I didn't realize was just how big that was going to be. Cassius predicted he would stop Banks in round four. The sports writers loved it! A fighter who predicted the round in which he would win. Great!

Cassius had fought outside of Louisville and Miami only once before, that was at the empty Las Vegas venue. This fight was different, we were in big league country now. This was the Garden and we were going into the fight a 5–1 favorite—partly owing to his record, but I think the "ballyhoo" also had a lot to do with it. How could anyone that confident lose?

For me it was like returning home. The Garden was my joint, but I realized that the atmosphere could give Cassius some pressure. I sensed his tension as he started round one. He was too square, giving Banks a lot of target. Then, halfway through the round, Banks unleashed a fast left hook, catching Cassius on the jaw. Cassius was down. He was on the canvas for the count of two, then he stood, taking the mandatory eight-count before being allowed to continue boxing. I looked in his eyes. For a couple of seconds they had been glassy, but they cleared and I could tell that Cassius was feeling less pain than astonishment at being decked. There was no question of his courage faltering. Cassius's pride had been hurt, that was all. In between rounds I told him to start moving laterally and stop standing so square—no fancy stuff, take the guy out.

In round two, Cassius went immediately on to the offensive. He showed his speed of foot and the machine-gun rapidity of his blows. He caught Banks with a left hook, putting Banks down for the short count. Cassius went after him relentlessly. The same determined attack went on in round three, until Cassius sensed that he could stop Banks. He let his courageous opponent finish the round, but in round four, as predicted, the fight was over, stopped by referee Ruby Goldstein, to save the helpless Sonny Banks. The experts were impressed, and so was I!

Clay was on his way, but Willie was nearly on the way out. I had to take care it didn't happen. I guess I had always known that Willie was a natural light-heavyweight, but when he first began boxing that division had no prestige and not a lot of fighters. A guy could have gone broke boxing as a light-heavy, so we had gone the heavyweight route. But times had changed. Archie Moore was a light-heavyweight, and Archie was fighting and beating heavy-weights too. The light-heavyweight division had gone through a similar situation as the middleweight division. In 1961 the NBA took away Moore's title for not defending it within six months against winner Harold Johnson. The New York State Commission didn't give its blessing to Johnson until about the time of the Clay-Banks fight. Now Harold Johnson, with the recognition of both boxing factions, was undisputed Light-heavyweight Champion of the World.

Where did that leave Willie? Well, I had heard on the grapevine that Archie Moore was looking to get back into action. If I could find a promoter who would like the Pastrano-Moore fight, and if Moore would accept Willie as an opponent, and if Willie could beat Moore, he would have to be in contention for a title shot with Johnson. I admit, there were a lot of "ifs," but if—there I go again. I got on the phone and rang a lot of people and subtly suggested that Moore against Pastrano would be a good idea. What did I do then? Wait.

Meanwhile, in March I had Sugar Ramos fighting in Paris, and in June Douglas Vaillant, another of my Cuban imports, was fighting in London. Plus I had Cassius going again in two week's time in Miami, then another bout in April. The month of May was completely untouched!

Being a fisherman, I knew that sometimes when you cast out your line you catch nothing, but sometimes. . . . I got a call from Aileen Eaton, a highly successful promoter from Los Angeles. She had an idea to match Moore and Pastrano in Los Angeles in May. She wanted to know what I thought, so I told her that she had a great idea. Then we discussed money, negotiating until we both thought we had a good deal.

Nobody gave Willie a chance. The story was going round that Moore had taken an easy fight on his come-back trail to a championship shot. To my way of thinking, Willie would never be an easy fight for anyone. Although I had to admit that Archie Moore was formidable. He had first won the light-heavyweight title in 1952 by beating Joey Maxim. He had knocked out the current champion, Harold Johnson, way back in 1954. Archie had even gone nine rounds with Rocky Marciano for the heavyweight title. He had lost that fight, but had gone straight ahead and won his next eleven fights, eight by knockouts. Archie was unbeaten in all his fights since the NBA had withdrawn their recognition of his title, and his last three fights had all been won by KOs. Yea, formidable is the right word.

I had to get Willie into top physical condition. Rodriguez and Clay were a good influence on Pastrano; they made training fun, and gave a competitive edge to getting fit. It became more interesting, and they learned from each other. I learned too—in boxing you are always learning. I began altering my training regimen and tried to make it more palatable for the fighters. It seemed to be having good results, because by the time we reached May 20, a week before the Pastrano-Moore confrontation, Luis Rodriguez had won two bouts and went on to remain unbeaten throughout the year. Cassius had three fights, and won all three by KOs. Friendly rivalry in the gym can be a good thing!

Even before we arrived in Los Angeles on May 26, two days before the fight, the press had taken an interest. Archie Moore had won his last fight in Los Angeles by knocking out Alejandro Lavorante and the media expected a similar result against Pastrano. I knew Willie was fit, but would his lack of ring time, nearly one year without a fight, affect his performance? Who could tell what could happen on the night.

Throughout the fight, Archie Moore was looking for that one knockout punch, the one that would put a finish to Willie and the fight. But everytime he threw a big punch, Willie wasn't there. Willie was dancing. I swear, if he had worn a top hat and tails he would have put Fred Astaire to shame. Nobody could accuse Willie of being a big hitter, but he sure could box. The fight could have gone either way. I thought Willie had sneaked it, but then I was biased. I guess the referee and judges gave the only suitable decision. It was a draw.

For Willie and me it was tantamount to a victory. Willie was back in the big league. He had to get a title shot, he just had to. Maybe not next week, or even next month, but it had to come.

The euphoria of the fight had died away and I was back in Miami, scheming and hustling for my fighters. I was handling and working with a lot of fighters. Working with all their individual personalities was like being a juggler. The difference was, if a juggler drops a club or a ball, so what. The guy just made a mistake. If I goofed, I could ruin a young man's career and break his heart. I guess I worked like crazy because I felt a responsibility for these guys. Sitting on my butt wouldn't earn any of us a living. I wanted success for them nearly as much as they did for themselves.

I may have been known as a manager, a trainer, or a corner man—but to work with fighters I had to develop other attributes. I was also psychologist, nurse-maid, and father figure. the problem, and the beauty of it, was that every fighter was different. As we reached the end of 1962 I was involved with sixteen fighters: Cassius Clay, who was managed by the Louisville syndicate, consisting of ten men and women, headed by Bill Faversham; Luis Rodriguez, who was co-managed by Ernesto Coralles; Florentino Fernandez, co-managed by Higinio Ruiz; Sugar Ramos, who was now ranked Number One contender in the featherweight division, co-manager Cuco Conde; Harold Gomes, whom I took over after he lost the NBA junior lightweight championship title; Gomeo Brennen, who in the following year would win the British middle-weight championship, and in later years would walk out on me; Carlos Hernandez, ranked Number Two in the lightweight division, who within months would be snatched from under my nose before I could confirm a permanent arrangement, by the astute, fast-talking manager Willie Ketchum. I was advising and working the corner of the young and promising Jose Napoles, and involved, either as manager, co-manager or trainer, with Tony Padron, Kid

Fichique, Sol Fuentes, Chico Morales, and Robinson Garcia, all Cuban fighters trying to make a name for themselves in the USA. I was still looking out for Jimmy Beecham and Ralph Dupas, and I was also co-managing the Number Three-ranked lightweight, the "wild boy" of the bunch, Douglas Vaillant. That's a lot of fighting talent, and every single one of them was a completely different individual. The only thing they had in common was that they were all boxers. They were all talented, but Cassius had that extra indefineable magic that is as rare as plutonium, and of course he had absolute dedication.

Douglas Vaillant was also very talented, but when they dished out good sense he went missing. Doug had it all except attitude and lifestyle. No matter how hard I made him train, he would dissipate his efforts with wine, women, and worst of all—drugs.

I would prefer my fighters not to drink alcohol. A social drink now and then is something I can live with, but heavy drinking is taboo. Vaillant had won the lightweight championship of Cuba in January 1960, but at that time he only had one vice, women. Once he hit the States he started drinking away his career.

One time he was fighting in Mexico City and as I could not be there with him I sent Luis Sarria, Rodriguez's trainer and later to be in the Clay camp, to watch over Douglas. The night before the bout I called Sarria in Mexico City to check up. I got no answer. The following morning I called again and got Sarria on the phone. After the usual "How you doing?" I asked why I hadn't got any answer to my call on the previous night.

"Gee, Angelo, I'm sorry. You see, what happened was Douglas hung one on last night. He got so goddam drunk you wouldn't believe it. Man, he was wild."

"That's terrible, Luis. The kid's gotta fight tonight. Couldn't you stop him?"

"No way, Angie. You know what Douglas is like when he gets going."

I thought for a moment. Something didn't add up. "Hey, Luis, I understand why Douglas didn't answer my call. He was either out of his head or dead drunk, but why didn't you take the call?"

"Well Angie, I tried to stop the kid, and when I could see I was busting my head for nothing, I thought to myself, if you can't beat 'em, join 'em. So I got smashed too."

Strangely enough Vaillant won that fight, knocking out the other guy in nine rounds. But booze takes its toll, and when you add late nights, and the use of drugs, you're on a one-way street and the only place you're going is down. Vaillant had his opportunity to become world champion. He fought Carlos Ortiz for the title, a fight he could have won, but his lifestyle caught up with him and he blew his big chance. It never came round again, and shortly afterwards Douglas Vaillant went out of boxing. He lives and works in Miami, and I sometimes see the kid and we rap about old times. I am pleased to say that he is clean and straight now, but I'll always think, what a waste of such a big talent.

Boxing is a profession that demands dedication, and invariably it pays off. Cassius Clay is proof of that. If in 1962 he had been anything but in top condition his fantastic career might never had happened. Keeping himself fit was a way of life for Cassius even when there was no immediate bout on the horizon. After Cassius had beaten Alejandro Lavorante in June 1962, I hadn't any fight lined up for him. I was waiting to get Archie Moore. I had spotted Moore in the Los Angeles auditorium watching Cassius fight Lavorante. When Cassius KO'd the guy in the fifth round, I grabbed him in an embrace and told him that Archie Moore was out there, and to throw out a challenge then and there. Cassius grabbed the microphone from the bemused television commentator who was trying to interview him, and went into his "thing."

"Archie Moore, I know you're out there." Cassius stalked around the ring until he saw Moore sitting at the ring-side. Pointing his glove at Moore, Cassius went on: "I want you next, old man. Moore will fall in four." I winced at the rhyme. Then I aided the announcer in taking back his microphone.

That had been in June, and I had heard nothing from anyone about a Moore-Clay confrontaion. Bill Faversham called me from Louisville asking about Clay's next fight. I told him the story. He went along with my ideas. We would wait a little longer if we had to. I wanted Moore.

I remember how Willie Pastrano's mobility and speed had troubled Moore. I believed that the taller, heavier Clay, with his lightning reflexes, would give Moore all sorts of problems. Willie hadn't the punch to nail Archie, but Cassius had. I wanted this fight!

Cassius carried on training as if his next fight was going to be for the world title. It paid off. When Aileen Eaton called with a deal for Clay to fight Archie Moore in Los Angeles on November 15, Cassius was ready.

Sure enough, we had time to prepare for the fight. It was only August 1962, and the Moore-Clay fight was over three months away. But it is so much easier for the trainer and so much better for the boxer if he is in good shape when he starts the strict disciplined training regimen required for ten or more rounds of professional boxing.

The publicity began to build up. It was the kind of a bout made for the press. The flamboyant, cocky kid, Cassius Clay, against the wily big-punching, experienced Archie Moore. For the first time Cassius was going against a name fighter. Would the confident, flashy upstart get his come-uppance from the old warhorse? The newspapermen were beginning to realize that Cassius Clay was a character who was giving some badly needed color to boxing. Sure, Patterson and Liston were news but they were kind of negative, whereas Cassius was bright, humorous, and controversial. A little scheme I had laid on helped too.

In September I had taken Cassius to the Liston-Patterson press reception in Chicago. Patterson, the world champion, sat tight-lipped, and the bulking Sonny Liston stared murderously at the young, handsome Clay as he taunted and teased them. Who is this crazy guy? Coming to somebody else's press party and insulting the world champion and the leading challenger! How dare he? What's the guy's name? The Olympic Champion—oh, yes, I know him. And they were buying tickets to see what he could do against Archie Moore.

Prior to the fight I was slightly worried that Cassius might find the pressure too much; after all, the kid was only twenty years old. I need not have worried.

The more publicity he got, the better he liked it, and if the coming night was causing him sleepless nights, I never noticed it. I had my own problems with getting to sleep, and it was nothing to do with tension.

The first night in the hotel, after making certain the two Clay brothers were in bed, I went to my adjoining bedroom and crashed out. I was awakened by an eerie moaning sound that got progressively louder. My sleep-ridden eyes opened slowly and tried to focus on the apparition that had materialized at the foot of my bed. The room was dark, lit only by street lights seeping through the curtained windows. What was it? The moaning got louder. I sat upright in my bed fumbling for the bedside light. I found the switch and the room burst into light. Standing at the foot of my bed were Cassius and Rudi, completely covered, except for their eyes, in white bed-sheets. Their moans turned into hysterical laughter. What could I do but join in? The night before the fight I waited up until I knew they were asleep!

Cassius had made his prediction: "Moore will go in four." I helped Cassius with the "poems," but with rhymes like Moore and four who wants to take credit?

I knew there was no love lost between Moore and Clay. But it was against Cassius's nature to bear grudges. He saw good in everyone. To illustrate my point, later in our careers a well-known hustler tried to hit Muhammad, as he was known then, for some bread.

"He's a thief," I told Muhammad.

"Yea, I know that, but he can't help it. And he is a good thief," Muhammad answered. As far as I know, he gave the guy the money. So, I didn't believe that the earlier clash of personalities between Clay and Moore would affect the fight. Cassius knew that I always believed in getting the other guy out as soon as you could, and that is what I expected of him.

On Novmember 15, 1962, in Los Angeles, the young upstart Cassius Clay knocked out Archie Moore, the aging warhorse, in the fourth round. Cassius was now a name fighter.

In 1963 my biggest problem was one that I couldn't solve. It was just impossible to be in two places at once! Cuco Conde wanted me to come to Mexico City to work with Sugar Ramos, who had won all his seven fights during 1962. Now he was getting a title shot! Cassius was fighting in Pittsburgh on January 24, and that was near Philly. I might be able to get to see my brothers and sisters. Luis Rodriguez was boxing in Miami on January 19, a warm-up fight before his long-awaited title shot against Emile Griffith. Just to make things more difficult for me, Willie was going against leading contender Wayne Thornton in New York on February 9, and Ralph Dupas was fighting on January 14, in Harvey. I don't know about "two places at once." I needed to be cloned!

In spite of the workload I still found time to spend Christmas with my family in Macon, Georgia, at Helen's parents' beautiful home. Listening to the kids talk and hearing the views of George, Mildred, and their friends, I realized that Cassius Clay had captured the imagination of a whole lot of Americans, and he wasn't even in line for a title shot yet. Sure, fight fans were excited about Ramos fighting Davey Moore for the world featherweight title and Luis Rodriguez fighting Emile Griffith for the world welter-weight title—both on the same night in Los Angeles—but ordinary people who were not fight fans were interested in the extrovert, outrageous Cassius Clay. I still didn't realize just how much his appeal would develop.

I worked in the corner of Luis Rodriguez, who won in Miami, and I was with Cassius in Pittsburgh, too. I didn't say "worked the corner" for Cassius, because for two rounds Cassius did his clowning thing and in the third round he knocked out the outclassed Charlie Powell.

I did get a chance to see my brothers and sisters in Philly. I took a limo after the fight and stayed with Jimmy. Most of the family came round, and I got a chance to say hello to my nieces and nephews. Phyliss, Mary's daughter, was now a grown-up young lady, and she reminded me of the days just after the war when I used to take her to see the Italian puppet shows and try and teach her how to dance. I asked her if I had changed.

"No," she said. "You're just as nice and funny as you were, even though you're famous." When I left, Jimmy, who knew me better than anyone said, "You're doing OK, considering you are only Chris's kid brother." He gave me a hug and said laughingly, "Don't tell Chris, but I heard someone call him Angelo's elder brother." We both thought that was funny—not fair, but funny.

I made a quick stop in Miami to see Helen and the children and flew off to Mexico City. Cuco Conde had moved his whole operation to Mexico City. He had a number of Cuban boxers with him, notably his star attraction, Ultiminio Ramos, otherwise known as Sugar Ramos, and the promising youngster, José Napoles.

Cuco's office in the Virreyes Hotel was a nice setup. He and I would spend many hours there over the years, talking, planning, and working out deals for Ramos and Napoles. Even then, way back in 1963, we felt that both boxers would become world champions.

The next few weeks I flew back and forth from Miami to Mexico City, overseeing the training and working on tactics with Ramos in Mexico and Rodriguez in Miami. I also fitted in the time to work with Cassius, who was fighting on March 13 in New York against a very useful contender, Doug Jones, and to oversee Willie Pastrano's training. Willie had lost on points to Thornton on February 9, but it had been close and a great fight. The return match was fixed for March 23, two days after the Ramos and

Rodriguez scheduled title shots. I think the fact that Sugar and Luis were going to fight for world titles encouraged Willie. He was sharp, determined, and fighting at a comfortable weight. I expected him to win the re-match. But before I could worry about that I had to give my efforts to Cassius, who was facing Doug Jones in New York.

If a fighter wasn't nervous before a fight, I would think that the guy had sawdust in his head instead of brains. Of course, any fighter gets either on edge, anxious, highly strung or scared before the fight; sometimes all four. Each guy handles it differently.

Cassius wanted to arrive at the Garden early so that he could loosen up. We arrived two and a half hours before he was due to fight. Cassius loosened up and worked out for the whole two and a half hours in the dressing room. But I could sense that he was still tense when the bout began. The smaller Doug Jones' style upset Cassius, but it was more than that: Cassius was sluggish. He had left his energy in the dressing room!

The bout went the full distance and Cassius took the decision, but it was not one of his better performances. He learned from that fight, and never repeated his marathon workout.

A win is a win, and the press and television coverage was amazing considering that Cassius was not yet a champion. The heavyweight division was completely dominated by the brooding, menacing Sonny Liston. In September 1962 he had demolished Floyd Patterson in one round to become Champion of the World. Liston was giving Patterson a return fight in July 1963, but no one was giving Patterson any chance of winning, including me.

I was a little concerned about Liston. Not because I thought he couldn't be beaten although the media suggested that he was invincible, but because I had wanted Patterson to be champion. I had always thought that Cassius could take Patterson, but now I had to re-think tactics. It was impossible to be around Clay and not believe that he would become world champion. He believed it and so did I.

Being caught up in the excitement of having two fighters going for world titles, and working with the pulse-quickening Cassius Clay, left only a portion of my energy and time for my other fighters. Willie Pastrano was always of prime concern to me, but he always seemed to end up one rung below the top. Maybe he would beat Thornton this time, and then we would try for the top rung again.

But Ralph Dupas and the other guys did suffer because I could not devote all the time needed for their maximum benefit. Back in 1962 Ralph Dupas had his chance to win the world welterweight title, but Emile Griffith snatched the decision after fifteen hard-fought rounds. That night in Las Vegas was another heart-breaking one for Ralph. He had had two cracks at world titles at two different weights, and lost both.

A manager and trainer can only do so much. They can help the boxer get in condition, carefully select the opponents, and give advice on how to fight them; but when the bell goes for the first round, the manager, the trainer, and the corner man are out of the ring and the fighter is on his own. If he wins, it is his victory and no one else's.

I had arranged another fight for Ralph that was coming up shortly on April 29. He would fight Denny Moyer for the NBA, junior middleweight title. Maybe it would be third time lucky. Who knows in boxing!

We were reaching make or break time, March 21, 1963. Would it be the night of the champions or the night of the vanquished for Ramos and Rodriguez? That night in Los Angeles turned out to be one of unforgettable glory and tragedy.

CHAPTER FIFTEEN

HAIL TO THE CHAMPIONS

"Some fighters you could tell what to do, others needed a different approach. Cassius Clay could never be told. I would sow the seeds and let him believe he had thought of it."

The last time that Luis Rodriguez had fought Emile Griffith, it had been in New York in 1960. He had lost that fight, outpointed in the ten-round contest. At least, that was the decision. I thought Luis had won. Gil Clancy and Howard Abert, Griffith's co-managers, laughed good-naturedly at me as I relived the fight round by round.

We were in Los Angeles. It was March 21, 1963, and once again Rodriguez was fighting Griffith, this time for the Welterweight Championship of the World.

The weigh-in was over, the fighters were resting, conserving their energy for the confrontation that would take place that evening. Clancy, Howard, and I were checking out the ring. It passed our scrutiny. We sat for a moment looking at the vast empty auditorium, imagining how different it would all look in a few hours' time. "Did you bring your own referee?" Gil teased me.

"I left that job to Aileen Eaton, she's the matchmaker. I told her, 'I don't care where the referee comes from as long as he's from Cuba.'" The guys laughed. They knew that both my fighters, Rodriguez and Ramos, were from Cuba.

"You gotta watch this guy," Gil said to Howard, meaning me. "Do you know the story about Angelo and Bill Bossio?" Howard shook his head. "Well," Gil continued, "Bossio is getting a hammering in the first round, then he caught the other guy with a lucky punch. The guy goes down. He's groggy, but not hurt. When the ref reaches five counting out the sucker, Angie jumps into the ring and puts the dressing gown around Bossio's shoulders as if the fight is over. The ref sees this and falls for it. He starts speeding up his counting. Seven, eight, nine, ten. The guy is counted out before he could get up! That's my pal, Angie. He knows more tricks than a hooker." Howard laughed.

I did too. "When Luis hits Griffith with his new special punch, I won't need to work the dressing-gown schtick," I said half-seriously. "Emile can kiss his title goodbye."

"What new special punch?" Howard asked.

Gil Clancy put Howard's mind at rest. "Forget it, Howie. He's trying to do a number on us. That's Angelo, always good for a laugh."

It was that kind of atmosphere. Fun. It was exciting too, of course, but the Los Angeles fight fans who had packed in to see the two world title clashes were a good-humored bunch. I liked the feel of the night. Was tonight to be the one? Would I realize an amibition I had nurtured for fifteen years? My own world champion! It could even be two world champions, both crowned on the same night. It was a mind-shattering thought. I'd take one step at a time. First, Luis Rodriguez had to beat Griffith. Then I would think about Sugar Ramos beating the featherweight champion, Davey Moore.

Before we left the dressing room I think I was more nervous than Luis. He always seemed relaxed before a fight. He hid what nerves he had well. I guess Luis believed—and it proved correct—that he would never be badly hurt. Luis was very fast and moved out of danger more times than not. He was a brilliant defensive boxer. He might get knocked out but he would never take a beating. At the end of his career, Luis had fought 121 bouts, had lost thirteen and had been KO'd three times.

The Rodriguez-Griffith bout went the full fifteen strength-sapping rounds. It was a gruelling action-filled battle, with both boxers refusing to lose. It was close, very close, and I anxiously awaited the decision. I had Rodriguez in front, but would it be another bad decision? This time the decision went against Griffith. Luis Rodriguez had won. He was the new Welterweight Champion of the World.

I had only a short time to enjoy the moment of victory. My heart was pumping like crazy with emotion, but I had to take a hold of myself. I watched from the corner as the new champion left the ring to the roar of the crowd. I was so happy for the guy. He had done his job, now I must finish mine. I had to get ready to work the corner again—this time with Sugar Ramos.

Led by Cuco Conde, Sugar entered the arena. When I had wrapped his hands in the dressing room, just before his entrance, I sensed his anxiety. He had warmed up. His body was covered with sweat, but he was tense. I wanted him loose.

Sugar did some stretching exercises in the ring as the champion, Davey Moore, made his entrance. Moore, five foot two and a half inches tall, was approaching thirty and had held the title for four years. He had won his title here in Los Angeles. I wondered if he would lose it here, too. The referee gave the two protagonists their pre-fight instructions. They touched gloves, symbolically shaking hands. The fight was on. Sugar was too tight in the early rounds, and the experienced Moore was building up a lead. The pressure of the occasion was affecting the twenty-one-year-old Ramos. During the middle rounds of the fifteen-round contest, Sugar began to find his rhythm and was giving as good as he was getting, but I still had Davey in front. Round nine ended. The stool was there waiting as Sugar reached his corner. I began working on the kid, holding the waistband away from the body with one hand, and lifting the abdomen with the free hand, to aid the breathing, as I had learned way back in my New York days. After wiping Sugar's face with the towel I patted his back for good luck as the bell sounded for the start of round ten.

There was a flurry of blows. Ramos threw a right to the champion's jaw. The champion fell, his head striking the bottom strand of rope as he went down. The referee started his count. Moore couldn't make it. The fight was over. Ultiminio Sugar Ramos was the new Featherweight Champion of the World.

The crowd went wild. A chief had fallen to a young warrior. I rushed across the ring and grabbed Sugar at the same time as Luis Rodriguez jumped into the ring with the same idea. Together we lifted the new champion and paraded him around the ring. When the tumult and the wild enthusiasm had abated slightly, the proud, sportsmanlike Davey Moore came over and thanked me for a good fight and asked for a return bout. I ruffled the little man's hair and told him, "You've got it."

We were back in the dressing room, a bunch of sports writers, Luis Rodriguez, Cuco Conde, Sugar, and me. We were ecstatic. I don't know who was the happiest—Sugar, Luis, or myself. Two world champions in one night. Unbelievable!

There was a knock on the dressing room door. I opened it. One of the Los Angeles newspapermen stood there. "Come in, pal," I said, not remembering his name. He shook his head. "Davey Moore just collapsed in his dressing room."

As he was being interviewed the ex-champion suddenly collapsed and was taken to the hospital. Davey Moore lay in a coma for two days. Ramos and I prayed together for his recovery. I was filled with an empty, horrible feeling. The one thing I wanted most in the world was for Davey to recover.

After waiting all those years for my own champion, now I had two, but it didn't mean a thing. I was numb with dejection, and the feelings I had were magnified a hundred times when I received the news that Davey Moore had died without recovering consciousness.

Doctors established that brain damage occurred when he struck his head on one of the ropes as he fell. It was a fatal accident. It was almost a year to the day since the tragedy of Benny Paret, a former world welterweight champion who had died under similar circumstances. It was after defending his title against Emile Griffith—the same Griffith who had boxed on this other tragic night. Benny Paret had lain in a coma for ten days before he died.

The death of Davey Moore sparked off a storm of protest against boxing. No one outside of Davey's family could have been more heartbroken over the tragedy than I, but in all honesty I couldn't blame boxing. There are tragedies and accidents in many sports. It is a sad fact we must live with, and die with.

Managing two world champions and training the up-and-coming Cassius Clay made me feel good. I can't say that I felt like a big shot or a very important person, I just felt sort of pleased with myself. Sure, I knew that I was only co-manager, but Cuco Conde was living in Mexico and Whitey Esneault hardly ever left New Orleans, so I think it is fair to say that I was the commander-in-chief at the front. Believe me I wasn't looking for personal publicity. Any publicity that was going, I wanted for the fighters. Nobody was going to pay to watch me work the corner. The fighters are the stars of the show; the rest of us guys only make up the cast. But I wasn't going to avoid a pat on the back or hide from the respect of my peers. I have to admit, I kind of liked it. As far as my partners were concerned, there were no problems. Just for the record, Cuco Conde and I never signed a contract. We just shook hands on the deal. It worked out OK. There are good guys around!

In April of 1963 there was a possibility that I would be handling four world champions. Both Ralph Dupas and Douglas Vaillant had title shots. I was in San Juan with Vaillant for his fight against the champion, Carlos Ortis. I wasn't feeling too good. Ever since the Davey Moore tragedy, I had been getting shooting pains in my back, and if I got unduly excited my face would break out in red blotches and swell up. As I watched Vaillant begin to fade in the fight against Ortis, and his title hopes fade with him, I felt even worse. Vaillant lasted thirteen rounds before he was KO'd. I tried not to think of what the kid might have achieved if he had looked after himself. After all, I only managed his boxing career, not his life. Anyway, that was one championship that had escaped. In the same month Ralph Dupas was getting his third chance at winning a title. All the signs were good. He was fighting at his best weight, 154 pounds, and he was unusually full of confidence. The time was right. Ralph Dupas made it right! He outpointed Danny Moyer to become Junior Middleweight Champion of the World. I couldn't believe it. Ralph had done it! You wanna talk about hanging in? Here was a guy who had fought for the World Lightweight Championship, and lost; fought for the World Welterweight Championship, and lost; fought for the Junior Middleweight Championship, and won. You want to talk about tenacity, talk about Ralph Dupas.

Ralph lost his hard-earned title in September of the same year in Milan, Italy, to Sandro Mazzinghi. In a return bout, the Italian once again KO'd the dejected American, who was no longer the same hungry young fighter with dreams of achievement. Ralph, after a third-round KO by Emile Griffith, became disillusioned and at the end of 1964 he announced his retirement and moved to Las Vegas.

He made a short comeback under a new manager in 1966. After five bouts in Las Vegas he finally hung up his gloves for good. He had been a fine and talented fighter who had given all he had in his quest to be Number One. Out of 134 fights, he was only beaten twenty-two times.

So there I was in April 1963 with three world champions on my books, Sugar Ramos, Luis Rodriguez, and Ralph Dupas, and a past that included being chief second to double world title-holder Carmen Basilio. Not bad for an ex-aircraft inspector from South Philly. The phone in the office was continually busy with newspaper guys ringing up for stories, but to my surprise it wasn't for stories about my champions, it was for "anything at all" on Cassius Clay.

I knew, and the sports writers knew, that the kid was a one-off. It would only be a matter of time before he faced the man who was standing over the heavyweight division like a colossus, Sonny Liston. But before I put Cassius in the ring with Liston, I wanted a couple more bouts and a little more time for Cassius to reach physical maturity. Remember, he was only twenty-one years old. I didn't think I'd get all the time I wanted, but I would try and stall. I knew time was on our side. I had an offer for Cassius to go against the British champion, Henry Cooper. I passed on the information to Bill Faversham, who worked out the deal. The fight with Cooper was set for June 18, in my old hunting-ground, London.

London! I remembered the first few times I had gone there with Willie Pastrano. How well he had done. What was I going to do about Willie? He was always so near and yet so far away from achieving his goal. Would he ever be champion? Would he ever get the chance? Things had been happening for Willie Pastrano. On March 23, two days after the dramatic night of the two championship fights, he held Wayne Thornton to a draw. We got a third, deciding bout against the highly ranked Thornton on May 4 in Las Vegas. Maybe Willie was inspired by the victories of Ramos and Rodriguez; at any event he sparkled on the night and took the decision, to the surprise of the media and to the astonishment of Thornton.

About the same time as the Clay-Cooper fight was confirmed, I got an offer of a bout for Willie. It was the offer I had waited years for. Willie was getting a title shot. The twenty-eight-year-old Pastrano was going to fight the Light-heavyweight Champion of the World, Harold Johnson. The bout was scheduled for June 1. We only had three weeks to prepare, but Willie was fighting fit from his three fights against Wayne Thornton in February, March, and May, so I concentrated on getting his mental attitude right. I had to instill confidence and an unshakable will to win.

In all honesty, I think I did a good job of using applied psychology with fighters. I had been known to give a tired fighter half an aspirin during a fight, telling the kid that it was a pep pill and that he wouldn't feel tired any more. It worked. I would never use the word tired when working a corner. I would never say, "You look beat, kid." If my guy looked exhausted I might say that the other guy looked beat. I would try any approach to motivate

my fighter. Flatter them and instill confidence, or shout at them
and insult them—as long as I could motivate them I'd say
anything. Some fighters you could tell what to do, others needed
a different approach. Cassius Clay could never be told. I would
sow the seeds and let him believe he had thought of it. The years
I had spent in New York listening to the great trainers and
managers paid off. I wonder whether, if I had never known
Charlie Goldman and the other wise fight men, I would ever have
been able to work with and understand Cassius Clay and Willie
Pastrano.

When Willie and I arrived at Las Vegas, I knew that he was
mentally right and physically fit. The rest was up to him. Let me
tell you, I knew that Willie had one hell of a fight on his hands. I
can't honestly say that I believed he would win. But this was his
chance, probably his last, of ever winning a world title, and he had
to go for it. Was I worried about it? Sure I was. The thought of
Willie taking a whipping haunted me. The betting boys, who are
pretty good judges, were laying 5 to 1 against Willie winning.
They're some odds! Harold Johnson had won his last fifteen fights.
His last defeat had been back in 1955, eight years ago! You can bet
your life I was worried.

Worried or not, in boxing anything can happen. I knew that
Johnson was good, and I knew that he punched like a kicking
mule, but Willie was Willie. To knock him out the champion would
have to catch him, and that was no easy thing to do. As the hours
ticked away before the fight, I kept uppermost in my mind the
knowledge of something I had known for an awfully long time—
Willie Pastrano is one hell of a fighter.

I gave Willie a light tap on his rear end as he went out to
confront Harold Johnson in the first round of their title fight.
Before Johnson had time to realize there was a fight going on,
Willie had caught him with a couple of rapid left jabs. Johnson
threw a great left hook, but Willie wasn't there. That's how the
fight progressed: Willie scoring points, and when Johnson threw a
punch Willie was someplace else. Harold Johnson, a great and
experienced fighter, began to suffer from frustration. He didn't
know how to handle the elusive Pastrano, who danced in and out
of range, scoring points with his accurate jabs. Round after round
Willie boxed like a man inspired, slipping punches, weaving, and
then attacking in savage bursts.

I began to feel a surge of confidence. I thought that Willie was
going to pull it off, and then in the fourteenth round he got hit
with a wicked right-handed shot. Willie's legs wobbled, but he

didn't go down. He kept his cool. He grabbed Johnson into a clinch and held on for precious seconds while his head cleared. The referee broke them, but Willie surprised Johnson by attacking venomously until the round ended. As he slumped on the stool, I could see that he was a little groggy and completely exhausted. "C'mon, baby. Three more minutes and you're Light-heavyweight Champion of the World. C'mon, for Faye—your kids." I named his children for him, emphasizing their names. "Little Frankie . . . Johnny . . . Donna . . . Nickie . . . baby Angelo. Three more minutes. You are gonna do it for them."

Willie found the energy and strength from somewhere deep inside himself. He finished the fight in style. We stood together in the middle of the ring, and I was holding his right glove, ready to raise his arm in triumph. The decision was announced. Willie Pastrano had won. At last! After being an "also ran" for so long he had finally achieved his goal. Unashamedly, tears ran down his handsome, battle-scarred face. I was finding it hard to talk, dead-heating between the emotional gagging back of tears and the overwhelming desire to shout and scream with joy.

Two days later, back in Miami, there was a very happy manager and an ecstatically happy fighter sitting in the office giving interviews to the local media in person, and interviews to sports writers over the phone nationwide. I watched the deliriously happy Willie handle the interviews with ease. How far he had come from those early years when most of his answers consisted of a nod of his head! I was proud of the guy. I was very happy for myself—you know what I mean, another world champion, another kid I had believed in had made good—but I was more happy for Willie. I got pure enjoyment out of watching him soak up his well-deserved success.

It would have been nice to sit around and soak up the glory and all the happiness, too, but I had things to do and places to go. I checked my daily journal, it was kind of full. From May 6 until June 20, 1963, I would cover 19,678 miles by plane.

So far my schedule went like this: *May 6:* leave Miami to set up training quarters at Tamarack Lodge, Greenfield Park, New York, for Luis Rodriguez's defense of title in June. *May 9:* return to Miami. *May 23:* leave for San Juan for Florentino Fernandez against Torres—my guy Florentino won. *May 29:* Miami to Las Vegas for Pastrano-Johnson on June 1. *June 3:* off to New York to put finishing touches to Rodriguez's training at Tamarack Lodge for title defense on June 8.

Well, that's where I was up to at the moment. Today I would

leave Miami around lunchtime and fly up to join Luis Rodriguez at his training quarters. I would work the corner on June 8, then fly off to London with Cassius for his fight against Henry Cooper on the 18th. I would arrive back home in Miami on June 20.

Now I could just fit all that in, but I was missing out on Ralph Dupas's title defense on June 7 and Douglas Vaillant's bout on the 4th. As I said earlier, I needed to be cloned!

I had a hunch about training in the mountains. I didn't like it. Luis Rodriguez was training at Tamarack Lodge, up in the mountains, for his return fight against the talented and resilient Emile Griffith. I wished he had trained in Miami.

The fight was at Madison Square Garden, and once again the two fighters went the full fifteen rounds, and once again it was a very close fight. This time the decision went against Luis, and Emile Griffith was once again champion of the world. I have nothing against Emile, I just wish he had been born ten years earlier, so that my guys could have missed him! OK, that's the way it goes. You win some and you lose some. Of course it is much better if you don't lose some!

I was off to London with the uncrowned king of boxing. Or as some of the English press put it, the clown prince of boxing. I gotta tell you, they loved him. Those British press guys knew a good thing when they saw it. This Cooper-Clay fight was made for the British press. Clay was outrageous—funny, but outrageous. It wasn't that he was rude or cruel, it was that he was so different. Nobody had seen or heard anything like him. To predict that the British champion, the talented and popular Henry Cooper, would fall in round five, was like waving a red flag at a bull. The British public went crazy. Not in a nasty way, but in their own particular humorous way. Clay was big news. There were even skits and impersonations of him on British television, and the guy wasn't even a champion!

At the time Cassius was champion of absolutely nothing. The well-respected English reporter, Peter Wilson, asked if I thought Clay would ever be champion. I answered that he'd better be. I didn't want to be driven crazy for nothing.

The British attitude of humorous tolerance towards Cassius changed just before the fight night. He had called Henry Cooper a bum! After that statement the British public wanted to see Clay whipped by Cooper. I didn't think that would happen in a million years, but the British fight fans wanted it badly. It was a question of respect!

As for the fight, it should have been no problem. By round four

Cooper had a bad gash over his left eye, with blood cascading out of it like Niagara Falls. It was just a matter of time before the referee, Tommy Little, would have to stop the fight. There were just a few seconds to go to the end of the round. Cooper, smarting from the taunting of Clay before the fight, was furious as Clay, with both hands down at his sides, tried to humiliate him in front of the British fight fans. Henry squinted at his opponent through the red waterfall of blood. He led with a soft left jab. Clay instinctively moved away from the predictable right cross. Cooper surprised him. He threw a long left hook. The Cooper bombshell, the famous left hook, known as 'Enery's 'Ammer. Clay's eyes glazed over, his legs turned to jelly. He was down. He was being counted out. The referee reached the count of four as the timekeeper rang the bell for the end of the round. Was Cassius saved by the bell? I didn't think so, but obviously all my British friends did.

Somehow Cassius dragged himself to his feet—that proves that he would have got up, whether the bell had gone or not—and staggered around aimlessly. I ran along the ring, outside of the ropes, and grabbed Cassius's arm, helping him maneuver his way back to our corner. Slumped on the stool like a sack of potatoes, Cassius looked like he was out of it. I knew better. I gave him a whiff of smelling salts, doused his head with cold water, and slapped his face until I saw those eyes clear. And I shouted at him—boy, did I shout at him!

As I was loosening and stretching his arms, getting the blood flowing through the tightened muscles, I saw a small split along the seam of the boxing glove. I had noticed the tear after the first round. It wasn't big, but it was there, and it shouldn't have been. I stuck my finger in the split, helping it along—now it was a bigger split. I yelled for Tommy Little, the referee, to examine the glove. I yelled at Teddy Waltham, the secretary of the British Boxing Board of Control. I yelled at Jack Onslow Fane, the President of the B.B.B.C. I yelled at everybody. I wanted a new pair of gloves, but hopefully not too quickly. I wanted time for Cassius to get himself together more! I don't know how many minutes I gained, and I admit it was gamesmanship, but it was advantageous to both fighters.

The very skillful Danny Holland, Cooper's cut man, had those extra minutes to work on the bad cut over Henry's left eye. How many fights had I been in where I would have given my back teeth to have had extra minutes in between rounds to work on my badly cut and bleeding fighters?

It didn't work out for Henry. The fifth round started minutes late with his cut still seeping blood and with both fighters wearing their original boxing gloves. The officials had decided the split in Cassius's glove was no threat and was not to be changed. In fact they had no extra gloves. Nowadays there is always a spare pair kept under the ring in readiness. It is mandatory—I guess I started that!

After a minute of the fifth round Henry's cut was furiously pumping blood, making it impossible for him to see. If the referee hadn't stopped the fight, they would have heard me yelling once more. But Tommy Little did his job and the fight was over. A fight I had thought would be routine had turned out to be a veritable nightmare. My guy nearly got KO'd!

After the fight Cassius withdrew his remark about Henry Cooper being a "bum." He gave the game British boxer full respect. I knew of course that most of Cassius's hype was just that—hype—but sometimes he could go too far. He had entered the ring wearing a crown and flowing robes, like a king, but I wouldn't let him leave the ring afterwards wearing the royal regalia, especially after decking the British champion. I don't think the British public would have appreciated that. Although it wouldn't have been meant, it might have looked insulting to the Royal Family, and we might have ended up in the Bloody Tower!

On the same card as the Clay-Cooper bout was a fight between Johnny Halifihi and a kid from Cassius's home town of Louisville, Jimmy Ellis. It wasn't much of a fight, Ellis stopping Halifihi in the first round. I thought that Ellis, a tall middleweight, had a good left hook. I remembered his name.

I think you will agree that I was carrying a pretty heavy and demanding workload. By the end of June the emotional traumas and the amount of traveling I had gone through since March had left me exhausted.

I was lucky to be able to spend the summer of 1963 with my family. I put my time in at the office and gym, but there were no big fights I had to travel to, and for the first time in my life I had time to go fishing. Not to catch fish to eat because it would save me money, but because I enjoyed it. Helen and I would drive down to the "keys," a paradise for fishermen, hire a boat for the day and revel in the warmth and solitude of the Florida Keys. I caught some fish, too! We had another hobby that was pretty big in our life at that time—country and western dancing. I didn't say too much about my country and western dancing to my boxing friends and associates. I could imagine entering the 5th Street Gym to shouts of "Here comes Hoppalong Angelo," or "It's Wild Bill Dundee, the dancing manager," or "Look, it's Sundance Dundee, from the South Philly ranch." No, I didn't mention the country and western dancing too much!

I was spending a lot of time at the office, so I was seeing Chris more often. Chris was really established as a promoter now, and was getting his share of the big fights in Miami. At the end of the summer, Bill Faversham accepted the Sonny Liston fight and Chris got the bout for Miami. Liston and his advisers were shrewd. They wanted Clay as soon as possible, before he became too ring-wise and experienced. I would have preferred to wait, but once the fight was set for February 25, the only thing to do was make sure Clay won it. I'll never forget the date of the fight, because it was Chris's birthday.

So, Cassius was going to fight for the world heavyweight championship—the big one! It had all come around so quickly. The enormity of the situation hit me. The Heavyweight Championship of the World! There was nothing bigger. This could mean big bucks for Cassius. I wasn't too conversant with how Bill Faversham and the Louisville syndicate cut up Clay's purse, but I believed they were straight and that Cassius would get his fair share. As for myself, with a world title looming on the horizon, I realized that I had made an error of judgement in my financial arrangements with the syndicate.

When I had taken over as Clay's trainer in 1960, the syndicate had offered me a wage or a percentage. I hadn't given Faversham an answer right away, I wanted to talk it over with Chris. He advised me to take the money. "Who knows how the guy will do? You need the bread. Take it. You gotta find the expenses for here and for your home. Why d'you need to gamble? Take the money." I couldn't blame Chris for giving me the wrong advice, I didn't have to take it. Besides, to have been helpful and instrumental in getting Cassius to a world championship bout was worth more than money to me.

You have to understand, I liked and admired the kid. I knew, too, that Cassius was far more talented than most people realized. They were blinded by his personal charisma and way-out personality. But I believed that he was perhaps the greatest heavyweight boxer the world had ever seen. When Cassius said, "I am the greatest," I believed him and eventually so did a great number of other people.

But he would have to prove it. First of all he must face and defeat the champion, Sonny Liston. We trained, me doing the suggesting, Cassius doing the sweating. 1964 arrived. The title shot was getting nearer. On January 10 Sugar Ramos, the Featherweight Champion of the World, was defending his title in Los Angeles against Vincent Derado. Naturally, I had to be there. Cassius decided to come to watch the fight. Sugar won on points over ten rounds and got some nice coverage, but the main story to hit the press was the one about Cassius Clay, challenger for the heavyweight title, charging the fans money for his autograph.

The press and the public had fallen out of love with Cassius. Stories had been circulating about Clay's involvement with the Black Muslims. The young American Olympic hero had tarnished his image. Once these stories broke in the newspapers, Cassius's popularity waned. People I hardly knew were telling me that they had known about Clay's involvement with the Black Muslim movement for years. It seemed that Cassius had been attending meetings for a couple of years. He had been seen at a rally applauding the leader of the movement, Elijah Muhammad, and that was not what the vast American public wanted from their fighting hero. Liston, the original "Mr. Nasty" became "Mr. Nice Guy," and Cassius was cast in the role of "Mr. Bad Guy."

As for the unpleasant story about Cassius charging fans for his autograph, that was true. But what nobody knew at the time or bothered to find out, was that Cassius was giving the money to a black hospital in Miami. No one can ever convince me that Cassius was cheap and mean. He was generous to a fault.

I never discussed Cassius's religious beliefs. I never discussed mine either. Whatever he believed was his business. I knew the man, he was sincere. If he wanted to follow the Muslim faith, and if he identified with the Black Muslims, that was no more my business than my religious philosophies were his, or come to that, anybody else's. That is what America is supposed to be about!

So we carried on training in the midst of what was to become worldwide news, resulting in Cassius changing his name and eventually refusing to fight for his country in Vietnam because of his religious and moral beliefs.

It wasn't all problems. Cassius had fully recovered from a hernia operation and was in excellent shape. He had filled out a little and was going into the fight at over 200 pounds—that's what I wanted. Mentally Cassius seemed OK. Of course he was affected by the Black Muslim publicity, but the syndicate, at my instigation, had given him a present of a tomato-red Cadillac, making at least one of his dreams come true. Cassius's other dream, of buying his mother a house, he made come true himself. He was that kind of guy.

To be frank, the Muslim publicity hardly touched me at all. To be simplistic, if Cassius wanted to be a Muslim, fine, let him be a Muslim. But Chris took it a little harder, because Chris was getting hurt where it hurt most—in the wallet.

The bad guy image was not helping the gate. It would be the advent of closed circuit television that would make the bout a financial success. Jerry Perenchio, one of the first guys in closed circuit television, told me it would revolutionize boxing. He was so right.

The promotional side of boxing never held a great interest for me. I have a single-track mind: I concentrate on the job in hand. If there are many things to attend to, I become a one-job-at-a-time guy. I have seen Chris hold two telephone conversations and negotiate a deal with a guy across the desk at the same time. If I'm talking on the telephone and somebody in the office asks me a question, I find it hard to switch thoughts and answer. Sometimes I won't even hear the question because I am concentrating on what I am doing. Being that way isn't an asset in business, but it sure helps when I'm working a corner, and it is a personality trait that can help a boxer. Cassius Clay has it. When he is in the ring he has full concentration. He was going to need that concentration against Sonny Liston.

Let me tell you, I thought Cassius could do it. The public and the media had been mesmerized by Liston's two wins against Patterson. So he'd KO'd Patterson in the first round both times. What did that mean? Nothing.

Cassius was big and strong, weighing in around 210 pounds. He could move, had a great jab and a good right cross. I really wasn't worried. Let Liston worry. I think that Patterson froze in the first fight against Liston, and he got himself so keyed up about not freezing in the second fight, he froze again. Don't get me wrong. I told you before, Patterson was a very good fighter, but being psyched out, if that was indeed the case, can happen to any fighter. It isn't a question of being afraid, because there is no boxer that I would call a coward. To have the guts to climb into that ring is bravery enough. Suffering from a tension that can numb the reflexes and immobilize the brain is a hazard of the fight game and can happen to the bravest of athletes. Normally, it only happens for a second or two, and then the boxer begins to act on instinct and fight his way out of his tension. But if you happen to get a solid punch on the jaw during that second or two, you are in trouble. I tell you, many first round KO decisions might have been reversed if the fight had gone on.

So, when the bell went for the first round in the Clay-Liston title fight, I was not unduly worried about Cassius. He would do just fine. The first round was pure Cassius Clay. Granted, he didn't do a lot, but he showed style and confidence. In the second round, for reasons known only to Cassius, he went the orthodox route. Hands held up, textbook style—he stank! He didn't do anything right from that stance. He had to do it his own way. The third and fourth rounds were better. Cassius didn't land any worthwhile blows, but, more important, Liston couldn't hit Clay. He tried— believe me, he tried. But Clay was too elusive.

When the bell went for the end of the fourth round, Cassius was slow getting back to the corner. He was blinking and grimacing with pain. As soon as I had him sitting, and had taken out his mouthguard, Cassius screamed at me, "I can't see, Angelo! My eyes are burning." I sniffed and tasted the towel I had just used to wipe around his eyes. There was something wrong. I tasted a strange substance. Perhaps something from Liston's glove or hair. Maybe a jet of perspiration had caused the stinging, blinding sensation in Cassius's eyes—I didn't know. All I knew was Cassius yelling that he couldn't see. I acted instinctively. I began washing out his eyes with a cold water sponge.

"Cut my gloves off. I can't see. We're going home," Cassius yelled.

"No way," I snapped. "Get in there and fight. If you can't see, keep away from him until your eyes clear. This is the big one. Nobody walks away from the heavyweight championship."

The bell sounded for the fifth round. I shoved Cassius forward into the ring. "Get in there. This is what we came for, baby." Cassius kept moving. Even with impaired vision he managed to avoid all Liston's punches. The round ended with Clay confident, with clear eyes, and Liston frustrated, with worried eyes. The sixth round confirmed Liston's worst fears: not only could he not hit Clay, but Clay, who had gone on the attack, could easily hit him. A cut opened beneath Sonny's left eye. As I watched the round I saw despair written all over Liston's face.

The bell sounded for the start of round seven. Cassius was up, eager. There was no move from Liston's corner. He still sat slumped on his stool. What the hell was going on? The referee seemed as puzzled as everyone else. There was a quick conference in Liston's corner. I couldn't believe it. Liston was doing what I had stopped Cassius from doing. He was walking away from the heavyweight championship. Liston stayed on his stool. The fight was over, Cassius Clay was the Heavyweight Champion of the World.

What happened next? Pandemonium! That's what happened. It wasn't the way I wanted Cassius to win the title, it didn't do him justice, but what the hell! You can't do better than come in first. I went over to the deflated Sonny Liston corner, and I offered some words I thought they might like to hear. Sonny didn't listen, he was wailing, "My arm feels like it's full of water." He was a sorry figure. I immediately thought that a balm applied to Liston's shoulder could account for the foreign substance in Clay's eyes, but it made no difference now, and I let the thought go. Nobody but Sonny knew how he felt, knew if he could have fought on or not. It is easy to condemn, not so easy to understand. Rocky Marciano finished off Ezzard Charles while fighting with a broken nose. So? Every fighter is different. And the same fighter can be different at different times!

The press crowded into the new champion's dressing room. Cassius, the king, held court. Red Smith, one of the great sports writers, cornered me. "Congratulations, Angie. I didn't think Clay could do it. I was beginning to think that Liston was unbeatable."

"You were seeing Liston through Floyd Patterson's eyes, that's why, Red. Cassius wasn't intimidated. Way back in 1962 Cassius and I went to Chicago to see the Patterson-Liston fight. He knew then he was gonna fight one or the other of them and was gonna beat 'em."

"OK, Angie, I know you think Cassius is God's gift to boxing, but you had to be concerned about Liston's punching power?"

"Come on, Red, I told about forty newspaper guys six days ago how this fight would go. Who did Liston knock out? Al Westphal, that's all. Cleveland Williams was on his feet and Besmanoff was stopped on cuts. Forget about Patterson—he was psyched out. Boxing beat Liston. Boxing and Cassius Clay."

"OK, OK. Clay's boxing is what beat Liston. Clay's boxing and you keeping Clay in the fight. Right?" Red laughed. "Come on, Angie, take me over to the champ. I wanna hear what he has to say. Do you think he'll talk?"

"Talk? They don't call him the Louisville Lip for nothing!"

Once again there was no time for me to put my feet up, smoke a large Havana cigar, have a whisky on the rocks, and soak up some of the glory. I was off to Tokyo, where Sugar Ramos was defending his featherweight title against Mitsumori Seki.

Don't ask me about Tokyo. I saw the airport, the hotel, and the auditorium, and that's about it. On the day of the fight I followed my usual practice and checked the ring and facilities. Everything seemed fine, but something was not quite right. I couldn't figure out what was bothering me. What was wrong? The ropes were just right, not too loose or too tight. It wasn't that. I asked my Japanese interpreter if the gloves could be inspected. With a slight bow he displayed the gloves, the bucket, the dressing room, everything was in order. What the hell was bugging me? Then I knew. The auditorium was empty. There were no chairs. No way could they be set up before the fight. There wasn't time. Trying to keep the panic out of my voice, I said, "Hey pal, there ain't no seats. You got no chairs. No seats." I spoke slowly and loudly, hoping the guy could understand me, because so far the interpreter hadn't said very much. He just kept bowing. "Capice?" I said. I don't know why I thought he might understand Italian better than English. I just gave it a shot. I tried English again. "Understand? No chairs!"

The guy went into his bowing routine again but this time he spoke. "Ah, so! No chairs. Japanese people prefer floor." He explained once more to make certain that I understood. "Sit on floor, no chairs."

What can I say! Sugar knocked out Seki in the sixth round. As Seki lay on the canvas I said to Cuco Conde, "Japanese people prefer floor." He didn't see the joke.

On a plane, off a plane. Flying here, flying there. What a way to live! I loved it. The months flew by, and as we reached the end of the year my most persistent problem got solved.

Bill Faversham had suffered a heart attack, and the syndicate lawyer had taken over. Now he was ill too! The syndicate decided with Cassius Clay, who was now known as Muhammad Ali, that I would take over as manager. That meant that I would be doing virtually the same as I had always been doing for the last few years, but I would get an increase in salary. Fine! They knew I had made a terrible mistake in not taking a percentage, and they also knew I could walk out any time I wanted. I had never signed a contract with any of them. I had shaken hands on the deal, and I guessed they knew that my word was as good as the most binding contract ever written. I liked money as much as the next guy, but I never made money the major criterion for what I did. As I said, I liked Muhammad, I enjoyed working with him, and I was proud of the job I had done. The syndicate showed their appreciation. With Muhammad's blessing they gave me a $20,000 bonus. And in the year 1964 that wasn't peanuts! It ain't bad now, either.

Before I could get hit upon, Helen and Mildred convinced me to invest in property, in case of a rainy day. I never worry about rainy days. I've had so many I'm used to them. But it was a good feeling starting another new year with an umbrella! As I keep telling you, anything can happen in boxing.

CHAPTER SIXTEEN

IT RAINS ON MY PARADE

"Sonny had his last fight in June of 1970, and on December 30th of that same year, Sonny Liston died in Las Vegas. Controversy followed him to his grave. His body was found five days after his death by his wife Geraldine, who had been away ... on a trip. A small quantity of heroin was found in the house, and needle punctures were discovered on Sonny's arm."

I left the office early. I didn't go to the gym, I went straight home. Too many things were happening. If I wanted to sound dramatic I could say my world was crumbling. There wasn't a lot I could do about it, except worry. That would have to wait until tomorrow. Today was my daughter Terri's tenth birthday, and I was going home to spend it with her. We were having a party.

I got home. No kids, no party, and Terri in tears. Helen gave me the picture. As we had just moved into our house, Terri had no neighborhood friends. OK! I got back in the car and drove to our old neighborhood, where I rounded up about twenty of Terri's old friends. Then, in a convoy, me leading the way, we drove to my new home. The mothers—there wasn't one dad in the group—went crazy about our new home, and I got a kick out of showing off the swimming pool. All the kids had heard of Muhammad Ali, and a few had even heard of me. Of course, Terri told all her old friends that her Dad was Muhammad's manager! It was a great afternoon, and Terri had a fun birthday.

The occasion made me realize one thing. No matter how well I had done with my other fighters, even those who had become champions, I was known and perhaps would always be known as Muhammad's manager. He was the spotlight that shone on whatever talent I had. Pastrano, Basilio, Rodriguez, and Ramos were stars, but Ali was the moon. D'you know what I mean?

I was still involved with many other fighters. José Napoles was becoming a title contender; and Jimmy Ellis the middleweight from Louisville, whom I had first seen fight on the same card as Ali in London, was now a fully-fledged heavyweight and a contender for Ali's title; but I was still known as Ali's manager. Believe me, I am not bitching, but you gotta admit, it was kind of strange—especially as I was no longer Ali's manager!

As I told you, I did take over the reins in 1964, but when the syndicate's contract with Muhammad ran out in 1966, Muhammad, who was deeply involved in the Muslim religion, chose Herbert Muhammad to manage him. Was I upset by the move? No way. My relationship with Muhammad transcended any argument over my official title. Manager, trainer, corner man? What the hell. If Muhammad wanted me, I was there. I worked with Muhammad. That was it! The newspapers gave a lot of space to the "Black Muslims take over" type of story, and unfortunately there was an underlined reference to the fact that I was the only white guy in Ali's entourage. Let me tell you, during the twenty years or so I was involved with Muhammad Ali I never heard a racist comment leave his mouth. He had deep feelings for his race, and believed that Allah had made him great for the purpose of helping his people. The exact amount of money he gave away to charity will never be known, but believe me it is a mind-shattering sum. He had love for all people—black, white, yellow, or whatever color of skin covers the person inside.

Contrary to news reports from reporters that I had never met, I got on fine with Herbert Muhammad, Ali's new manager. Herbert bought me an inscribed, custom-made diamond ring that matched one Muhammad had given me, and when he gave me that highly prized gift, Herbert told me that I was a valuable part of Ali's future. I liked that. Herbert was the son of Elijah Muhammad, the leader of the Muslim movement. I could understand Muhammad Ali's desire to have the guidance of his religious leaders in his career.

Sure, for the first few months I felt a little awkward when Herbert called the shots, but I had never ordered Ali, only suggested, right from the beginning, so it wasn't any big deal to me who suggested the warm-up time, or quitting time. After a few months we settled in and found a workable routine. The transitory period from Clay to Ali caused a few waves but no storm. I personally thought it was a pity that the name Cassius Marcellus Clay was no longer used. I had liked that name. It had a fine ring to it. I got used to the name Muhammad Ali, and that name began to take on its own identity, becoming synonymous with its owner. I was never asked to call Cassius Muhammad. I just did it. You have to respect people's religious beliefs, even if you don't understand them.

Rudy Clay, Cassius's younger brother, had also become a Muslim. He told me that he too had a new religious name like Muhammad. I said jokingly that I would call him Rocky Muhammad, but Rudy saw no humor in my remark. "Oh, no," he said. "Elijah Muhammad gave me my name, I would never change it."

The two brothers, Rudy and Cassius, were sincere. It was not a topic for jokes. You called Muhammad Ali by that name or you lost a friend. Muhammad had some heavy words with his idol Sugar Ray Robinson because Sugar was reluctant about calling him Muhammad, and the Ernie Terrell bout turned into a "hate" fight because Terrell refused to use the name Muhammad Ali. Terrell continually referred to his opponent as Cassius Clay, and all through their fight Muhammad would snarl at him, "What's my name?"

The Ali-Terrell fight took place on February 6, 1967, in Houston, Texas. Muhammad Ali chased Ernie Terrell for fifteen rounds to win the untidy and not particularly exciting fight. Now, in April 1967, only two months later, I was helplessly witnessing what could be the end of Muhammad Ali's career. Why? Because in late March, only weeks ago, Muhammad had been stripped of his world title for refusing to accept his military draft. If he continued his refusal he would be liable to be fined and perhaps sent to prison. Not a happy thought. Not a happy time!

Let me tell you what had happened since Ali (then known as Clay) had won the world title in 1964. You know most of it; the involvement with the Muslim religion; the changing of his name to Muhammad Ali; the end of the Louisville syndicate's contract and the taking on of Herbert Muhammad as his manager in 1966. That's the background, but I couldn't let all those events get to me. There were fights to be won!

Sonny Liston had a return fight clause in the contract when he fought and lost his title to Muhammad in 1964. We gave him his return in May 1965.

Some fight fans thought that Liston had thrown the first fight to get a big payday in the return fight, when he would show his real power and stop Ali. Any fight fan who did think that, thought wrong! Liston wanted to win that first fight with Ali. I have never known any champion who wanted to throw away his title, and

Liston was no exception. It was going to be a lot harder winning his title back than defending it. Ali liked being champion, and was not about to give it away. I thought the return fight would be a lot easier for Ali, because he had torn away Liston's cloak of invincibility and with it a chunk of Liston's confidence.

So, the first title defense by Muhammad Ali took place in Lewiston on May 25, 1965, against Sonny "the Bear" Liston. The one-sided fight only went one round. Muhammad had done to Liston what Liston had done to Floyd Patterson: psyched him out and KO'd him in one round.

No one could believe the result. Liston KO'd in one round by flashy, loud-mouthed Muhammad Ali! The guy who changed his name and became a Muslim!

The press did not like it. Boxing got some bad publicity. There was an outcry for federal control, and there were the usual innuendos about crooked fights, but nothing came of it. The Ali-Liston fight caused a lot of controversy. It was first scheduled for the winter of 1964, but it had to be postponed. On the night before the fight, I left Muhammad safely relaxing in his hotel room, watching the movie *Prince Valiant* on television. I went with John Crittenden, a sportswriter on *The Miami News.* to see a closed-circuit telecast of the University of Miami–Boston University football game.

I'm a football nut. And with my adopted home team playing, there was no way I would miss watching the game. During a time-out the commentator announced that Muhammad Ali had been taken to a hospital. How could that be? I had only left him an hour or so ago, and he had been perfectly OK. But it was true. Suffering with pain, Muhammad had called the hotel doctor, who had immediately checked him into a hospital. Within hours, they operated on a strained hernia. Obviously the Liston fight was off.

It was rescheduled for May, 1965. Muhammad was as fit as he had ever been. He dominated the fight from the very beginning. He was too fast and talented for Liston to handle. He began to taunt the ex-champion, a habit I am not fond of, but psychologically it was hurting Sonny nearly as much as the punches. The fight ended dramatically in the first round with Liston being KO'd once again by the young, flashy champion.

Some people, who obviously never saw the fight, or if they did were not paying enough attention, said that Liston went down without being hit. They said he had not been counted out and that the fight had been fixed. Horsefeathers!

In round one, a tense and cautious Liston threw a long left jab, was badly off balance, and kept his left arm hanging out in front of him. Muhammad slid to the right, threw a short right over the top of Liston's outstretched left, and caught him on the temple. The punch was so hard, Liston's left foot came off the canvas involuntarily as he rocked back before collapsing in a heap.

Muhammad stood over Liston, taunting him to get up and fight. But Sonny couldn't get up. He couldn't even move.

The referee, the ex-heavyweight champion Jersey Joe Walcott, waved Muhammad away and in the process omitted to begin counting out the floored Liston. Luckily, one of the ringside officials did begin the count, banging his palm on the canvas to emphasize the numbers.

"One, two . . . ," the voice yelled out, and still Walcott ignored Liston and gave his attention to Muhammad, who was taking his time moving away from the prostrate figure on the canvas. Then the ringside officials captured Jersey Joe's attention and he began to count out the ex-champion.

The ringside official reached "ten, and out," and the fight was officially over. But Walcott was still counting—enabling Liston to stagger to his feet. Ali was ready to pounce in for the kill, but the outcry from the officials and my own yelling held him off. I was in the ring, holding him back before any damage was done. Sonny bravely stood there, completely bemused and dazed. Within seconds, Walcott realized that Sonny had indeed been counted out, and that the fight was over.

I was relieved, not only for my fighter, but for Liston too, because when I went over to pay my respects to the dejected figure who was slumped on his corner stool, Sonny's eyes were still glassy. He was in no fit state to continue boxing.

If there is any doubt that Liston had been hit with Ali's right-hand punch, there is a photograph of the blow being landed showing Liston's left hand hanging out and Ali's right hand landing square on the temple.

Sonny Liston was a complicated and controversial figure. He had been arrested at the age of eighteen for robbery and did three years in prison. It was in prison that Liston was persuaded by the prison priest to take up boxing.

After he lost the title to Muhammad and failed to win it back, Liston dropped out of boxing for awhile. But he began fighting again and won five out of six of his bouts. Sonny had his last fight in June of 1970, and on December 30th of that same year, Sonny

Liston died in Las Vegas. Controversy followed him to his grave. His body was found five days after his death by his wife Geraldine, who had been away with their adopted child on a ten-day trip. A small quantity of heroin was found in the house, and needle punctures were discovered on Sonny's arm.

Foul play was suspected, but nothing was ever substantiated and the autopsy report could not come out with a definitive cause of death. Sonny had a bad reputation and associated with alleged gangster figures. Throughout his career, he was never allowed to box in New York because of reputed mobster connections. People had called him a bully and an unpleasant character, but beneath his tough exterior there was a sensitive, caring man. This was shown to be so by the friends who attended his funeral. Unfortunately, I was not there, although I wanted to be.

The list of mourners at Sonny's funeral included: Ed Sullivan, Ella Fitzgerald, Jerry Vale, Jack E. Leonard, and Doris Day; one of his pallbearers was Joe Louis. Quite a testimony. In my opinion, Sonny Liston was a very good fighter, and under different circumstances he might have been remembered as a great and respected champion. As it is, he always will be remembered as one of the most feared heavyweights in the annals of boxing.

After two months of touring the world giving exhibition fights, we came home from Scotland at the end of August 1965 to get ready for the Floyd Patterson fight. At last they were going to meet.

I do not like "hate" fights. Boxers are professionals and should not let personalities enter into their contests. But it often happens, and there ain't much you can do about it. I am not suggesting that Ali and Patterson really hated each other, but there was an undercurrent of personal differences. On Muhammad's part, he resented the fact that Patterson, like Ernie Terrell, continued to call him Cassius Clay. I was a little apprehensive about the fight. I had no fear of Muhammad losing under normal conditions, but personal feelings could affect his judgment, and I always say you can never tell what will happen in a boxing match.

On November 22, 1965, in Las Vegas, Muhammad Ali outboxed, taunted, and, I am sorry to say, humiliated the brave and talented Floyd Patterson, finally knocking him out in the twelfth round. Not a good fight, but Muhammad had demolished the two boxers who had dominated the heavyweight division for the last few years. Patterson and Liston were finished as world champion contenders.

Throughout 1966 Muhammad defended his title successfully five times. I traveled to Canada, London, Frankfurt, and Texas with the Ali entourage. I got a lot of personal publicity throughout the year. Unfortunately, many times the articles were slanted, with the emphasis on the fact that I was a white guy in a virtually all black setup. Maybe one or two of the guys in the ever-increasing circle of "helpers" that surrounded Ali didn't feel too happy about having a "honky" close to the champion, but I never heard anything said, and heck, I was working for Muhammad, not them, and I could live with the fact that I was no longer the manager. You can't eat ego!

The spring of 1967 was a time of important events. A month before Terri's birthday I had been in New York with Muhammad Ali and Jimmy Ellis for their respective fights against Zora Folley and Johnny Persol. Jimmy put Persol away in the first round, and Muhammad stopped Folley in seven rounds. That was on March 22, 1967. Muhammad Ali did not fight again until October 26, 1970.

Almost immediately after the Folley bout, Ali was stripped of his world title by the governing bodies of world boxing for not accepting his military draft. In Houston, Texas, Muhammad refused induction on April 28, and on June 20 he was convicted of draft evasion, fined $10,000, and sentenced to five years in prison. He was appealing against the ruling and was still ostensibly a free man.

I guess you may be wondering how I felt about Ali refusing to be drafted. A very difficult question to answer. I'll give it a shot, but if it doesn't fully satisfy you, you have to understand that I, like millions of other Americans, didn't understand the whole goddam Vietnam situation. All we knew was the American boys were getting killed out there, and we weren't even certain if it was our fight!

I am proud of being an American, and I would have accepted my own draft, but I can't honestly say how I would have felt if my son Jimmy had been drafted. I thanked God he was too young and prayed he would never have to go to war. As for Muhammad, I respected him and I respected his religious beliefs, and I couldn't help feeling that if the media hadn't hyped up the "Black Muslim" issue, the authorities might have treated the whole affair differently. Muslims were not too common in America at that time, and maybe it was a case of being scared of the unknown. As for the "Black" bit, as far as I know the Muslim religion has no color.

I had been told of well-known Hollywood film actors who had for one reason or another escaped the draft. I closed my mind to the Ali controversy—no, not closed my mind, but isolated the problem in the back of my mind and carried on the best way I could with my own life.

Although my life was dominated by the charismatic Muhammad Ali, I did have other fighters who were equally important to me. I guess I had better bring you up to date on my other guys. To do that we have to go back to the fall of 1964.

Sugar Ramos, the Featherweight Champion of the World, defended his title in Mexico City on September 26. Cuco Conde and I watched Ramos go through his workout in the Mexico City gym before he went in against Vicento Saldivar. Ramos looked sharp, but to my mind he had two strikes against him: first, the pressure of knowing he had been in a fight in which a man had died; and second, his trouble making the weight.

Sugar Ramos was KO'd by Saldivar in the twelfth round, and lost his World Featherweight Championship title. Cuco was thinking of a return, but when I brought up the fact that Ramos would only weaken himself trying to keep in the featherweight division, Cuco agreed to let time decide at which weight Ramos would fight. Time decided that Ramos should fight with a little more weight on his small, hard-muscled body. He fought as a lightweight.

After three fights—all wins—in 1965, I arranged a world title fight with Carlos Ortiz for the lightweight championship. So, on October 12, 1965, in Mexico City, Ramos fought Ortiz. Ramos went only five rounds before he was KO'd. The great little battler ran out of gas and was beaten by the better guy.

After long and drawn-out negotiations, a return fight was set for July 1967 in San Juan. I was there with Sugar Ramos when that game little guy was once again KO'd by the champion, Carlos Ortiz. This time, the fight was over in four rounds. I hoped that Sugar, who was comfortably settled in Mexico City, would call it a day. He did remain inactive throughout 1968, but decided to make a comeback in 1969 as a lightweight. He won his first fight in two rounds, but the old magic and desire were no longer there. Sugar fought spasmodically for another two years, and in Los Angeles on April 25, 1972, after being KO'd by Caesar Sinda in ten rounds, Sugar Ramos hung up his gloves. A great fighter whose career was marred by a tragic accident.

That other great Cuban fighter, Luis Rodriguez, was still going strong. As I mentioned before, his brilliant defensive qualities made for durability and longevity. After he lost his world title in 1963, and suffered another defeat at the hands of Emile Griffith in 1964, he won all his eleven fights during 1965. It looked a sure thing that Luis would get another shot at the title, but in April and July of 1966 he lost two important fights against Percy Manning and Curtis Cokes. I began to wonder if Luis had missed his chance at another title fight. Luis obviously didn't think so, because he went through 1967 and 1968 undefeated and looked real good. He was carrying a little more weight, and after six straight wins during 1969 he earned himself another world title shot—this time as a middleweight.

The fight was in Rome on November 22. Luis took on the world champion, Nino Benvenuti. For ten rounds Luis moved, jabbed, and boxed his way to a lead. Benvenuti was tired, but a strong guy who couldn't be taken for granted. In round eleven Luis, for some reason only known to him, decided to slug it out with the tough Italian. Although nearing exhaustion Benvenuti found the strength to throw one good shot to the jaw of Rodriguez, who was also tiring. That was it. The fight was over and Luis missed out being the Middleweight Champion of the World.

That's the way it goes! Eight fights in 1970, all wins for Rodriguez, four won by KOs. Could he make it back to the championship? It wasn't to be. Two losses in 1971 and another two defeats in 1972 dispelled any title hopes. In April 1972, after his loss to Donato Poduano, Luis retired. What can I say about Luis? His record speaks for itself. Out of 121 bouts, he lost only thirteen. He was a world champion, and deservedly so. We still see each other and he knows I have and will always have great respect for him both as a fighter and a man. A true champion.

You must be asking yourselves, "What happened to the Errol Flynn of boxing?" Well, after his glorious night of victory on June 1, 1963, when Willie Pastrano won the World Light-heavyweight Championship, Willie had a month off to enjoy the fruits of his labor. He fought again on August 31, easily outpointing Ollie Wilson, but then, Willie being Willie, he coasted through a bout against Gregorio Peralta and lost the decision. OK, he knocked the guy out in six rounds seven months later in April 1964, but I wasn't happy.

I've told you before, I never interfere in the private life of a fighter, but Willie was like family and I had to speak out. You see, he was messing with some bad dudes. Willie attracted bad guys like honey attracts bees. I would see these weird guys hanging around the gym and I didn't like it. I barred them from going into the dressing room. They went crying to Willie, calling me a "square bear." Willie knew I was no "square," but I didn't go for those weirdos. I told him how I felt about his so-called friends, but he just laughed it off, saying that the guys were OK, just a little "way out." Later, he would learn it was no laughing matter. I was glad when we left Miami for the Terry Downes fight in London; it would get Willie away from his weird friends and bad habits.

You can imagine the kick it gave Willie to return to Britain as world champion, after all the successes and failures he had had in that country. He was fighting a tough opponent, the former World Middleweight Champion, Terry Downes, who, although an Englishman, had fought many times in the States. The guy knew his way around. He would be a determined and experienced opponent. The venue was in Manchester, a city which I knew to be very sports-oriented. They had two big soccer clubs, a speedway team, and a great cricket stadium. I was sorry that it wasn't the cricket season. We were in November, and a local guy by the name of Tommy Burke, who became and still is a close friend of mine, told me that cricket is only played in the summer, because the weather is good then.

I think he must have been kidding, 'cause I've been in England during the summer too! Why do you think those English guys always carry an umbrella?

The Manchester crowd gave Willie a great welcome as he entered the ring. I think it must have gone to his head, because instead of doing his work he was posing for the first half of the fight.

We reached round ten—only five more rounds left—and Willie was way behind on points. Terry Downes had hustled and bustled, doing all the work and piling up the points. Willie was lazy and indifferent to the whole deal. I saw the title slipping away.

When round ten ended and I had Willie sitting on the stool I started in on him. Boy, was I mad! Willie was throwing away the fight. I called him every name in the book and some that weren't in the book! I blush as I remember. "What the **** are you doing, you ****! This guy is only a **** puffed-up **** middleweight and you are the **** world champion. Do you want to throw your **** title away?" During this rather heated monologue, I was working on Willie.

Carefully removing his gum-shield, which ain't as easy as it sounds, because if you do it incorrectly you can cut a fighter's mouth, I'm sponging him, then wiping him with the towel, and cleaning him up. He is sitting there burning at my abuse. Calmly I carry on with my work, but my voice is loud and excited: "You're fighting like a **** bum. You're the **** world champion. You lazy ****! Go out there and **** fight!" The bell sounds. I slap him hard on his buttocks.

Willie raises his arm as if to hit me. I say to him, "Don't hit me, you ****! Hit him!"

Willie knocked out Terry Downes in that round and retained his title. He thanked me for the pep talk and for enlarging his vocabulary! In the following year, 1965, Willie fought José Torres. This time there was nothing I could do to pull out a victory. Willie lost his world title and, against my advice, he decided to retire. I am not a believer in premature retiring. I have noticed that those fighters who retire before it's necessary find that they miss the glamour and make an invariably unwise comeback. It is so much harder to make a comeback. Getting back into shape is a tough discipline to take. Better, the fighter carries on, soaking up the glamour until the end. Gradually fading out and becoming mentally prepared for the completely new lifestyle awaiting him.

So, Willie retired. I heard stories that he was taking drugs and slowing killing himself with that sinister habit. I called him, and although he was always flip when we spoke, he knew that I was concerned and I was there if he needed me.

He did need me. He would call all hours of the night, sometimes when he was hallucinating. Once he called me to come round because there were "things" in his garden. Of course, the "things" were only in his mind.

Willie had the choice: carry on, and sink deeper into the ugly and destructive pit, or give up booze and drugs and rehabilitate himself.

It takes a lot of courage and determination to carry out the latter, but thank God, Willie did it. He pulled himself right around and built a new life for himself in New Orleans where he now works with children. Willie still has his sense of humor. When I told him about this book and asked if he minded being in it, he replied, "Don't leave the bad bits out, I wanna show it to the kids so that they'll know that when I say a thing is bad, I sure as hell know what I'm talking about."

One by one my special fighters were leaving the game. But, it is in the nature of the fight manager's life that the fighters he has

worked, struggled, and triumphed with are replaced by new eager
young men. Willie the fighter may have been replaced, but
nothing will ever replace the affection I hold for him, locked in my
memories.

Although I have looked ahead to the end of the careers of Willie
Pastrano, Ultiminio Sugar Ramos, and Luis Rodriguez, my story is
still in the year of 1967, the year Muhammad was stripped of his
world title and faced charges for refusing to fight in Vietnam. I
have tried to tell how I felt about that episode and explain it in
relation to my life at that time. Remember, I was involved with so
many fights and fighters. I had my own private life, a wife and
children to think about. I was working with my brother Chris,
sharing an office and involved in the now famous 5th Street Gym
on Miami Beach. I was traveling thousands of miles—guiding,
training, and managing fighters. So, you must try and understand
that the Muhammad Ali drama was just another drama. OK, a
major one, but every goddam fight was a drama!

In 1968, I had Jimmy Ellis fighting for the vacant heavyweight
title: the championship that had been held by Muhammad Ali was
up for grabs. After a series of elimination fights, it was Jerry
Quarry, the fighting Irishman from California, against Jimmy
Ellis, the quiet kid from Louisville who had plenty of ring savvy.

Jimmy, just a skinny middleweight with a good left hook when
I had first seen him fight in London back in 1963, had developed
into a very talented fighter. Although he was boxing as a heavyweight, he would have been a sensational, awesome light-heavyweight. But you know how it goes—"food, glorious food!"— the
guy loved his food!

When Jimmy had written to me asking for help back in early
1966, he had been on the verge of giving up boxing. I took away
the worry and strain of day-to-day living. He needed guidance and
some bread coming in, and I took care of both problems. I made
the kid eat well and sleep good. He was a clean living, church-
going young man, and I was delighted with the way he was
developing. I took Jimmy to London in May 1966 to fight Lewina
Waga on the same card as the Ali-Cooper return bout, and I was
also using him as a sparring partner for Muhammad.

It was a wonderful trip to London, even the weather was
delightful. Muhammad and Jimmy did their roadwork in Hyde
Park and some mornings they had an extra runner, the famous
football star turned screen actor Jim Brown. He was over in

England making a movie and, although back home in the States he was a big name, in England nobody knew who the heck he was! The newspaper pals of mine thought he was just another sparring partner until I put them wise.

I love it when stars like Jim Brown turn up at a big fight. It gives boxing some glamour and creates an atmosphere and excitement that infects the fighters as much as the star-spotting crowd.

Whatever stars, and whoever else, happened to be at the Arsenal football stadium in North London on May 21, 1966, saw Jimmy Ellis stop his opponent in one round, and Muhammad Ali knock out the likeable British champion in six rounds, dashing all hopes of a world title for "our 'Enery," as the British fans called Henry Cooper.

A passing thought: back in 1962, the famous William Morris Talent Agency had the then Cassius Clay under contract, but they let him go. They thought that he had no future. Something tells me someone blew it!

It was April 1968. I was in the gym working with Jimmy Ellis. His world title fight against Jerry Quarry was only weeks away. Muhammad Ali came into the gym. He hadn't fought for eleven months, except for some exhibition bouts, and they had been eight months ago. His appeal against his conviction was still being handled by his lawyers. His life was in turmoil, but he looked good. "Hi, Angie," he said as he waved hello to the other guys in the gym.

"How ya doin'?" I asked him. He looked like he didn't have a worry in the world. He was in Miami to make a commercial, and was staying at the Four Ambassador Hotel with his lovely wife Belinda and his children.

"Is it OK if I work out in the gym?" he asked in that soft voice of his.

"What are talking about? You gotta ask?" I said. "Come on! Please, the gym is yours." I had an idea! "You wanna work with Jimmy?"

"That'll be great, Angie. Be like old times." Muhammad smiled.

"Great! A hundred bucks a day OK?"

"Hey, I don't want any money."

"Jimmy got paid when he sparred with you." I held out my hand.

"You got a deal," he said laughing. We shook hands.

When the advertising agency stopped paying his hotel because the commercial was finished, I did. It was my pleasure.

Tactical talk between rounds can be helpful, but when the bell sounds Sugar Ray Leonard must make his own decisions.

The WBC Manager of the Year Awards at Madison Square Garden, 1980. *Left to right:* Gomez, Holmes, Dundee, Leonard, Suleiman (WBC president), Arguello, and Lopez.

Left to right: Don King, Angelo Dundee, and "Sellout" Moe Fleischer.

ith Sugar Ray in the Los Angeles Superdome on the night of the second
:onard-Duran fight, November 1980.

Just a few of the guys. Sitting between Muhammad and Ray is Ray, Jr.

My circle of champions. *Front row, from left to right,* Willie Pastrano, Muhammad Ali, Carmen Basilio, Sugar Ray Leonard. *Back Row, from left to right,* Ralph Dupas, Luis Rodriguez, Sugar Ramos, Jimmy Ellis, Pinklon Thomas, José Napoles. Hopefully the circle will get bigger.

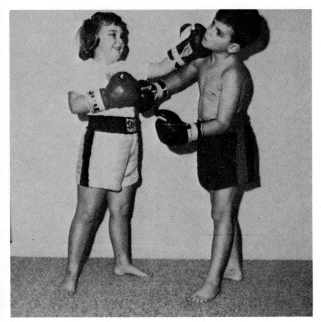

My other two champions, Terri and Jimmy, 1961.

Who said romance is dead?
A happy day with Helen.

My beautiful family—at Terri's wedding.

At the Touchdown Club of Washington, D.C. Award Dinner with Jerry Lewis and Judge Sirica.

Me as Grand Marshal riding with Governor Jay Rockefeller in the West Virginia Italian-American Heritage Parade in Clarksburg, West Virginia, 1983.

Who does Mr. T. want as his personal trainer?

Doing the broadcast with Al Albert for USA Cable, 1983.

With World Champion Pinklon Thomas at a press conference after
Thomas beat Tim Witherspoon for the title, August 1984.

The press and the bookies gave Jimmy Ellis no chance against Jerry Quarry, but they didn't know Jimmy had "the Greatest" for a sparring partner!

April 27, 1968: the night of the Ellis-Quarry fight. The venue was in Oakland, California. A Los Angeles sports writer had just asked me if this fight was Black versus White. I remembered how Muhammad Ali had answered a reporter in London who had asked the same question about the Henry Cooper fight: "Don't be childish. It's a fight between two professional boxers." I gave the same answer. Maybe that's one quote of Muhammad's that never made the papers!

Jimmy was laid back. If he had been tensed up I would have known. We had our game plan and I knew Jimmy would stick to it. It promised to be a lousy fight to watch, with Quarry waiting for Ellis to go forward and throw punches so that he could counter-punch, and Jimmy under instructions to stick and run. I wasn't after the best fight of the year award, I wanted to win. Jimmy was making $125,000 for the fight, win or lose, so the will to win had to come from inside himself, with a little help from me.

The fight, as far as the spectators were concerned, did turn out pretty bad. That was a shame, but what can you do? If we had fought the fight to suit Quarry, Jimmy would have lost. As it was, Jimmy did as we planned and it made for a dull fight. Nobody forced Quarry to fight the way he did. He could have changed his style any time he wanted to—if he had had the ability to change gears. It was no good me telling Jimmy to throw overhand rights if he couldn't throw an overhand right. No point asking Jimmy to jab and move if he didn't have the talent to do it. Do you know what I'm saying? The fighters make the fight! In this fight, I gave the right instructions because I had the right fighter.

By the thirteenth round I had Jimmy well ahead on points. I told Jimmy to stay out of trouble for the last two rounds. Jimmy won the fight on a split decision. Two of the three judges voted him the winner. Jimmy Ellis was the new Heavyweight Champion of the World!

To be honest—and I know Jimmy agrees with me—his great achievement was slightly marred by the controversy over the taking away of Muhammad's title. Some people still considered Ali the world champion, and there were five states who considered Joe Frazier the champion. It was a time of confusion, but no one will ever be able to take away the fact that Jimmy Ellis was, for the majority of organized boxing, the world champion. It was a title he had earned through his skill and endeavor.

My personal stock was high. I had been manager of two consecutive world heavyweight champions. Everyone likes a pat on the back, the acknowledgement of a job well done, and I am no exception. I was thrilled and grateful when the New York Boxing Writers voted me the Al Buck Award, named in honor of my late pal who was a great sports writer, for Manager of the Year. I narrowly beat Yancy Durham, Joe Frazier's manager, for the award. I had great admiration for Yancy and I like the guy a lot, but I was sure glad it was me instead of him! To be chosen by those hard-bitten, knowledgeable sports writers was a big honor for me. They were my kind of guys—good professionals. I can't pay anyone a better compliment than that.

I received my award at the New York Sports Writers 44th Annual Dinner in February 1969. It was the year that saw the loss of one of boxing's legendary heroes. On August 31, 1969, the day before his 46th birthday, Rocky Marciano was killed in an airplane crash. I was devastated. It wasn't because I had known the man so intimately. It was because Rocky epitomized all my struggling years, all the fine friends I had made in those early days in New York, and all that can be attained through endeavor and the will to be good at what you do. It was as if a whole chunk of my life had died with him. My heart went out to Rocky's family and to little Charlie Goldman, the man who had always believed in him.

A few years later Charlie Goldman died, alone in a hotel room. No nieces this time. When he died he was wearing an old worn dressing gown many sizes too large for him. The dressing gown had once belong to Rocky Marciano.

CHAPTER SEVENTEEN

IF THE CROWN FITS

"Foreman didn't know how to handle the situation. Being a big and muscled man, he was better suited and more used to punching *down* and hooking. Muhammad blocked the hooks, his amazing reflexes allowing him to pick off the blows; and it wasn't possible for Foreman to punch down, like he did to the shorter Joe Frazier, because Muhammad was as tall as he. At the end of round seven I said to Muhammad, 'Go and take him out, he's ready to go.'

"Muhammad did just that."

Chris had just left the office. He was in a lousy mood. The 5th Street Gym was losing money. What did he expect? You didn't run a gym for boxers and hope to make money. I told him that it was part of the promotional expenses, and it didn't come to any goddam fortune anyway. The dues for the boxers was floating around twenty dollars per month and sometimes when a name fighter was training there, Chris would charge a dollar or two for spectators. Big deal! I needed the gym as much as Chris. My fighters used it and it was near the office, which made it convenient. Also, since Muhammad Ali had trained there the gym had become kind of famous. It was a dump, but it had an atmosphere and all the fight guys congregated there.

No one can out-talk Chris. The way it worked out, I ended up paying all of the expenses to run the gym and Chris kept the dues! If someone ever tried to sell Chris the Brooklyn Bridge, it would end up with Chris selling the guy the fishing rights to the Hudson River!

It had been one of those days. Before the conversation with Chris I had spent hours with Paul Safer and Betty Mitchell, my accountants. Betty and Paul were the result of one of Chris's money-saving policies. They were his accountants and he was paying them for one week per month to come around and do his books. He decided that I needed them two days per month, and he would get by with three days per month. That way their fee was split. It worked out OK, because since Betty and Paul joined us, way back in 1964, I really started to need accountants.

Betty Mitchell dealt with my account, and she was a nice lady. She was bright too, with a good sense of humor. She sure needed it, dealing with me. That morning she had said to me, "Look, Angelo, I read English pretty well, but I do not read Egyptian hieroglyphics!" She placed in front of me the sheets of paper containing the figures of my month's expenses.

"I'm sorry Betty," I said. "You know I can't help doodling." The papers were in kind of a mess. Covered with my doodles, they were practically impossible to read—even for me.

"What are those figures?" she asked. On the side of the indicated paper were the names Juan, José, Gene. Against the names were the figures 200, 300, 600. I put on my glasses; I couldn't read the sucker without them.

"Oh, those figures," I answered. "They're loans to fighters."

"That's eleven hundred dollars this month. I'm glad to see you are building up your loan business. It was only five hundred last month." She stared at me and slowly shook her head. "It's a great business you've got. Not only do you not get any interest on your money, you don't even get the money back! By the way, there is a statement for two thousand dollars from Caesar's Palace. Shall I send them a check?" I nodded my head, feeling as dumb as I knew I had been. Betty began gathering up her papers. "Well, you may as well gamble your money away instead of giving it away. See you next month." As she left she said, more to herself than to me, "Loans!!" There was a note of disgust in her voice.

Not a good day! I thought that I had better go home. That would cheer me up. Maybe Helen and I would go out to eat. Yea! We would. Often I would say to her without any warning, "OK, hon, let's get dolled up and go out and have a meal." Yea, I'd go home, but I wouldn't mention the gambling.

The children were growing up. We didn't have to worry about babysitters any more. Terri was a teenager now, a bright and lovely girl who was doing great at school; and Jimmy, at sixteen, was already towering over me. He was around six foot two, slim and muscular, and one hell of a tennis player. His tennis coach had told me that Jimmy would probably get a tennis scholarship to college. I would be very proud, but I would have preferred Jimmy to make his way in life with sport as just a hobby rather than a business. Still, he was my son, and I would be proud of him whatever he decided to do.

Being with Helen and the children always made me feel good. Sure we had arguments. If you can't argue with your wife, who can you argue with! Right? And kids are meant to give parents some aggravation. After all, they give so much pleasure. I know it doesn't happen in every family, but I was lucky and I counted my blessings.

While Terri was telling me about her future plans to help retarded children, how could I worry about Muhammad's legal battles, or Jimmy Ellis fighting Joe Frazier? Come on!

When I was back in the office the following morning, *then* I worried. There was nothing I could do about Muhammad. His problem was in the hands of his lawyers, but Jimmy Ellis fighting Joe Frazier was something I could work on.

I really didn't want the fight. I tried to talk Yancy Durham, Joe's manager, into letting Frazier fight Al Jones first. Al was a six foot two inch heavyweight that I represented. He was a big strong guy and would have caused Joe all sorts of problems; but Yancy was too smart, he wanted no part of Al Jones. He wanted Ellis. He wanted the champion and the championship! You couldn't blame the guy, that's what it is all about! Poor Al Jones missed out on a big payday and a chance of fame. Shortly after, Al quit boxing, the result of broken hands.

So, it was going to be Frazier against the champion, Jimmy Ellis. I respected Joe: he was so darn strong, and had the heart of a lion; I felt he would be a very tough opponent for Jimmy. I told myself that Jimmy would be too fast for Frazier, but I also remembered the old saying that the *Titanic* was faster than the iceberg!

The fight was set for February 16, 1970, in New York. On the night before the Ellis-Frazier bout, José Napoles was fighting Ernie Lopez in Los Angeles. Cuco Conde had not asked me to work with José for this fight. Napoles' trainer, a guy everyone called "Rapidez"—I guess that was his name, but I don't know whether it was his first or last name—would work the corner with Cuco. Knowing how thoughtful Cuco was, I suspected he hadn't asked me to come to Los Angeles because he was aware that I had to be in New York with Jimmy Ellis and he hadn't wanted to give me problems. As it worked out, José won and I wasn't missed, but maybe the owners of the Hotel Alexandria in Los Angeles wished that I had been there!

Rapidez, a nice enough guy, was into the "black magic" bit. The night of the fight, Rapidez was trying to cast a winning spell for Napoles. He left some ceremonial candles burning in the hotel room. The candles caused a fire and nearly burned down the hotel. It must have been some hot spell!

So I missed out on the Napoles-Lopez fight, but I had been with him on April 18, 1969, when he got his world title shot at last. Napoles fought Curtis Cokes in Los Angeles. It was a lucky city for José, he was never beaten there, and on that night his potential blossomed. Curtis was a good, talented fighter, and it took a better fighter to take away his championship. José Napoles had a touch of greatness. He KO'd Curtis in the thirteenth round to become the Welterweight Champion of the World.

As I wasn't in Los Angeles, Cuco Conde gave me the Napoles-Lopez result over the phone. So, on the night of the Ellis-Frazier fight I was still involved with two current world champions, Ellis and Napoles, and the "people's champion," Muhammad Ali. Unfortunately, Muhammad wasn't being allowed to fight, so whether or not he was really champion was academic.

By the end of the night of February 16, my tally of current World Champions went down to one fighter only. Jimmy Ellis fell to Joe Frazier. Frazier was too strong for Jimmy, and I stopped the fight at the end of the fourth round to prevent further punishment. A disappointed Jimmy asked why I had stopped him from starting the fifth round.

"Gee, Angelo, I was OK. I was only put down once. I was a little dazed but I was fine," Jimmy said.

"You were put down twice, but you only remember once. That's why I stopped the fight," I told him.

Jimmy had never been KO'd before, and he hated the thought of being stopped. I understood how he felt, but I stop a fight when in my judgment my guy is not capable of defending himself properly. Better that I am wrong than my fighter sustain an irreparable injury. To me boxing is a very tough sport, but a ring is not the Roman Coliseum and boxers aren't gladiators who must fight to the death.

Stopping a fight is never an easy or pleasant thing to do, but I always have to follow my conscience. A few days after the fight I received a very warm letter from Edwin B. Dooley, the chairman of the State of New York's Athletic Commission, and I would like to quote part of it.

You used excellent judgment and I know it took a lot of courage to make that decision. Jimmy Ellis is one of the finest men boxing has ever seen. Emotionally and philosophically he is above the run of boxers. In fact, above the run of most men and it would be a pity if he were hurt permanently as he might have been under the circumstances which prevailed at the Garden Monday night.

The letter made me proud to be a part of professional boxing. I knew that I worked with many fine people, and it was reassuring to know that there were men in control of the sport who had feeling and sensitivity toward the often maligned boxers.

There was a new heavyweight champion, Joe Frazier. After his victory over Ellis, Frazier was the undisputed king, except for the man who lost his title outside the ring, Muhammad Ali. But Muhammad was not out of the game yet!

Legal battles were still going on over the draft evasion conviction, and a lot of people didn't think it right to stop a man earning his living in his chosen profession until the conviction was upheld. One such person who felt that way was Governor Maddox of Georgia. Muhammad Ali and Herbert Muhammad kept me informed on how things were progressing. By the end of September 1970, a bout had been arranged for the undefeated ex-champion, and once again I was training with Muhammad, getting him ready for his fight against Jerry Quarry in Atlanta, Georgia, on October 26, 1970.

For the brave Jerry Quarry it was a night of defeat. He was KO'd in the third round. For Muhammad Ali and his followers it was a glorious night of victory, and it was celebrated at a big lavish party held by Muhammad after the fight. Winning so decisively after such a long layoff called for a celebration. Helen, Mildred, and George joined me after the fight for the party. They had deep affection for Muhammad. Paradoxically, this family of mine from the deep south, where racism was strong, had no prejudice against anyone's race or religion, and when the chips were down it was the governor of Georgia, not a professed liberal northern state politician, who gave Muhammad his license to box once again. On June 29, 1971, the US Supreme Court overturned Ali's draft conviction by an 8–0 vote.

After the Quarry fight in October 1970, Muhammad Ali was back on the track. Other states began to give him his license to box. It was arranged for Ali to go in against Oscar Bonavena in New York, but before I could start working on that fight I had to get Jimmy Ellis right for his bout in Miami, on Chris's promotion.

The Frazier fight hadn't diminished Jimmy's talent or determination. He KO'd Robert Davila in seven rounds. I began to see an

Ellis-Ali fight as inescapable. I would think about it after the Ali-Bonavena fight.

With Ali fighting Bonavena on November 7, I would find it very difficult to work with José Napoles when he fought Billy Backus in Syracuse on the 3rd. Billy Backus was a relation of Carmen Basilio, and Carmen was working the corner for Billy. I would have liked to have been in the Napoles corner. For the second time Cuco Conde hadn't called me to ask for my services. As usual I had no contract, only an understanding. If Cuco felt he could manage without me, outside of feeling hurt there was nothing I could do about it. I wanted to call Cuco to wish him luck with the fight, but I felt a little embarrassed to do so in case he felt I was pushing. I sent José a telegram wishing him luck and left it at that.

José Napoles got badly cut and the fight was stopped in the fourth round, so Billy Backus became Welterweight Champion of the World. I was sorry that José had lost, and felt that if I had been there I might have been of use. Losing a fight because of cuts was a situation I didn't appreciate. I also believed that Napoles could beat Backus. I hoped I would be in José's corner if there was a return bout, which I thought was inevitable, knowing Cuco's astute business sense. He would never have allowed Napoles to fight, with the title at stake, without a return fight clause in the contract.

I couldn't let a touch of false pride get in the way; a couple of days after the Backus fight, and the night before the Ali-Bonavena fight, I put in a call to Cuco in Mexico City. I got through to Cuco's home. After he had given me his version of the fight, he brought up the subject of the return fight.

"We settled on June 1971. Now, you got plenty of time to plan your life. I want you with me. I understand that you had to be with Ellis for the Frazier fight and you wanna be with Muhammad at this time, but you had better be with José and me in Los Angeles in June. Understand, Angie?"

Fancy me thinking Cuco didn't want me. I guess I'm just a sensitive guy!

On November 7, 1970, the Garden crowd saw Muhammad defeat the durable Oscar Bonavena who was decked three times in the fifteenth round. Muhammad was still not back to his devastating best, but for my money he was still "the Greatest." I looked forward to the New Year. There were sure to be some great fights ahead. Before the year ended, Herbert Muhammad informed me that an Ali-Frazier fight was arranged for March 1971. Ali would have another shot at the world championship!

I called my brother Jimmy to wish him and his family a Happy New Year. He could tell by my reluctance to hang up that something was on my mind, plus the fact that it was a little late for New Year wishes—it was the first week in March!

"OK, Angie, what's bothering you? A difference of opinion with Chris?" he asked.

"No, Jimmy, nothing like that. Jimmy Ellis knocked out Tony Doyle last night here in Miami."

"That's great. He must be back in line for a title shot. Maybe you can get him in with the winner of the Frazier-Ali fight."

"That's what's worrying me. If Ali beats Frazier on the eighth, Jimmy will want a shot at the title, and if Ali loses, Jimmy will have to beat him to get another shot at Frazier. If Ellis goes against Ali, whose corner do I work in, Jimmy?"

There was silence at the other end of the wire. I knew Jimmy was thinking. He didn't believe in making rash statements. He thought before he spoke. He then answered my question. "As I see it, Angie, with Muhammad you are no longer his manager. You are his friend, sure, but with Jimmy you are the manager, trainer, friend, the whole bag of tricks. It's a professional decision, and you are an old pro, Angie, you know the thing to do. You don't need me to tell you. All I'm gonna add is this: if you make a professional decision, both Jimmy and Muhammad will respect it. Now, you take care of yourself. Love to Helen and the kids. Say good luck to Muhammad for me for the Frazier fight."

I always liked to talk over my problems with Jimmy. He was my personal "guru." Somehow he made me see what was the right thing to do. I would worry about Ellis fighting Ali later; right now I had to worry about Ali fighting Frazier.

It was another chance for the championship for Muhammad, but Joe Frazier was no Sonny Liston. Joe had no image to keep up. He was a tough, talented, hard-hitting fighter who would carry on punching until he dropped—if he dropped!

On March 8, 1971, Frazier and Ali fought for fifteen strength-sapping rounds. The prize was the Heavyweight Championship of the World. It was the first multi-million-dollar purse fight. Frazier went to work, but Ali grandstanded, fooling more than fighting. Muhammad showed the world he could take a good punch. He got up after being knocked down in the fifteenth round, only to lose a unanimous decision to the relentless Frazier. Muhammad had lost his chance of regaining the title. He would have to wait until another chance came round, and that would only happen if he kept fighting and kept beating the opposition. The immediate opposition was waiting. Jimmy Ellis was ready, willing, and able. The fight I hoped would not take place was here. Ali was going against Ellis in Houston on July 26, 1971. I had made up my mind in which corner I would be.

The Ellis-Ali fight took place at the Astrodome, Houston on July 26, 1971. The 32,000 spectators that came to watch the fight may have been a little surprised when they saw the two protagonists standing together receiving their fight instructions from the referee. It looked like a mismatch. Ali towered over Ellis. It wasn't the difference in height—Ali was only just over two inches taller—but Muhammad had come into the fight at 220½ pounds, as against Jimmy's 189 pounds. Over 30 pounds' difference in weight!

Bundini Brown and I nodded at each other as we stood behind our fighters listening to the ref's instructions. We went with our respective fighters back to our corners to wait for the bell for the first round. Bundini was in Ali's corner, I was in the corner of Jimmy Ellis.

There was little Bundini or I could tell our fighters because they had sparred and worked together so many times in the past. I felt that I knew both fighters' styles better than they did. I was looking for Jimmy to catch Muhammad with his dangerous right hand, but I was aware that Muhammad knew my thinking and would take no chances on getting nailed by that punch. It was a Catch-22 situation.

During the fight I was one hundred percent behind Ellis. I didn't let my personal feelings for Muhammad intrude one little bit. I had told Muhammad of my decision to work with Jimmy, and explained my reason. Simply it came down to this: with Muhammad I was the trainer, only part of the team; with Jimmy I *was* the team, and Jimmy paid me one third of his purse—he was entitled to my services.

Muhammad understood and respected my decision. Some of the newspapers took literally Muhammad's remarks about this being the end of our relationship, and that he had found someone far better than me to work with. He also told the press that he would take me back if I didn't talk too much!! Imagine that! You've got to know Muhammad and understand his offbeat sense of humor and his dedication to hyping a fight.

Halfway through the twelfth round, I knew the result was inevitable. Ali was too good, too strong, and too much for the thirty-one-year-old Jimmy Ellis. With only fifty seconds of the fight remaining, the referee stepped in and stopped it, awarding a technical knockout decision in favor of Muhammad Ali.

All I can tell you is that after the fight the two Louisville fighters and old sparring partners were good pals again, and I was back in Muhammad's corner for his next fight and every other fight throughout his amazing career.

There were two more bouts for Muhammad in 1971. They were as far apart as Houston, Texas, and Zurich in Switzerland. Ali won both fights. He ended 1971 firing on all guns.

I was looking forward to April 1972. I was going to Tokyo again, this time with Muhammad, who was due to meet Mac Foster. But before I tell you about that trip I must tell you what happened to José Napoles in his return fight with Billy Backus back in June 1971.

I had given my word to Cuco that I would be with Napoles in his lucky city of Los Angeles for the Backus fight on June 4, 1971, so naturally I was there. You know, sometimes in life you really feel as if you have done a good job. I got that feeling that night in Los Angeles. José had lost his title because of cuts, and—would you believe this—in the first round of the return bout he came back to the corner covered in blood from an ugly cut above the eye. I got to work, with compresses, coagulant, and other goodies from my little black bag. Anything to stop the flow of blood before the referee stopped the fight. I only had a minute to perform a miracle. I had skill, sure, but we needed luck too, lots of it. When the bell rang for the second round, I told José, "No problem," No one would have known from my manner that José even had a scratch, let alone a badly cut eye! José went back full of confidence. The Mexicans called Napoles "Mantequilla," because he fights as smooth as butter. Well, he spread havoc all over Backus. The referee humanely stepped in after one minute, fifty-three seconds of the eighth round to stop Backus taking further punishment.

I went across to Backus' dressing room after the fight to offer my respects to his skill and courage, and to say goodbye to his manager, the man who gave me my first taste of big-time boxing, Carmen Basilio, the former Welterweight and Middleweight Champion of the World.

The dressing room was quiet, with only one reporter present— a nice guy, Bud Furillo of the *Los Angeles Herald Examiner.* Billy was sitting there, legs dangling over the bench. His face had been patched up, but he didn't look pretty. Carmen and Furillo, pad on lap, pencil in hand, were sitting opposite each other on two hard-backed chairs. I took in the scene: the graying white walls of the dressing room, the naked light bulb hanging from the ceiling, the smell of ointments, sweat, and linseed oil.

It reminded me of another time—the time I had first met Carmen, under similar circumstances and in a similar environment. The Napoles dressing room which I had just left had been jubilant, packed with reporters and well-wishers. There the smell was one of success. No one noticed that the walls were dirty and that the hanging bulb had no shade! This was the fight game! Most guys can dish it out, only the best can take it too! You had to learn to swallow the sour taste of defeat, wash out your mouth, and get ready to take another bite at success.

Carmen made me sit down. He wanted to know how I treated Napoles' cut eye. Bud Furillo called me the Dr. Christian Barnard of the fight game. As I left the dressing room, Billy Backus said, "You did a great job on José, Angie."

Carmen added, "I wish to hell you had been in our corner." Two great winners, both reaching the very top of their profession. They were gracious losers, too!

My reputation as a skillful cut man seemed rather ridiculous about ten days after the Backus-Napoles fight. My son Jimmy, like most young men in their late teens, was learning about life from experience, and not all experiences are good. Jimmy was attending North Miami High School, confident in the knowledge that he was going to college in the following year. Driving home from school one day in the Volkswagen Carmen Ghia that I had bought him for his sixteenth birthday, he swerved to avoid hitting a car that had jumped a red light, and crashed into a telephone pole, and also hit a fire hydrant, doing plenty of damage to the car and unfortunately to himself. He was taken to the hospital, where he had the presence of mind to ask for my good friend Dr. Julian Groff.

Julian rushed over to the hospital. As he was so emotionally involved, he was relieved to be able to leave the necessary medical attention to the highly competent hospital staff. He called me, and knowing about my sensitivity when it came to seeing my family hurt, gently told me what had happened. I immediately headed for the hospital.

Julian warned me before I entered Jimmy's room: "Listen, Angie, Jimmy is going to be all right. He was bleeding pretty badly from a cut bottom lip, but he is OK."

"Is that all? A cut lip?" I said, putting on a brave and confident face.

"Well," Julian paused before he continued. "He has a broken toe, dislocated back, torn left knee, and multiple bruises." He saw me turn pale. "But, he is going to be all right." I entered the room and looked at my son swathed in bandages. I felt my legs turning to jelly.

"Hey Dad, look!" Jimmy huskily croaked at me as he removed the blood-stained gauze pad from his lip. I fainted.

When I came to I was lying on a cot in a tiny room somewhere in the hospital. Dr. Julian Groff was leaning over me. "You'll be OK. You fainted. It happens to the best of us." Once again the famous cut man had taken the count at the sight of a bloody cut!

Just for the record, Helen refused to enter the hospital room after Julian had told her the extent of Jimmy's injuries and how badly bruised his face was. She spent hours pacing up and down the hospital's corridors, finally taking me home and waiting until the following morning before visiting our banged-up son.

Thank God, Jimmy recovered, but will always carry a small scar on the left side of his bottom lip, to remind us all that cars are lethal weapons.

The incident confirmed my belief that in life, as in a fight, anything can happen!

Preconceived ideas can get unexpectedly shattered too! I had my own opinions on Japan, formed from my very short visit to Tokyo in 1964. I wasn't too crazy about the place—an opinion based on my observations from my hotel room and a boxing auditorium! In 1972 I had the opportunity to visit Tokyo again, for the Ali-Foster fight, and I can't say I was looking forward to the trip.

You know that I have done an awful lot of traveling. I've spent so much time up in the air, I am surprised I haven't sprouted wings! That trip to Tokyo is one hell of a long flight. Muhammad and I were flying first-class, but that didn't prevent us arriving in Tokyo wiped out. Altogether we had been traveling for twenty hours.

Muhammad had ten days to get over jet lag, promote the fight, and completely acclimatize before the bout. Enough time? Well, it was going to be the same for his opponent Mac Foster. Rocky Aoki, the promoter of the bout, expected a sellout. "Everybody knows Muhammad Ali in Japan," he had told me back in New York when we had last met. I asked him if he was putting in chairs for the spectators. When he asked me what the hell I was talking about, I told him the story of my last visit to Tokyo back in 1964, when I had been with Sugar Ramos. Rocky laughed, and said, "This time you will find things a little different, and you must see Tokyo. I think you will enjoy it."

Rocky Aoki was so right. On the second night of my stay we had supper together. I left the choice of restaurant to him. Yea, letting him choose the place to eat seemed like the right thing to do, considering he was a restauranteur and a Japanese!

Rocky took me to a very elegant restaurant off Nihombashi, a very fashionable street. By the way Rocky was welcomed, it was obvious he had eaten at the place before, and after I had eaten I could understand why he had decided to come again. We ate what I was told was called Kaiseki cuisine. The meal consisted of many dishes. There were vegetables and fish, with mushrooms as a seasoning base—and seaweed. Yea, seaweed! I must say it was all delicious. There would be no hamburgers for me while I was in Tokyo!

I attended the gym and press conferences with Muhammad, but I could hardly wait for some free time so that I could get out and explore Tokyo, not to mention its restaurants! During the ten days or so that I was there, I must have eaten in at least twenty different restaurants. They were all good. Hey! I ate sushi! That's raw fish eaten with a spicy sauce. I don't think it would be a big hit in South Philly, but in Japan it works! I sampled Soba and Udon—sounds like a magical act from Vegas! In fact, it's Japanese pasta! No kidding. I wasn't the only guy in the American contingent who was really digging Tokyo and Japanese culture, but I suppose I have to own up to being the one who ate the most Japanese food!

The Ali-Foster fight took place on April 1. Muhammad was relaxed. I would have preferred him to have been a little more excited. Muhammad isn't ever at his best if he's bored. He even talks slower, so you can imagine what he's like when he's fighting. It takes a long time for him to wake up to the fact that he might lose!

Mac Foster never got the credit he deserved. He was a good strong kid with a lot of smarts. His record of thirty KOs in thirty-one fights says it all. Everybody expected it to be a walkover for Ali, but I didn't. At the top level of boxing there are no walkovers.

Rocky Aoki had been right. The Nippon Budokan Hall was packed with fifteen thousand Japanese boxing fans who had come to see the famous Muhammad Ali fight another big tough American. I don't think they really cared which big American it was, they'd come to see Ali. Many of the Japanese fans still called him Cassius Clay—maybe it is easier to say in Japanese!

Muhammad entered the ring wearing a beautiful embroidered silk Japanese robe. That was nice. He was carrying a large banner saying that Foster would fall in round five. That was not so nice, as it worked out! Muhammad started as if his prediction would fail, because Foster would fall in one! Foster had other ideas. He was still around at the end of round five and, although behind on points, he was still dangerous. The Japanese fans were disappointed. Ali had boasted he would win in five rounds, by round six the crowd began to yell at Ali, "Taoshite Kure," which translates roughly to "Come on sucker, knock him out!" The fight went the full fifteen rounds and I had no worry about the decision, it was Muhammad by a mile. It had been a tough fight, but Muhammad made it look easy. It is never easy fighting for fifteen rounds against a big, strong, professional fighter who really wants to win. But the two Japanese judges, Takeo Ugo and Hiroyuki Tesaki, and the American referee, J. E. Crowder, gave the fight to Ali unanimously. You can't do better than win!

I had enjoyed my trip to Japan and hoped to return. I did, in 1976. Once again I was with Muhammad, for perhaps the strangest fight of his career.

For some reason, unknown to me, Muhammad decided to fight the famous Japanese wrestler, Antonio Inoki, considered the best in the world. Maybe it was an "ego" thing—you know, proving to himself that he was not just the best boxer, but also the best *fighter* in the world. I really don't know. Still, I was delighted with the chance of visiting Tokyo again. Rocky Aoki had told me about "Yakitori"—chicken meat, liver, and vegetables skewered on a bamboo stick and grilled on an open fire. I admit it was a long way to go for a meal, but what the hell!

The fight was a little unbelievable. Muhammad standing up trying to box, and Antonio lying on the canvas kicking the heck out of him. We had set up the rules before we had left the States, but no one seemed to remember what the rules were. No doubt Inoki would have been phenomenal if allowed to fight in his natural style, but he didn't know what was allowed. Muhammad would have been Muhammad if Inoki had stood there trying to box, but the Japanese champion was no fool. After trying to grab Muhammad and getting caught by some hard jabs, he reverted to his wrestling style, using kicks from a safe position on the canvas.

This went on for ten rounds! Halfway through, Muhammad wanted to forget the whole deal and go home. I reminded him that he was the world champion and talked him into finishing the farce. At the end, the American referee was trying to decide on the decision. I went over to him. "Hey pal, let's call it a draw." The referee was wise. That was the official decision—a draw. Nobody lost face, but Muhammad sure collected some serious bruising on his legs that turned into dangerous blood clots. I was worried, and wanted to get him back to the States to be checked out. But he had an exhibition to do in the Far East, and he foolishly went through with it. He never wanted to break a promise. I don't know how he got through the exhibition, because he could hardly walk. Once back in Los Angeles he had to go to the hospital and spend some time recuperating. If the clots had traveled to the upper body, the Ali era might well have ended there and then.

Helen had come with me on the trip. She, too, fell in love with the magical qualities of Japanese life and culture, and we both enjoyed *Yakitori*. Two overweight Dundees returned to Miami!

It was inevitable that Muhammad would get another shot at the world title. He had beaten all the opposition. Seventeen fights, fifteen wins, two defeats. Joe Frazier and Ken Norton had taken decisions from Ali, but in return fights, Muhammad had reversed the verdict each time.

Now, ten years after he had first won the world heavyweight title from Sonny Liston back in 1964, Muhammad was fighting George Foreman, and once again the world championship was at stake. Muhammad had not lost his title in the ring, it had been taken away from him through legislation. This was his chance to win it back in the place where it really counts—the ring.

The venue for this fight feast was Kinshasa, Zaïre. In case you are wondering, as I did, where the hell that is, Zaïre, formerly known as the Belgian Congo, is situated right in the middle of Africa, on the equator. Kinshasa, the capital city, is in the west of Zaïre, near the mouth of the Congo River, which is now called the Zaïre River. The training quarters for both Foreman and Ali were about forty miles from the capital, in a government complex called N'Sele.

Why Zaïre? It was a unique situation. The government of Zaïre was the "promoter" of the fight! President Mobutu and his advisors believed that staging a boxing promotion of such proportions—Ali and Foreman were dividing a $4,500,000 purse—would bring his country credibility, respectability, and a viability for overseas investment. Ain't nothing wrong with that! People promote fights for a lot less good reasons.

I have seen promoters come and go, and no matter how powerful a promoter may become, there always seems room for another promoter to come along and take over as top dog.

Back in the late forties, Jim Norris was the big-time cookie promoting at the Chicago Stadium and Madison Square Garden. During the fifties and sixties, Babe McCoy had a lot of clout out on the west coast, but I think George Parnassus and his co-promoter Aileen Eaton, who later became Boxing Commissioner of California, were the fat cats. My old pal Mickey Davies was matchmaking for the Olympics in Los Angeles, and brother Chris was a big-time operator too. Chris promoted a lot of world championships in Miami, and when you promote the championship fights you are big-time all right.

There are still some powerful promoters around: Don King, Bob Arum, Dan Duva, head of Main Events, and Phil Alessi, from Tampa, who is rapidly growing in stature. There are lots of good local promoters, and the fight game needs those guys, because that is where the boxer learns his tricks, on those local boxing promotions. Today, the biggest power in boxing, as I see it, is television. That creates the stage for the boxer and gives him an audience of millions. Television, with its new various forms of communication including satellite, closed circuit, and the growing cable system, is the boss. For a promoter to make it today he or she must be tied into a television deal.

The government of Zaïre had such a deal, otherwise it would have been lunacy to promote a fight like that. Four and a half million dollars for two fighters!

The fight was originally arranged for September 25, 1974, but Foreman cut his eye and the bout was postponed until October 30. Muhammad and his entourage, which included me, arrived three weeks prior to the fight date to acclimatize and put the finishing touches to the training. Muhammad was fitter than he had been for many a fight. This was one fight he badly wanted to win. The challenge of such a gigantic undertaking motivated him. For six months he had slowly conditioned himself at his Deer Lake hideaway, where he had taken off most of his fat. I was pleasantly surprised at his physical change when we began working out in our Zaïre training quarters.

The training accommodation was kind of strange; the encampment was two miles long. Foreman had one extremity, Ali the other, and the press and television people separated the two rival camps. The living quarters were villas, small but comfortable for the entourages of both fighters. Muhammad shared his with his friend Pat Patterson; Bundini, Muhammad's close companion and assistant trainer, had his own villa; and I shared mine with Luis Sarria. Foreman, who was broody around the encampment, moved into the Inter-Continental Hotel, and the change of scene lightened him up.

The training started, the buildup began. Both camps kept their training sessions under wraps. No one wanted the other people to know what was going on. I attended Foreman's sparring sessions unofficially. I peeked through a gap in the lattice-work wall surrounding Foreman's sparring and training area. If you don't try, you don't get!

Watching Foreman spar confirmed my opinion of how the fight would eventually finish. Muhammad would win by a knockout. Muhammad and I had watched films of Foreman in action, and although he looked great against Frazier and Norton, their styles were made for him. He had never met anyone like Muhammad— but then who had?

I was being interviewed by Skip Myslenski, who asked me for my fight forecast. I told him, "Well, Muhammad has been saying for months that he'll knock out Foreman in eight rounds, but I don't think so. I think it's gonna take ten or eleven rounds."

Skip smiled. I don't think he believed me. "So you think Ali will knock out Foreman?" he said. He scratched the back of his head, "I don't suppose you can look into your crystal ball and tell me how?"

"Sure. Get your pad and pencil ready." I gave him a run-down on how I thought the fight would go.

It was understandable that Skip, along with most of the sports writers, thought that Muhammad and I were whistling in the dark. Foreman looked unbeatable to them. I remembered the run-in to the first Liston fight, when the news guys only believed what they saw. They were earning their living by writing about boxing, but I earned my living in it. I could see things that their eyes missed. At least, I hoped I did, because although I didn't have a one hundred percent record in picking winners of fights, I just hoped my considered judgment was more on the ball than theirs. This was one fight I wanted to be right about, because this one could be Muhammad's last chance to win back the title.

It was the morning of the fight. No, that isn't quite right. It was the morning of Tuesday, October 29. The fight was taking place at 4:00 A.M. on Wednesday the 30th. After doing a thousand trivial duties I went to inspect the ring, accompanied by Bobby Goodman, who handled publicity and public relations for the fight promotion, and Murray Goodman, another good guy in the public relations business.

I always check out the ring before any of my guys fight. Most times it isn't necessary, but I'm sure glad I checked this sucker out. The ring was leaning to one side—that would mean the fighters would be boxing up and down a slope. Come on! The safety padding under the canvas had to be sized, and there were twenty-four-foot ropes sagging nearly to the canvas because it was only a twenty-foot ring.

Now, you have to picture this. I wasn't in New York or Los Angeles, where I could have gotten on the phone and got things put right in no time flat. This was Kinshasa, and the government complex where we were staying was a forty-five minute drive away in N'Sele. The officials and workmen were not the most experienced boxing "setup" men I had ever worked with, and it was hot. Boy was it hot! And humid. I would have liked to have had a bet, a double, that Ali would win by a KO and that it would pour with rain within an hour!

What can you do! Bobby and I supervised the fixing of the ring. I borrowed a two-edged razor blade and began cutting and refitting the ropes. I corralled a couple of the local workmen, who had been watching me with looks of amazement and horror as I began cutting the ropes, into finding some strong wooden blocks so that the ring could be straightened up. I eventually got them to do this, but they weren't too happy about it. They didn't expect the fight to take place in a ring that was tilted, did they? Maybe they knew something I didn't!

I won the first part of my Zaïre double: it rained solidly for an hour. Eight hours later a tired and wet Angelo Dundee arrived back at N'Sele. I wanted a hot shower and ten hours' sleep. I settled for a lukewarm shower and two cups of black coffee. Who could go to bed! The fight was starting at 4:00 A.M. and there were things to do. I checked my black bag, and double-checked my list of required equipment. If they couldn't construct the ring properly, you couldn't be sure that little things like a water bucket and gloves would be available. I was prepared, I had everything with me—plus a spare set of gloves for Foreman, just in case.

We arrived at the open-air arena. Thank the Lord, the rain had stopped, but the sky looked menacing. I was told by the sports writers that the president and his official party would not be at the fight, they would watch it on television from the comfort of the hotel. I looked up at the threatening sky. Was the president telling us something?

It didn't rain, and the early morning was less oppressive than it had been during the day. The cooler early morning wasn't the reason this ungodly time had been chosen for fight time. The television people picked the time, they wanted their enormous American audience to watch the fight at a more congenial hour, and allowing for time differences, four o'clock in the morning Zaïre time suited the media best.

Let me tell you about Muhammad's opponent, the reigning Heavyweight Champion of the World, George Foreman. He was a twenty-six-year-old kid, from the slums of Marshall, Texas, who learned to fight in the back alleys of the black ghetto in Houston, Texas—a very tough city, and this is a guy from South Philly talking! Before George could get into any heavy trouble on the streets, he began boxing as an amateur. He was big and strong, and he realized that boxing could be an avenue of escape from the ghetto. George worked hard at getting himself in condition. There wasn't much time for laughs, but then, living in a crowded, violent, and impoverished slum didn't make you feel much like laughing.

In 1968, Foreman fought his way to the Olympic Heavyweight Championship, winning a gold medal for America. In the following year, he turned professional, managed by the astute and knowledgeable Dick Saddler. In that first year, George fought thirteen times. He won thirteen times. By the time 1972 came around George was ready for a shot at the title. The champion at that time was Joe Frazier, who had beaten Ali in 1971. The Foreman-Frazier championship fight lasted only two rounds. Foreman KO'd Frazier and became world champion.

George had the pleasure of fighting in Tokyo in 1973, and the pleasure of knocking out his challenger, José Roman, in one round. Next, George fought in Caracas, against the only other boxer to have beaten Muhammad Ali—Ken Norton.

Ken, who had twice gone the full distance with Muhammad Ali, once beating him, lasted just two rounds against George Foreman! George had fought three leading contenders and had demolished them all in only five rounds of boxing. He had fought forty times as a professional and had never been beaten. Next on his agenda was Muhammad Ali.

Foreman was a 2½–1 favorite with the bookmakers, but the Zaïre crowd that packed the arena was pro Muhammad Ali. As Doctor Ferdie Pecheco, who was now part of the Ali entourage, said,"In Kinshasa, there are more people with the name Muhammad or Ali than George or Foreman." At my instigation, Muhammad had taken on the services of Ferdie. He was a valuable asset and a good friend. He fitted in with the other guys with no problem, and, with Gene Kilroy, who had befriended Ali during his enforced retirement, made up the white members of the Ali entourage into a trio. The entourage numbered at different times between thirty and fifty people.

A roar from the crowd welcomed the reigning champion, George Foreman, into the ring, but the volume of sound didn't compare with the ear-shattering outburst that had erupted a minute earlier for Ali's entrance.

The two massive gladiators glared at each other. Bundini Brown, towel around his neck stood near me, impatient for the fight to start. "That's some mean-looking man," he said.

I answered, "I don't know, the ref looks OK to me." Bundini smiled. He knew that I knew he had meant Foreman. I agreed with him: Foreman did look mean, and powerful too. His muscle definition would have given Charles Atlas an inferiority complex.

It was time to go to work. The bell sounded for the first round. I lightly slapped Muhammad's rump, a good luck gesture, as he left the sanctuary of the corner to enter the battlefield.

The dressing room was like a furnace, Muhammad was holding court. And why not? If a king can't hold court, who can? His loyal subjects consisted of ten percent well-wishers, ninety percent sports writers. I was emotionally drained, and the locker room was too damned hot. I edged towards the door. Ali was talking. "That couldn't have been me out there, 'cause I can't punch!" He was taunting the newspaper guys who had written that he didn't have a knock-out punch. I slipped out, and the door closed behind me, cutting off the laughter Muhammad's remark had evoked. Then the door opened again, and for a moment the noise from the locker room came bursting out.

"Hey Angie, hot in there ain't it?" I turned to see who had spoken. It was Skip Myslenski. "You sure called it right, Angie, except you said it would be round ten."

I grinned and answered, "Yea, I did, didn't I? Sorry about the round, though. Muhammad thought it was gonna rain so he decided to finish it." I was being glib, but I had called it right. I had told Skip how the fight would go, and I had been as right as any fortune-teller could hope for. I had said that Muhammad would move, throw a couple of punches, then move in close, not giving Foreman room to punch. Muhammad would land a punch, then grab. Foreman could knock down an oak tree, but oak trees don't move. Muhammad's hand speed would bewilder Foreman, he would become discouraged and get tired of hitting arms and air. By round ten Muhammad would have softened him up, then wham—it'd be all over.

I had been nearly right. It went very much as I had predicted. Muhammad did his own thing in his own way. He lay on the ropes, letting Foreman expend his energy hitting his arms and gloves. Then, from a defensive position, Muhammad would move in, invariably catching Foreman with good shots. Foreman didn't know how to handle the situation. Being a big and muscled man, he was better suited and more used to punching *down* and hooking. Muhammad blocked the hooks, his amazing reflexes allowing him to pick off the blows; and it wasn't possible for Foreman to punch down, like he did to the shorter Joe Frazier, because Muhammad was as tall as he. At the end of round seven I said to Muhammad, "Go and take him out, he's ready to go."

Muhammad did just that. He knocked out the formidable George Foreman in the eighth round and became only the second man in the history of boxing to win the World Heavyweight Championship for a second time. Fantastic! Wonderful! Yet, somehow deep inside of me I knew that Muhammad would not be satisfied to only equal Floyd Patterson's record. The idea of being the second man to win back the title would diminish the achievement in Muhammad's eyes—he would want to be the first and only! I wondered what Everest Muhammad would set himself to climb next.

CHAPTER EIGHTEEN

AND THEN
THERE WAS ONE

"Betty Mitchell put the telephone on hold and said,
'It's a Mike Trainer. He's a lawyer from Silver
Spring, Maryland. He says he represents the Olympic Champion, Sugar Ray Leonard. Do you want
to talk to him?' "

It was a strange but pleasant feeling, having my own office. It was
no big deal, but at least I wasn't sharing with Chris—or anyone
else, come to that!

The move had taken place while I was in Zaïre. Betty Mitchell
had taken care of all the arrangements; all I had to do on my
return to Miami was walk into the office and sit down behind my
desk. Why had I moved out of the office with Chris? I guess you
could call it a set of circumstances. I'll give you a rundown on the
background that led to my move.

In 1970 Betty Mitchell retired from the Paul Safer firm of tax
accountants, and Chris and I tried to get her to come and work for
us—we knew a good thing when we saw it. Betty had been
invaluable since she first began to set up our books in 1964. Bit by
bit we had unloaded more and more responsibility onto her
shoulders. Chris had her paying out the fighters and tallying the
ticket sales at his promotions, and I gave her the responsibility of
Muhammad Ali's and Jimmy Ellis's checkbooks. She paid out their
training expenses and sent financial statements to their tax
accountants.

We needed her to carry on, and after a couple of months of
sweet talking we eventually talked her into working for us—Chris
Dundee, Fight Promotions, and Angelo Dundee, Manager/Trainer.

At first Betty only put in three days a week, but that stretched into five, and when Chris became involved in the closed circuit television promotions for Ali's fights, Betty was the natural choice to run it. She became a fixture in the office. I guess she was the first woman to invade our male-dominated premises. We warned the more vocal of our visitors to watch their language, and if the odd Anglo-Saxon oath slipped out, Betty always gave the impression that she hadn't heard. Maybe she hadn't, but it was an awfully small office! Let us just say she was a very cool lady.

In 1972, Chris lost his contract with the city of Miami Beach for boxing promotions. Another guy had put in a better bid and was given the contract. Chris still had an exclusive on the wrestling promotions for the city, but we were advised by the Beach Commission that we would have to vacate our office in the Auditorium to make room for the boxing promoter. We moved to 420 Lincoln Road, a stone's throw from the Auditorium. We bought two new desks and chairs, a couple of new filing cabinets and carried on business. After nine months, the new boxing promoter went out of business. The Miami Beach city authorities contacted Chris and he was welcomed back into the fold with open arms.

The Auditorium was in the throes of being turned into the Theatre of Performing Arts. We were offered offices next door at the Miami Beach Convention Center. So, with our new office furniture, we moved to the Convention Center. I was hardly ever at the office, I was too busy flying all over the place with my fighters, so Betty's day-to-day contact was all with Chris. Now Chris is the first to say that he is not the easiest guy in the world to work for, and after five years of sharing the office with him, Betty decided to call it a day. She was gonna walk!

I was a big boy now, and I had often thought about having my own office, where I could have some privacy and where I could be driven crazy by the sound of only my *own* phone ringing! The thought of trying to find someone else to take over Betty's work and responsibilities finally made me decide to make the move. I moved to a room two doors down from Chris's office in the Convention Center, and I persuaded Betty to come and work for me on a trial basis . . . see how we got on. Find out whether or not she could put up with me as a boss. Find out whether I could afford to pay her!

It worked out OK. Betty Mitchell is still my office manager, and an invaluable friend. We have a good working relationship—she doesn't wrap hands, and I don't do the books! After three summers of break-ins and broken air conditioning in our Convention Center office, in 1979 we moved to a new office complex in Miami, where I had my first office with windows and my name hand painted on the door.

I turned the responsibility of the 5th Street Gym back to Chris. I had been paying the expenses for a few years and trying to keep it in good condition, but I didn't have the number of fighters who would use the south beach gym to make it worthwhile being involved. After a couple of years on his own, Chris turned the gym over to Tuto Zabala, a Latin promoter who is doing a good job promoting boxing on Miami Beach.

By the end of 1974 I knew that the careers of Jimmy Ellis and José Napoles were nearing their end.

Jimmy, after a run of four wins, had a bad loss at the hands of hard-hitting Ernie Shavers. On June 18, 1973, in New York, the stocky Shavers sent Jimmy crashing out in one round. In December of the same year Jimmy lost a fight he would have won a couple of years earlier. I didn't say anything to Jimmy, he would know himself when it was time to quit. Two defeats in 1974 against good opposition, Ron Lyle and Joe Bugner, didn't mean too much. He lost both fights on points and didn't take much punishment. At the beginning of 1975 I was glad Jimmy hadn't quit because he had a big payday coming. He would be fighting Joe Frazier in Melbourne, Australia, on March 1. This was a fight I hoped he would win. It was an outside chance but one Jimmy had to take. When they had met before Frazier was too strong and Jimmy forgot to hit and run and got nailed when he stopped running. This time Frazier was still strong and Jimmy's legs were getting a little old for lots of running! I still felt it was a fight that Jimmy, at this stage of his career, could not pass up.

I flew out to Australia to be with Jimmy in the final stages of his training and in his corner the night of the fight. March 1975 was a hell of a month for traveling. Melbourne, Australia, on the 1st, fly back to Miami, then on to Cleveland for Ali's fight against Chuck Wepner on March 24. Back to Miami, then fly down to Acapulco, Mexico, to be with José Napoles for his fight against Armando Muniz on March 30.

To get to Melbourne I went from Miami to Los Angeles, changed planes, then out to Hawaii. From there it was on to the Pacific island of Fiji, then it was the last 3,000 or so miles to Melbourne. Quite a trip!

The young promoter John Thieme and his promotional team

were nice people, as were the American production company, Global Ltd., who were involved in the deal. Jimmy Ellis picked me up at the airport in a chauffeur-driven car. He told me that the car and chauffeur were at his disposal, compliments of John Thieme. I thought, I'm gonna like it here in St. Kilda, Melbourne, and I did. A beautiful city, Melbourne was a hybrid of England and America. The result was wide boulevards, big stores, stately homes, and a cricket ground! The Australian people are fanatical sports fans and they really got behind the Frazier-Ellis fight. The fight was being called the "Showdown at St. Kilda." (A few years later the Leonard-Hearns fight was called "Showdown at the Palace." You can't keep a good name down!)

The last boxing promotion to capture the imagination of the discerning Melbourne sports fans was in 1969 when the great Aussie world champion Lionel Rose defended his bantamweight title against the tough Englishman from Liverpool, Alan Rudkin. Over 14,000 people went to see that fight, but to put things in perspective, back in 1961 over 90,000 fans packed into the Melbourne Cricket Ground to watch a cricket match between Australia and the West Indies. I was dying to catch a cricket match, but my Australian pals told me that March was the wrong month. It was the same as in England, they only played in the summer. Maybe one day I will actually see a cricket game, or is the whole thing a myth? A devious rumor put out by the English to keep us ex-colonials in our place! Come on!

Everything was so nice. Jimmy and I were having a ball, it was a pity that Frazier had to ruin the trip. The "Showdown at St. Kilda," proved to be a knockdown for poor Jimmy. Smokin' Joe Frazier, better than ever, methodically wore down the thirty-five-year-old Ellis, finally putting him down and out in the ninth round.

It was time for a showdown with Jimmy with regard to his career. I never like telling a fighter it is time to hang up the gloves, and I didn't with Jimmy. But, I didn't want him taking any beatings or getting that one blow too many, so I suggested we go for one more fight and see how it went.

In May 1975, Jimmy fought Carl Baker in Orlando, Florida. It was a fight that Jimmy won effortlessly, KOing Carl in one round. I thought that Jimmy would be raring to go on the comeback trail, but I was wrong. The thought of going through the rigors and discipline of a training regimen was daunting enough, but knowing the classy opposition waiting for him at the top of the heavyweight division was too much for the thirty-five-year-old Ellis, who wisely decided to call it a day.

I was glad that Jimmy took the decision to quit on a winning note, just as I was glad that I had been fortunate enough to have been instrumental in his successes. I had grown to respect and have great fondness for Jimmy, and his quitting fighting didn't and wouldn't ever change that.

I still see Jimmy. In fact, about a year ago I asked for his assistance and he came to Miami to work with Jim Tillis, a young heavyweight I had an interest in.

Jimmy is a classy guy, and should always be involved in boxing because he has good rapport with fighters. There haven't been many professional boxers who fought at top level into their late thirties. Jimmy Ellis was an exception, as was Muhammad, but in the end age always takes its toll.

José Napoles could beat practically every welterweight in the world. From April 18, 1969, when he won the world welterweight title from Curtis Cokes, until he eventually lost it in Mexico City on December 6, 1975, he proved he could beat all comers. He even had a shot at the middleweight championship. The three musketeers, Cuco Conde, José Napoles, and me, went to Paris, France, in 1974 to take on the world champion, the very talented Carlos Monzon. Of course, Cuco and I made certain that José was the one who stayed in the ring with Monzon. When that bell sounded for the beginning of a round, we were always outside the ropes! I can't say it enough; managers, trainers, coaches, whatever, they can do a great job, but it is the guy inside the ropes doing the actual fighting who is number one.

In my opinion Carlos Monzon was one of the all-time great middleweights. During his career which spanned fourteen years, 1963 to 1977, he had 102 bouts. He lost only three and was never knocked out. The only question mark against his greatness was perhaps the lack of great opposition. He beat all there was around, including Emile Griffith, who moved up from welterweight to middleweight, Nino Benvenuti, Denny Moyer, Jean Claude Boultier, and Rodrigo Valdez, the Colombian fighter who eventually became world middleweight champion after Monzon retired undefeated champion. José Napoles, a great welterweight, was thirty-three years old when he fought Monzon for the middleweight title. José had fought at 147 pounds throughout his welterweight career. Even with extra weight added to his five foot seven and a half inch frame, Napoles was no match for the extremely strong Monzon, and he did well to stay in the fight until the seventh round when I stopped the fight in the corner because of José's cut eye and because I knew he had no chance of winning.

For Napoles it was back to the welterweight division. In August 1974, he was back on the winning track beating Hedgeman Lewis in nine rounds. Another win followed, against Horacio Saldana in Mexico City, and it seemed that José would end his career as the undefeated Welterweight Champion of the World.

He decided to carry on into 1975, and a month after his thirty-fourth birthday he defended his title successfully against Armando Muniz in Acapulco. Then would have been a good time to walk away, but it is hard for men like Napoles to refuse that one extra challenge. A tough Englishman who fought with patriotic fervor was crying out for a title shot. On December 6, José fought John H. Stracey, who had made the long journey from his native London to Mexico City to grab his chance at glory. There was hardly any difference in their weight, but Stracey was ten years younger and in his prime at just twenty-five years of age. Napoles had done it all; Stracey was consumed with the desire and the will to win. The veteran fell to youth. Napoles was KO'd in the sixth round by the gritty Londoner. I am not detracting from Stracey's performance one little bit, but Napoles fought two opponents that night, John Stracey and age. One, he might have beaten, the other—no chance!

José Napoles retired. A great champion. He had promised so much when he first started boxing in Cuba way back in 1958. I am proud to have been a force in helping José realize that early promise.

Another of my boxers had left the arena. A chunk of my life had been spent with my champions, a happy and exciting chunk of life. As I reached the year 1976 there was just one champion with whom I was involved. That could well be enough for anyone, because the fighter was Muhammad Ali.

The next three years of my life from 1974 to 1977 were hectic, exciting, and glorious fun. Helen called them "the Ali years," and they were. We were carried away on Muhammad's magic carpet that took us all over the world. I traveled to Kuala Lumpur for the Joe Bugner fight. Helen and our daughter Terri accompanied me to that exotic place. My son Jimmy was away at college studying optometry at Florida University. He had taken my advice and kept tennis as a hobby and was studying a really solid profession, otherwise he would have been with us. My family didn't travel everywhere with me, but Helen began to come along far more than ever before. In Germany, she shared a day's boat trip up the River Rhine with Muhammad's mother. We all got along well together and we had fun.

Muhammad fought in Las Vegas, Manila, San Juan, Tokyo, Landover, Munich, and New York. I was always with him in his corner, suggesting, cajoling, and occasionally demanding. These exhilarating times would one day turn into happy memories.

There were fights won easily and tough fights, too; some were made tougher than necessary because Muhammad hadn't taken the bouts seriously enough. What the hell! He won 'em all. There were great fights. Who could forget the fabulous third and final meeting between Ali and Frazier in Manila. They called that fight "the Thrilla in Manila"—and it was. Rivals before the fight, afterwards the two gladiators were friends and respectful of each other's skill and courage. There were the two nail-biting confrontations with Ken Norton, where the decisions were so close they had to be controversial. Exciting times!

On September 29, 1977, Muhammad had problems beating the shorter, hard-hitting Ernie Shavers. I never told Ernie but we had an edge that night in Madison Square Garden. Eddie Hrica, a well-known matchmaker and pal of mine, watched the fight from our dressing room, where we had installed a television set. Probably it was the only time on television that the commentator relayed the scoring of the judges. Eddie gave me the scoring after each round. He would run from the dressing room to the ramp where we entered the arena and give me signals: a thumbs-up sign if we won the round, a thumbs-down if we lost, and a wave of his hand, palm down, if it was even. I tell you, the information helped. Muhammad won on points.

Yea! Muhammad won 'em all, but there was one opponent he couldn't lick—Father Time. He was thirty-five years old when he fought Shavers in September. Muhammad's next fight was scheduled for February 15, 1978. A five-month layoff. A long time for a young well-conditioned boxer; a hell of a time for a fighter who would be thirty-six years old at the time of the fight, and who wasn't taking the bout seriously anyway!

Muhammad's opponent was Leon Spinks, the light-heavyweight champion of the 1976 Montreal Olympic Games. Leon had only managed a draw against Scott LeDoux in Las Vegas on October 22, 1977. Even an out of form Ali would be able to beat an inexperienced puffed-up light-heavyweight, I thought. Not for the first time, I thought wrong. But the Ali-Spinks fight wasn't until

February 1978, and I must tell you what had gone on in 1976—the time of the Montreal Olympics.

Betty Mitchell put the telephone on hold and said, "It's a Mike Trainer. He's a lawyer from Silver Spring, Maryland. He says he represents the Olympic Champion, Sugar Ray Leonard. Do you want to talk to him?" I thought for a moment before answering. I had first set eyes on Ray Leonard when he had come to meet Muhammad Ali before the champion's fight against Jimmy Young in Landover, Maryland, on April 30, 1976. Muhammad had told me that the kid was going to fight in the Montreal Olympics; I wished Ray good luck, and was pleased to read later in the year how well he had done. That time in Landover, Muhammad once again demonstrated his feelings for young aspiring athletes. He had taken Ray Leonard out of his seat and brought him close to the ring so that he could get a better view. He even had Ray take a bow, along with another amateur fighter. Muhammad didn't have to do that, he hardly knew the kid, but that's Muhammad.

I met Ray again at a party in New York at the time of the second Ali-Norton fight, around September 1976. Muhammad brought him over to say hello to me. Ray mentioned he would like to turn professional. Muhammad said, "If you want a good manager, here's Angie." Who needs a press agent!

Betty interrupted my thoughts, "Mike Trainer is still on hold. Are you going to speak with him?"

"Yea." I pressed down the button on the phone that transferred the call from Betty's line to mine, and said hello to Mike Trainer. We had never met, I didn't know him from Adam. Trainer explained that he was Leonard's lawyer and that he had formed a corporation to look after Leonard's potential earnings, and that he was calling around looking for a manager for Sugar Ray. "Yea," I said, in a noncommittal tone. Was he asking me if I wanted to handle Leonard, or what? Trainer finally got around to asking me if I was interested. Sure I was interested. I knew the kid slightly and liked him. He was an Olympic champion and was popular with the American people. The young man had promise. We discussed my involvement, and by November 1976 Trainer had sent me, to check out, a copy of the proposed six-year contract as personal representative, boxing advisor, and manager to Sugar Ray Leonard. My reward was to be fifteen percent of Leonard's earnings from boxing. Signing contracts isn't a habit I had developed over the years, preferring the word and a handshake of an honorable person. I didn't sign any damn contract just because I thought it would make me a lot of bread. Sure, I manage fighters, that's my job, but I choose the fighters I manage, believing that they are talented. Hopefully they will make money not only for themselves but for me too. If they do, great; if they don't, I am disappointed more for them than for myself. All I can do is try for them, the rest is in the lap of the gods—and the fighters' talent!

I went to Silver Spring, Maryland. Mike Trainer met me and dropped me off at a hotel for a night's sleep. I was kind of excited.

The following morning we had the meeting. There was Mike Trainer, Dave Jacobs, Janks Morton, Ray's dad, and of course Sugar Ray was there too. It went well, all very friendly, and we rapped about the best approach for furthering Ray's career. I felt strongly about Ray having a home base. If the fighter's home life is good, as Ray's was, it is a big asset for the boxer to have that security and affection that can only be found in a warm family life. Without that home base it sure can be a tough road to follow. Mike Trainer wholeheartedly agreed with me on this, as on all the other points that I raised. I signed the contract, which was dated November 16, 1976. We were in business.

The lawyer, Mike Trainer, had been introduced to Ray by a former insurance man, Janks Morton. It didn't take me long to realize that Ray held Janks, an old friend and a bright guy, in high esteem. Ray still worked with Dave Jacobs, his trainer from his amateur days. He seemed competent enough, and if a fighter gets on well with his trainer, I'm inclined to leave well enough alone.

I asked for Ray to come down with Dave and Janks to Miami, where I could evaluate his skills in the 5th Street Gym. There I got to know Ray better, and it was obvious to me that he had an awful lot to offer. He had great balance, lightning reflexes, and a potentially big punch. He needed to be nursed along.

The first hurdle the amateur boxer has to clear when entering the professional ranks is building up his stamina. Sugar Ray had never fought over three rounds as an amateur. After stamina-building exercises, long sessions of sparring, and shadow-boxing, Ray's first pro fight was arranged, a six-round bout against Luis Vega, to take place in Baltimore. Ray earned a convincing points decision: he was off to a winning start.

It was no big deal getting Ray the publicity every fighter craves for. Being the Olympic Champion was a big asset, but no guarantee that the press would give him coverage. But, I was a name in my own right. No point in being unrealistic—after all, I was still the man with Muhammad Ali, and my list of champions was kind

of impressive—even to me! So, when the news that I was Leonard's manager got out through our press conference, the sports
writers were immediately interested. I told them honestly that I
thought Leonard would one day be champion, and that was
before his first pro fight! Ray also had enormous likeability, which
wasn't lost on the sports writers. All the kid had to do was fight
and win.

Hank Kaplan, one of the world's foremost authorities on the
history of fights and fighters, was my promotional and publicity
consultant. He wrote up an exciting thumb-nail biography on
Leonard. I had it copied and sent to most of the fight promoters
and matchmakers. The offers for fights came in, sometimes
directly to me, sometimes to Trainer, especially those bouts
offered around the Maryland area. I checked out every opponent.
Those I hadn't seen fight personally I got checked out by buddies
of mine who knew the style and quality of the fighters. Things
looked good. Leonard was winning and improving, and that ain't
a bad combination.

As we came to the fall of 1977, Leonard, Ali, in fact the whole
boxing business, was put in cold storage for a few days. My son
Jimmy was getting married. After graduating from college—he
was the first in the whole family to do so—Jimmy had started his
career as an optician. It seemed that both father and son took care
of eyes. Of course, I was at my best when the eyes were cut! Then,
you know the story: boy meets girl, boy falls for girl, girl falls for
boy, etc. Well, that's how it was.

Cathy Vest, a lovely young lady, was to be my daughter-in-law.
Her parents, whom I had never met at that time, seemed nice
people. Jimmy had told me that during their courting days, Cathy
had kept telling her mom and pop that she was dating this nice
boy whose father managed boxers. As the dating became more
serious, Cathy's parents wanted to know a little more about us.
"Well, he manages Muhammad Ali," Cathy told them. They were
impressed. Later, she showed them a photograph of Ray Leonard.
"Jimmy's dad manages him too, that's the Olympic boxer, Ray
Leonard." Cathy was quite proud of the fact. Her parents smiled
and looked suitably impressed.

The next day Cathy's mom called her quietly to one side, and
asked very politely, "Is Jimmy black, Cathy dear?"

"No, Mom, why?"

"Oh, we just thought . . . Oh, nothing, darling. I was just wondering. I'm sure, whatever he is, he is a very nice boy." Yea, they
sounded like nice people.

The wedding took place in Clearwater, a lovely town on the west coast of Florida, and the place that Jimmy had chosen to work and live. About seventy of us flew over, and the night before the wedding I threw a big party at a wonderful, authentic Spanish restaurant, the Columbia, in the old Cuban section of Tampa. My brother Jimmy had flown down from Philly; sadly, my brother Frankie and my two sisters couldn't make it. I accepted and respected their reasons, and I knew that their good wishes, love, and affection were sincere.

It was a lovely wedding. Helen and I were proud of our handsome son and delighted with his choice of bride. I don't know about anyone else, but I enjoyed the whole marriage bit. I said to Terri, "You're next, my girl. No big rush, when you finish college will be fine. I love weddings."

"Well, why are you crying?" she said, putting her arm through mine.

"Tears of joy, Terri, tears of joy."

By February 1978, Sugar Ray Leonard was fighting eight-round bouts. On February 4, in Baltimore, the young welterweight went the full eight rounds to win a points decision over Rocky Ramon. I was pleased and impressed with Ray, and surprised how quickly he was coming along. I knew that within a couple of months he would be making the big step up into ten-round contests. Still, I was in no hurry. Better to let Ray take a year longer to reach his goal than move him up into longer bouts and tougher opposition too fast, and maybe risk an unnecessary beating and a strength-sapping fight too soon. After all, it had taken Muhammad Ali four years before he won the title.

It was hard to believe that Muhammad had won that biggest of all prizes, the world title, way back in 1964. And now, fourteen years later, he was defending his title once more. The opponent was Leon Spinks, the date February 15, 1978.

For young Leon Spinks, that night in Vegas when he fought for the Championship of the World was a night he would remember all his life. It was a night of triumph, a moment in his life that was so overwhelming that it took time to learn to live with it.

For Muhammad, it was a night best forgotten. All the excuses for his defeat—and there were many—meant nothing. His title had gone. Last time, his title had been taken away because of a moral issue; this time because of indifference on his part, and his failure to understand that his mental youth was encased in the matured body of a man. The fight had one positive result for

Muhammad: it gave him the incentive and desire to try and win the title back.

Muhammad had laid off for five months before the Spinks fight. To win back the title, he would first have to rest to regain his strength, depleted by his fifteen-round bout, then slowly and methodically build up into top physical condition. A very tough and dedicated regimen to undertake. Immediately after his defeat by Spinks, there had been a lot of talk about retirement. I didn't think so. Muhammad wanted his title back. He would want to retire undefeated champion, and also, knowing Muhammad, he would now be determined to be the first and only heavyweight champion to win the world title for an unprecedented third time.

It was mid-May. Summer would soon be here. Helen and I had spent the weekend in the Keys, and the fish had been biting. I was feeling good. Muhammad was slowly getting into shape for his return bout with Leon Spinks—I always knew that the fight was inevitable—scheduled for September 15, 1978. Meanwhile Ray Leonard had continued to blossom, showing incredible skills and a lethal punch in both hands. Ray's last four fights had all been won by knockouts. On May 13, in Utica, he had KO'd Randy Milton in eight rounds. All in all, things were not at all bad.

I liked working with Ray. He listened, and had the talent to implement suggestions and ideas. I believed our personal relationship was growing; we would rap together and I thought I was getting to know the young man. He told me why he had turned professional boxer: his father had been ill, and Ray wanted to make some money quickly. He confessed that he hadn't really wanted to be a fighter. What Ray craved was education. I had learned early on that Ray was no fool, and I noticed how, in such a short time, he had acquired a poise and sophistication that were both admirable and a little disconcerting.

I believed that he would make sure his baby son didn't miss out on any opportunities, as happens to so many young black kids. We talked about families, and all kinds of little inconsequential things. It was just the rapping of two friends. I liked the kid, and foresaw a big future in store for him. Helen was fond of Ray, too, and we hoped that we were heading for a happy and successful association with another unusually talented boxer. Helen, said, half-jokingly, "Maybe we will have the Leonard years." We were already used to speaking of "the Ali years."

We should have been more discerning than even to think that

there would be another Muhammad Ali, and known that to have relationships with mutual respect and affection takes time. But most of all I should have known that my special relationship with Muhammad was unique, a "one of a kind" kind of thing that could never be duplicated.

CHAPTER NINETEEN

SUGAR AND SPICE

"The eighth round began. Ray, confident and fully in charge, began to taunt Roberto—not verbally but by his actions. . . . Once again Duran moved to go after the now out of distance Maryland marvel. Then he changed his mind. Duran turned his back on Leonard and raised his arms. What was he doing? Sugar Ray was astonished, he didn't know what to do. He couldn't hit the back of his opponent's head. Duran was walking away, waving his arms, shaking his head and saying, 'No more, no more.' "

The letter was dated August 8, 1978. It was from Mike Trainer. I read and re-read the letter. I felt sick. I sat at my desk staring at the envelope until Betty asked me what was wrong. I felt embarrassed and humiliated as I handed her the letter to read. She was shocked, too, but not embarrassed. Betty was mad!

"Is he kidding? What does he mean he's 'concerned by the lack of time and effort you've put into Sugar Ray'?" She re-read a little more. "Oh, this bit is good: 'As the second highest paid person in his organization (Ray is obviously first), we all expected more. To date your involvement has consisted of arriving approximately two days before a fight, meeting with the press, and working Ray's corner at fight time.' " Betty read on, " 'More was expected of you!' He's got to be crazy. What does he expect you to do?"

"What can I tell you? Ray hasn't been beaten. A one hundred percent record! Great rapport with the press, and in just over a year I've got him winning in ten-round bouts. How do I explain what I've done, what I do? That's the problem of being involved with people who don't know about the fight business. People not experienced in boxing have a different perspective. Trainer is a lawyer; Janks is a nice guy, but he's from the insurance business. Hell! Maybe Trainer wants me to clock in and report every day. I

246

know one thing, he wants me to adjust my . . . er . . ." Betty looked at the letter and helped me out. " 'Adjust your compensation so that it is more in line with your duties.' " She shrugged her shoulders and said, "Well, that's what the letter says. It is a good thing Ray hasn't lost a fight. Can you imagine what would have happened if he had got beaten? You might have been shot for dereliction of duties." It was a funny thought, but I was in no mood to laugh.

I had to answer the letter, but I found it hard to word the reply. I didn't want to defend myself. I thought that my record was answer enough. How could I explain all the judgments and evaluations I continually made in the fighter's interest? How did anyone evaluate the worth of that one specific instruction to a fighter in the heat of battle, that could turn a fight from a potential loss into a victory? What was the value of a repair on a cut eye that saved the fight and saved the fighter serious damage? How did you put a price on experience, knowledge, and expertise?

It was Trainer who had come to me with an offer. I wasn't hawking my talents! It had been agreed that I would receive fifteen percent of Leonard's earnings from boxing. When I signed the contract, Leonard hadn't fought as a professional, so I was then earning fifteen percent of nothing! I took a chance on how things would turn out. Ray had weak hands. Who could be sure then that, after only one fight, his hands, or any other injury, would not bring his career to an early end? I gambled on Ray's formidable talent and my own judgment. Now that Ray was approaching the big-time, Trainer had decided that I was too expensive!

Because of my involvement with Muhammad (it was the time of the Ali-Spinks fight) I didn't reply until September 20. I stated that I believed I was doing a great job for Leonard. I explained that my value was not to be dictated by other people's opinions, but was a proven fact. I also told him that I expected my proper remuneration; after all, boxing is my living!

And so the argument went on. Trainer wrote back. He informed me that, "Unfortunately, Ray Leonard's win-loss record is not the only measure of your performance." I couldn't understand the guy's thinking. What did he want from me? Maybe he should have chosen a manager who would work cheaper and have a string of losses on Ray's record! I know that Trainer wanted me to spend more time with Ray, but hell, the guy can only win the fight once!

From the very beginning I had difficulty in communicating with

Mike Trainer. Maybe the fault was mine. I found him a cold fish, and rather intimidating with his lawyer's articulation and his personal indifference to the camaraderie that I had experienced with other business associates in the boxing field. Whitey Esneault, Joe Netro, Ernesto Corralles, and Cuco Conde were a different breed of men. Herbert Muhammad, too. They had personal warmth, and a feel for and knowledge of the fight game. I could talk to them. With Trainer I felt ill at ease, and perhaps tried too hard at being friendly and accommodating, hoping it would make the working atmosphere in the camp more pleasant.

Throughout early September, I must confess the Leonard contractual problem hadn't been uppermost on my mind. It was time for Leon Spinks to defend his newly won world title against a determined and well-conditioned Muhammad Ali.

New Orleans, September 15, 1978. A date that will be remembered forever in the annals of boxing history. A record was set, and such a record that it will take a phenomenal man and extraordinary circumstances for it ever to be broken. Muhammad Ali comfortably outpointed Leon Spinks, to win the fifteen-round contest and to become the first man in the history of boxing to win the World Heavyweight Championship three times. After the decision was announced I felt a surge of happiness and pride flood over me. To have been involved with this magnificent athlete and to have assisted and played a part, however large or small, in his career, was to me an honor. I had worked with the best, the Greatest! Muhammad Ali, not for the first time, announced his retirement from the ring. I hoped that this time he really meant it.

The Leonard drama went on, and so did his run of wins. My value to the young fighter's career was being worked out in dollars and cents. I can't argue with that! But what about the contract we had all signed under two years ago? I really didn't know how to handle it. I tried to visualize how Chris would handle the situation, but Chris would never have ended up in this position. My brother would have stayed on top of Trainer right from the start, and wouldn't have given a damn who liked who!

Still, I had a job to do, and in spite of all the aggravation I intended to do it. About the time of the second Ali-Spinks fight, in September 1978, I had been unavailable for Leonard, I was too busy to be with him, but I was always at the other end of the telephone if needed. An old and trusted friend, Eddie Hrica, was arranging bouts for Leonard—with Trainer's blessing, of course.

At one time a bout had been arranged that I hadn't OK'd. I didn't want it. The opponent, who was big and strong, did not make sense to me at that time. I felt Ray could win, but it would be a tough fight—and why take a chance at this stage of his career? The two fighters had sparred together in the gym previously, and it had turned kind of heavy, resulting in a little bad blood. Ray needed a needle fight against a big, tough fighter like a hole in the head! Leonard was undefeated and was wrapping himself in the psychological cloak of invincibility, which in itself could psyche a fighter out before a blow was thrown. The wrong choice of opponent at this stage could blow the whole deal. I insisted the bout be taken out, and I had my way. I had stopped Ray fighting Tommy Hearns. They would meet, of course, but at *our* time, when Ray was ready. In the meantime Hearns became a name to be reckoned with. Having people say that we were ducking him did no harm—it was good for box office.

The contractual dispute remained unresolved and stayed that way into 1979 and in spite of the partially submerged tension, Leonard's career prospered. There was no denying his talent.

On February 10, 1979, Ray was fighting Fernard Marcotte on Chris's promotion in Miami. Trainer and I got together and talked things over. The conversation was amicable, but future events proved that although we both spoke English, we spoke a different language! Ray had now gone seventeen bouts without a defeat. He was featured on NBC televised fights and was maybe six months away from a championship shot. What the hell did they want from me! I had no choice than to leave the matter in the hands of my lawyers.

And so, the lawyers began writing letters and the band played on. Leonard, with me still in his corner and still acting as manager, won his next fight against David Gonzales in one round. There was no real pleasure for me. Satisfaction, for what I believed was a good job, yes, but pleasure, no!

The lawyers were hotting up their battle. It seemed that Sugar Ray Leonard Incorporated would agree to pay me fifteen percent of fight proceeds as long as Sugar Ray "chose to let me appear in his corner"! Leonard, Inc. wanted a fight-to-fight contract. That really made me think that perhaps Sugar Ray personally was trying to drop me. If he wanted me in his corner, why not just leave things alone? We had a contract that agreed to fifteen percent! If he didn't want me around, why not come out and tell me?

Why didn't I go ahead and ask him about the whole lousy deal? Well, I had been instructed in Trainer's letter of January 22, 1979, that Ray would prefer that Trainer and I resolved the dispute between ourselves, and Ray was very friendly and carried on as if nothing was happening. I guess I just hoped the whole thing would blow over. After all, no matter what anyone thought of my value and contribution, Ray was winning, wasn't he?

I do not want to plead my case here, it wouldn't be right. I would need another whole book to lay out all the attitudes, opinions, and points of view that were involved in the dispute. I have only tried to tell how it went down as far as I was concerned. In the end the dispute was solved in a rather irregular way.

Ray was fighting the British boxer, Dave "Boy" Green. I was in the dressing room before the fight with Sugar Ray, Mike Trainer, and his partner Jim Ryan. Janks Morton was there too. There was only a short time to go before Ray and I would have to make our entrance into the arena.

I don't remember the exact conversation in the dressing room. I do remember that Trainer produced a handwritten contract that everyone wanted me to sign. I knew that I should let my lawyers check it out first, but unfortunately I didn't happen to have one with me! Everyone assured me of their great affection. Sugar told me that he would like me to sign the contract. Trainer, unusually friendly and convincing, explained that it was in my best interests. I would get my fifteen percent! The only change from the original would be the contract's duration. They reminded me that I had always said that I hadn't liked contracts and that the fighter must have faith in his manager. What did I want a long-term contract for? Didn't Ray have great admiration, faith, and affection for me? I signed. The contract was for one year.

Leonard threw his arms around me, saying how glad he was that I had signed. Everyone was happy. I've got to be honest—even though I felt I had been suckered, it was such a relief to be in a pleasant and relaxed atmosphere, that I felt kind of happy too.

Leonard won the fight easily. I could see no one stopping him on the road to a title fight. But I left Landover with mixed emotions: pleased about the win, but a little sick at my premature signing of the contract.

Back in my office I explained the latest development to Betty. She wasn't pleased at all. "You were coerced. You should start legal proceedings."

I contacted my lawyers, who told me in no uncertain manner

that I had been a fool to sign any contract without legal advice. Did I want to pursue the matter? No I didn't. I had signed the damn contract because I couldn't stand the unpleasant atmosphere, and I had been talked into it like a little kid. No one broke my arm, I signed it, that was that. I had no intention of starting litigation, because I didn't want to damage the Sugar Ray image. You have to understand that all through this murky episode I still felt that Ray was a great kid. We were close. I had to believe that he was being led by Trainer. On second thoughts, maybe not "had to believe," more like "wanted to."

I knew that Ray had received copies of most of the Trainer letters, so there was really no way he didn't know what was going on. Maybe he had no faith in me as a manager! Perhaps he shared Trainer's opinion of me. It could be that he just didn't want to pay me fifteen percent! I didn't know what to think. I asked myself: "Could it be Ray?" No! Not Ray! The kid was too nice a guy. I left it at that.

I had a new contract and I would give it my best shot. I wanted a World Title for Ray. He was the best and he deserved it.

The atmosphere lightened and my relationship with Ray was like old times. I liked him, and hoped the feeling was reciprocated.

About three months after I had signed the new contract, Ray spent some time with Helen and me in Miami. When he returned to Maryland he sent me the following note which I'll always keep with fond memories.

Hello Buddies,
Just a few lines to say things are going well and I am very happy to say that not only have I found the world's greatest manager and wife but two dynamite *friends*,
Love Ya!
The Next World Champ, Sugar Ray.

What can I say! The world's greatest manager. Come on!

The end of the seventies was only a few weeks away. They had been turbulent but exciting, and I would always have the memories of the "Ali years" to warm me in my later years. Muhammad had retired, I hoped permanently, but with Muhammad, who could tell? Luis Rodriguez, Jimmy Ellis, José Napoles, and Sugar Ramos had retired too. It was as if my old friends had moved away to another neighborhood. My old pal and partner in the management of Sugar Ramos and José Napoles had died in 1979. I would miss Cuco Conde and always remember his kindness and friendship. Joe Netro had also passed away. Carmen Basilio's trusted adviser and co-manager would be missed too. His partner John de John and I are friends to this day.

The seventies had seen the meteoric rise of Sugar Ray Leonard and, notwithstanding the pain over the contractual problems, I was elated when on November 30, 1979, he fought for the world title.

Once again I was in Las Vegas, working in the corner of the fighter who was to become the champion. Wilfred Benitez, the reigning champion, fought well in this great and exciting bout. Sugar Ray fulfilled his early promise and was superb. For fifteen rounds the two well-matched boxers demonstrated all that is good in boxing. Finally Benitez was overcome by Leonard and fell, KO'd in the last round of the fight. Sugar Ray Leonard was the new Welterweight Champion of the World.

As for me and my feelings about the previous unpleasantness: when the master of ceremonies announced Leonard as the winner and the new world champion, I thought as I stood watching the jubilation in the corner, that for someone who had been told that he had "no credibility," and hadn't been doing his job, I must have been doing something right!

The Muhammad Ali–Trevor Berbick fight was now history. The debacle of a promotion had taken place on Friday, December 15, 1981. The bouts started hours late, which made the fans irritable and led them to wonder what the hell was going on. It was only a little luck and some fast thinking from a young lady that prevented the bouts from being bare-fist fights!

The morning of the fight I was in my hotel in Nassau. One of the promotion organizers asked me if I had any boxing gloves with me. I told the guy that I had one pair for Muhammad, plus one spare pair. I was then asked if Berbick could use the spare pair. I said, "Sure, no problem." But there was! The promoters had no boxing gloves for the rest of the card! I told the guy to call my office in Miami and ask Betty to sort out a few pairs from our MacGregor boxing glove samples, and to send someone over on the next plane to Miami—about an hour's trip—to pick them up. Their problem would be solved!

Betty Mitchell received a call at 9:30 A.M., and by ten o'clock the gloves were ready to go. Two hours went by, and no one arrived to pick them up. She took three calls from Nassau from three different people, including one from the government, all explaining that they had no gloves. What do you know! Betty patiently explained three times that the gloves were waiting in Miami to be picked up. Each phone call assured her that someone would be at the office by two o'clock, two-thirty at the latest. They thanked her and confidently told her that everything was under control. That's what Napoleon said at Waterloo!

At four-thirty, with no one from Nassau having arrived, Betty called it a day and went home. At five, someone from the boxing promoters arrived to find a locked and empty office.

Luckily, Shelli, who was still working in the leasing and management office next door to mine, was aware of the ongoing drama, and had the presence of mind to call me in Nassau. By some unlikely stroke of luck she caught me at the hotel. I told her to use her master key and go into my office and give the guy the gloves that Betty had prepared.

The guy and the gloves caught the seven o'clock flight from Miami, and the fights started two hours late. The way the evening went, I wish the guy had missed the plane and the whole deal had been canceled, saving Muhammad from a disappointing defeat.

I returned from the Bahamas a little teed off with the Ali result and the whole damn fiasco. I decided not to go into the office until lunchtime on Monday. I intended to sleep in. I called Betty and told her of my plans; otherwise she would be wondering, come Monday morning, where the hell I'd gone to.

When I did make my entrance around noon on Monday I was wearing my new sports jacket which I had picked up at a sale. I thought it looked good, but neither Betty nor Mike Winters, my business advisor, made any complimentary remarks. I don't think they even noticed it!

Well, they did have other things on their minds. They wanted to know about Muhammad. They knew the result of the fight. Berbick had won. But what would Muhammad do now? "He will retire now, won't he?" Betty asked. She liked Muhammad and was concerned for him.

"I think so. I really think so this time. The well has run dry," I told her.

"Why did he take the fight?" Mike asked in his clipped English accent. "I think it is quite sad."

"No, it wasn't sad. Sure, it's tough that Muhammad didn't or couldn't fight like he did, say, ten years ago, but sad? No.

Muhammad has been a great. He was a refreshing thing for boxing. He gave the game new life. If he wanted one more fight, one fight strictly for himself, he had to go for it. Muhammad knew, everybody in boxing knew, even Trevor Berbick knew, that in his prime he would have taken Trevor. Do you know, Trevor worships Muhammad, even tries to imitate him. That Muhammad! The guy is thirty-nine years old, and he still thought there might be a chance! No, I don't think it was sad."

I took off my dutch-boy cap, took a cigar from the box, lit up and settled back in my chair. I felt like talking. (In maybe thirty minutes the phone would start its frantic searching again. No time for conversation then.) "Now, the Holmes fight was sad. Muhammad could have won that one. It was October 1980, he was only thirty-eight years old then!" Betty and Mike smiled.

"Why was that fight sad?" Mike asked.

"Because he never fully confided in me. When I joined him for the final training sessions he looked terrific. No weight problems, and you know that he'd been having that trouble. Come the fight, he's got nothing. No reserves, no strength, no fatty tissues to burn up. Muhammad told me after the fight that he'd been taking thyroid pills to help him shed weight. I'm not taking anything away from Larry Holmes, who in my opinion is a great, classy champion. Very underrated. Doesn't have the personal charisma of an Ali or Leonard, but a good fighter, but I really thought that Ali, even at thirty-eight, had a good chance of winning. It broke my heart to stop that fight. It was the worst beating Muhammad ever took. Yea, that was sad."

"He must be a terrific chap," Mike said.

I had to smile. "Terrific chap"—I liked the way it sounded. "Yea, I guess you could say that, Mike. Muhammad gave away around three million dollars to charity. For a small instance he bought Houston McTear's parents a house."

"Who is Houston McTear?" Mike wanted to know.

"An Olympic track star, an amateur. His parents were living in poverty. They had sacrificed themselves for their son's amateur career. Anyway, Muhammad bought them a house. Another for instance: he gave $100,000 to an old people's home in Miami. They didn't have any television sets, so Muhammad bought them some. At one time, his payroll was around $3,500 a week. I asked if he was crazy or something. He said, 'I don't need them, they need me.' Muhammad is like that. He told me that the people in the ghettos needed him. Needed to see somebody like themselves winning. He believes it is his mission to help people. I remember Muhammad telling me, 'I'm gonna be in trouble when that judgment comes, if I don't help those I can.' Yea, I guess you could say Muhammad is a terrific chap."

My relationship with Ray Leonard was, as far as I could tell, just fine. Since the contractual dispute in 1979 a lot had happened. My contract had run out on March 24, 1980. I was offered a new contract for a two-year duration. I accepted Mike Trainer's offer and went to work with Ray preparing for his fight in Montreal against the formidable Roberto Duran.

The beautiful Canadian city was buzzing with anticipation. The fight was full of thrills and excitement, but for me it was disappointing. Leonard fought his own fight against Duran. He ignored my pleading for different tactics throughout the fight. He did his own thing, but he lost the fight.

Five months later in November 1980, Ray had his chance for revenge. The two contrasting personalities were meeting again, but this time Ray, Janks, and I had worked on a new game plan.

We practiced moving off the ropes, along with other moves, to negate the hustling, bruising style of Duran. Half jokingly I told the press, "Duran has three weapons, a left hand, a right hand, and a head." Duran was tough. He had beaten Ray once and was confident he could do it again. I didn't think so.

At their meeting before the first fight Duran had incensed Leonard by his rude, arrogant manner, even going as far as to insult Juanita, Ray's wife. Contrived or not, it had made Ray lose his cool. Result: defeat for Ray. This time it would be a different ball game.

Duran couldn't believe his eyes. Leonard and I arrived at the weigh-in wearing beards! You see, Duran never shaved before a fight. It made him look a real rough customer. It intimidated his opponents. Not this time. We burst that balloon, showing our contempt by wearing the false beards. This time, Ray wasn't the quiet, well-mannered gentleman. He treated Duran with disdain and contempt, and acted as if the result of the fight was a foregone conclusion, with himself the undisputed winner. It was psychological warfare.

The Superdome in New Orleans was packed. The interest in the fight was worldwide. It was rumored that the two boxers were splitting a $16,000,000 purse. That's eight million bucks apiece. Don't tell me about any fifteen percent—I don't want to hear it!

The fight had the classic ingredients for a "big fight," and fans all over the world wanted to know who the winner would be. For most people it was good guy Leonard against bad guy Duran, but for the millions of Latins it was the other way around.

As the two fighters listened to the referee's instructions and indulged in the staring-each-other-down game, I believe Roberto noticed that Leonard looked bigger than he had in Montreal. Ray was carrying a few pounds more, and besides the extra strength I hoped this would give, a bigger, confident, arrogant Leonard might create doubts in the mental attitude of his opponent.

During the first few rounds, Ray negated all Duran's bullish tactics. I could see Duran's frustration building up. It was showing in the way he turned and walked back to his corner at the end of a round, the way in which he shook his head when he missed a shot at the elusive Leonard. In a fight, frustration can be a dangerous thing. Ray began putting on pressure, moving in, delivering a flurry of blows, then retreating out of distance. Duran was looking ordinary, pedestrian. At the end of the seventh round I had Ray comfortably ahead on points. I was looking for a KO victory.

The eighth round began. Ray, confident and fully in charge, began to taunt Roberto—not verbally but by his actions. He was playing, displaying complete disrespect towards the street kid from Panama. Another quick combination by Leonard. Here, and then not there! Once again Duran moved to go after the now out of distance Maryland marvel. Then he changed his mind. Duran turned his back on Leonard and raised his arms. What was he doing? Sugar Ray was astonished, he didn't know what to do. He couldn't hit the back of his opponent's head. Duran was walking away, waving his arms, shaking his head and saying "No mas, no mas." I couldn't believe my eyes or my ears. "No more, no more," Duran was saying. He didn't look hurt, as far as I could tell. He went back to his corner, his seconds and handlers surrounded him. They were as surprised as everyone else. "No mas!" It was incredible. The fight was over. Sugar Ray Leonard had won, perhaps the strangest victory I had ever seen, but he had won!

There were so many different stories of why Duran had quit that it becomes a case of "you pay your money and take your choice." I don't know the reason, but it certainly wasn't because Duran was a coward. His record speaks for itself, and no guy who has the guts to put on those boxing shorts and shoes can be any kind of coward. You want my observations about the dramatic end of the fight?

Well, it was a similar situation to the first Clay-Liston fight. Ali got to him psychologically, and when things didn't go right for Liston in the ring, the mental assurance and strength needed to undertake any uphill climb was undermined.

Do you get the picture? Duran was no quitter, he stopped fighting against Leonard because, for reasons real or imaginary, in his mind he believed he couldn't carry on. Roberto retired from boxing, but like so many champions he made a comeback. I believe he did so to prove to himself and the fight fans that Roberto Duran was no quitter. He didn't need to prove anything!

After his victory over Duran in 1980, Sugar Ray had two more victories, one giving him the Junior Middleweight Championship of the World, when he defeated Ayab Kalule. Early in the year of 1981, he reached superstar status by beating Tommy Hearns—the same Tommy Hearns we had avoided fighting back in 1979—and reunited the welterweight title by becoming champion of both the WBA and the WBC.

After the victories over Duran in 1979, and Hearns in 1981, I thought my standing with Ray was pretty high. We were close, and I believed I had more than proved my value. I got on well with Janks Morton, too, which was fortunate because Janks was now Ray's trainer (as distinct from the other Trainer. Even Mike Trainer's name gives me a problem!)

I must give Janks credit. He had turned a hobby into a profession. When Dave Jacobs, Ray's old trainer from his amateur days, fell out with the champ and left, it was Janks who took over and he did a great job. In the few years we had worked together, he learned. He soaked up the "know-how," and Leonard's superb physical condition was evidence of that.

Business wise things were good and I should have been as happy as a pig in slop, but there was a dark shadow over my life, one that I couldn't ignore no matter how hard I tried.

My brother Jimmy was very ill. It was serious, it was cancer. He had been on a special diet for the last six months, and had his meals cooked on a butane gas grill. I knew nothing about the why's and wherefore's of the preventive treatment, but if Jimmy believed it was doing some good, that was OK by me. There was no hope anywhere else.

Just before Christmas of 1981, Jimmy and his second wife, Irene, came and spent some time with Helen and me in Miami. Helen and I bought the specific butane gas grill and the special food he wanted. Irene cooked his meals exactly how he liked them. I silently prayed that it was helping him, and that he would have a remission from the merciless and insidious disease.

The time we spent together was precious. We talked, spoke our innermost thoughts. The bond between us was strong, enabling us to speak of things that we could never share with anyone else. That his illness was terminal was never allowed to enter our thoughts. He would beat it. We had to think positively. We had to have faith.

When Jimmy left, to go back home to New Jersey, I forced myself not to believe that it would be the last time we would be together. But it was.

On February 14, 1982, James Mirena, my beloved brother, passed away. I was heartbroken. Helen was a great comfort to me, as she had been when I suffered the loss of my father. I am not a devout, religious person, but I do believe in an Almighty God, and I believe Jimmy and I will meet up again.

I received the news of Jimmy's death while I was in Reno with Sugar Ray. It was the day before Ray was scheduled to fight Bruce Finch. I kept my grief to myself and decided to work the fight *as Jimmy would have wished.*

Ray stopped Finch in three rounds, but it wasn't as easy a contest as the result suggests. Finch caught Ray some good shots and hurt him. Maybe I was wrong, but although nothing was said, I had the impression that Ray no longer had his old appetite for the fight game. I didn't dwell on the matter and dismissed the thought from my mind, telling myself that Ray needed a much bigger challenge to stimulate him.

On February 17 I went to Cherry Hill, New Jersey, to attend my brother Jimmy's funeral. It was for family and close friends only. I was deeply touched to see Ray and his wife Juanita standing among the mourners.

The day my contract with Sugar Ray Leonard Inc. ran out was March 24, 1982. It came and went, and still no news from Mike Trainer. Previous to that date I had OK'd Roger Stafford as Leonard's next opponent. I had videotapes sent to me of Stafford in action and was studying and working on tactics ready for the bout scheduled for May 14, 1982, in Buffalo. Ten days before the fight I was asked by Mike Trainer to join Ray for the final training sessions. There was no mention of my contract, but I wasn't too concerned. Trainer could be a tough, hard-nosed businessman, but I knew that he was a man of integrity and honesty. I had no doubt that I would be paid, but exactly how much remained a mystery. It was no good worrying about it, so I cast out all negative thoughts and left for Maryland.

Ray was friendly and looked in good shape, and I was surprised to learn that he had hurt his eye accidentally in a sparring session. It was a worry, especially with the fight so near. He saw a couple of local doctors, but the eye continued to give him trouble.

On Saturday, May 8 Ray went to Baltimore, where he was checked into a hosptial and was prepared for surgery. The eye problem had been diagnosed as a partially detached retina. When I heard the news, I left Buffalo and was at the hospital in Baltimore alongside Janks, Trainer, and Ray's immediate family, waiting to hear the result of the operation. When the doctor told us the result and his prognosis I felt some relief. At least Ray's eyesight would not be seriously impaired, if at all. Other boxers had undergone similar operations and had come back and continued their ring careers. Maurice Hope, the British former world junior middleweight champion had done so a couple of years back, as had the hard-hitting heavyweight Ernie Shavers.

The Stafford fight was canceled. Ray's career was up in the air: either he would be able to fight or he wouldn't. All future plans would have to wait until the doctor gave Ray the word, and it would be six months before any decisions could be taken. Whatever the doctor's verdict turned out to be, and I prayed that he would give Ray a clean bill of health, I didn't believe that Ray would ever choose to box again. However, in spite of everything that had gone down in the past, if Ray did decide to box again and he wanted me in his corner, I knew that I'd be there.

I tried to give my best efforts to my other fighters. Two of them, Jim Tillis, a heavyweight, and Ian Clyde, one hundred and twelve pounds of talent, were moving up into title contention, but my enthusiasm for the fight game had never been lower. The truth of the matter was I couldn't get over Jimmy's death.

Sometimes during the day, for no apparent reason, a wave of depression would wash over me, and I would seek out a quiet corner where I could be alone. Tears would come to my eyes as I remembered my brother. I had always loved and respected Jimmy and had accepted his wise counseling automatically. Now that he was gone I realized how much I had relied on his guidance. Never again would I be able to listen to his calm voice make sense from situations I considered senseless. My brother Jimmy had gone.

I wasn't completely alone; I still had the love and affection from Helen and my two children. Their strength and comfort helped me survive that sorrowful period of my life.

Two distinctly different events also helped me get over my sadness. The first was my daughter's wedding.

Terri's happiness took precedence over everything else. I became caught up in Helen's excitement and joined in the endless discussions trying to decide where the June wedding would be held. Terri wanted an informal, quiet affair and eventually we all agreed that the reception would be held at our home in Miami.

In this day and age, when for some people marriage seems to have lost its magic, Helen and I were thrilled that Terri was doing it the so-called "old-fashioned way." For the first time in many months I felt happy about something. At Helen's suggestion, we took a short vacation and visited Calabria, in Southern Italy, the birthplace of my parents, and we returned in the right frame to enjoy our daughter's wedding.

It was a small family affair, but I believe Terri and her husband James started their married life overwhelmed with love and affection—as if there had been a thousand guests.

The second event that helped shake me out of my depression was the visit of an old friend. Muhammad Ali came to town.

CHAPTER TWENTY

ANOTHER DAY, ANOTHER DOLLAR

"The last time I saw Muhammad was July 1984. He reassured me about the stories stated by the media that he was seriously ill and had brain damage."

Wednesday, November 2, 1982. Yesterday Mike Winters wanted to know if I could contact Muhammad Ali for him. He had a promotional deal to offer, and wanted to check to see if Muhammad was interested before he contacted Herbert Muhammad.

I didn't know where Muhammad was, but I took a chance and called his office number in California. Lo and behold, "the Greatest" was there. We spoke and, can you believe this, he was about to leave California for Miami. He wanted to work out, really sweat—he loved doing that—and get in some kind of shape before he undertook a tour of India, Pakistan, and Saudi Arabia, where he was going to box some exhibition bouts. I put Mike on to say hello and tell Muhammad about the deal. After a couple of seconds of conversation, Mike burst out laughing. He cupped his hand over the receiver and said to me, "I asked Muhammad, what do you think about the figure, meaning the money offered, and Muhammad said, 'Did you say figure, or nigger?'" Mike, still laughing, tried to carry on his conversation with Muhammad, but I could tell that Muhammad was in one of his joking moods, and that Mike had about as much chance of getting a straight answer as the Incredible Hulk had of becoming a Dallas cheerleader.

I arranged to pick up Muhammad at his hotel on the beach at twelve o'clock the following day and take him to the gym where he could work out in private. He would spar with one of my fighters. I was glad Mike had asked me to call Muhammad. I was really looking forward to seeing him.

The next day, as I drove Muhammad to the Allen Park gym, he asked me if the local TV stations would be coming. "I thought you wanted secrecy. I didn't call anyone," I told him.

Muhammad chuckled, "I asked Betty to arrange a little television coverage." He grinned at me. "But after today it's gonna be private."

The camera crew was waiting for us, but the interviewer hadn't yet arrived. Muhammad got changed. Over his tracksuit he wore a plastic zip-up jacket to make him sweat. I introduced him to Reiner Hartmann, the young, blond German boxer I represented. Obviously Betty had tipped him off that he would be working with Muhammad. He was thrilled. The awe and admiration shone in his eyes. Can you believe this: Reiner had with him Muhammad's autobiography, printed in German. Naturally, Muhammad autographed it.

The two strapping boxers, one a young potential, the other the greatest heavyweight boxer who ever lived—that's my opinion— sparred together in the ring. They wore no boxing gloves and never landed a blow on each other. They sparred and sweated. But Reiner probably learned more about balance and technique during those three three-minute rounds boxing with Ali than he ever will in years of practice.

After the exhibition, Muhammad sat on an old wooden chair, ready for the television interviewer who had arrived with apologies for being late. There were only a few people in the gym.

We all listened to the interview. Muhammad was in vintage form. When the cameras had gone, Muhammad still sat on the chair. His plastic shirt was doing its job; perspiration dripped onto the wooden floor. I placed a robe around him. I'd noticed a tear in his shorts—after all, there were ladies present!

Muhammad sat and talked to the gathering. He was funny, he was serious, he was compelling, he was Muhammad. Tony Green, one of my fighters who had been working out and had stuck around to renew his acquaintanceship with Muhammad, whispered softly to me, "He's phenomenal." I had to agree. Muhammad wound up his impromptu performance by asking the gathering to tell their friends that Ali was here, and that he would be in the gym every lunchtime for two weeks. "Bring the children," he said. So much for keeping his visit a secret! As I always say, soak up the glamour right till the end.

Muhammad went for a shower and I tagged along and waited, holding a large towel until he was finished. It was like old times.

Muhammad asked me how I was doing and I answered that I was not really interested in boxing anymore. I didn't know whether I really believed that or not. Muhammad certainly didn't: "You're talking crazy, Angie; I know you, you can't walk away from boxing. I tell you, Angie, boxing needs you as much as you need it."

I was warmed by his concern for me and I for my part was just as concerned for him. I was worried by his slurred speech although I knew perfectly well that hypoglycemia could be the cause. The disease creates an abnormal decrease of sugar in the blood which results in feelings of listlessness and fatigue. Muhammad needed something to do, something that would really charge him up. I hoped that he would find it. The last time I saw Muhammad was July 1984. He reassured me about the stories stated by the media that he was seriously ill and had brain damage. He did have a medical problem, but nothing that couldn't be controlled by medication. There was no brain damage and to show the world that he was okay he went on TV. Muhammad said that for the last few days he had more press coverage than Michael Jackson. And, with his usual humility, he was surprised at the interest in his condition considering all the big media stories happening worldwide. I pray that Muhammad regains his health I believe that he still has so much to give to the world.

Slowly but surely I came back to my old self and rediscovered my interest in boxing. Jim Kaulentis, a friend of mine from Chicago, asked me to evaluate Jim Tillis, a heavyweight he thought would interest me. How do I evaluate a boxer's skill in a gym situation? I watch them spar and make notes, normally on the back of any handy old envelope. Here are my exact notes.

JIM TILLIS

Right hand—don't punch. Elbow high
(meaning his elbow is too high when punching with right hand)
Only moves to left, never to right
(self-explanatory)
Puts hands on shoulders
(when going into clinch he places hands on opponent's shoulders. Very dangerous—leaves himself wide open for body punches)
Must be taught to slide to right
(self-explanatory)

Falls in too much when clinches
(he is losing balance)
Comes in too straight
(doing that makes him a bigger target)
Learn to double up on jab
(instead of using a single straight jab, the boxer will use two punches in rapid succession)
Grabbing because off-balance
(after missing with punch, falls off-balance)
Summary: Potential World Class Talent—providing he learns.

In late October 1982, out of the blue, Ray Leonard announced that he was going to hold a press and television conference. In Baltimore on November 9, in front of the news media, invited guests, and the general public, who paid an admission charge that went to charity, Sugar Ray Leonard announced his retirement from the ring. There was a presentation brochure entitled "An Evening with Sugar Ray Leonard," that included these comments:

"Angelo respected me as a man. That was one big reason why we got along so well. His input has been invaluable to my career"—Sugar Ray Leonard.

"Throughout Ray's professional career, Dundee's impeccable knowledge of the fight game, sage advice, and ringside savvy have helped build a champion"—Mike Trainer.

The following years were those of hard work with little success to show for it. Jim Tillis lost a couple of fights, including a title shot against Mike Weaver, and unfortunately he also lost his appetite for the fight game. Little Ian Clyde won some but lost the important one in Korea for the International Boxing Federation's world flyweight title. It was a long way to go for a defeat, and I tried to cheer up the dejected Ian. The bitter taste of failure takes some swallowing, but I told him that worrying over what might have been ain't worth a cent, you have to think positively and go right on living.

Another of my fighters, Tony Green, who had recently won the Cruiserweight Championship of Florida, sustained an eye injury and I was forced to tell him that he should retire. He was heartbroken, and so was I knowing how badly he wanted to continue boxing. But he'll do OK. He will make a good life for himself. Tony is probably one of the nicest and most likable guys I have ever worked with.

One bright shaft of success came from the blond German heavyweight, Reiner Hartmann, who I had been training and managing for two years. We flew from Miami to Frankfurt for a shot at the German title. This time the long journey paid off and for the first time in my career I represented a Heavyweight Champion of Germany.

As promising as my fighters were, I reached 1984 with the realistic feeling that none were ready for the highest honor—a World Title. Of course, I was fully aware that in boxing anything can happen, and as if to prove this point, late in April I received a call from Mike Trainer informing me that Ray Leonard was making a comeback, or as Ray put it, continuing his career in boxing. Was I surprised? No, not really. The temptation to come back is very strong. In some cases the boxer fights again for the money, but in Ray's case he missed the excitement and he wanted to prove to himself that he still had it. I had no doubt in my mind that if Ray's eye was OK and he had no other health problems he would win back his title.

He came down to Miami to train and I watched him improve and sharpen up as the days progressed. The atmosphere was good and the Allen Park gym where I always train my fighters was buzzing with excitement and had not been so busy since Muhammad had worked out there, last year.

The media were all over us making training that much harder. Ray, a supreme showman, split himself in two, performing for the press and television reporters and preparing for the fight and keeping to our training regimen.

Ray had looked good shadowboxing and sparring in the ring. He was relaxed enough to fool around with his sparring partners, and got laughs and cheers from his fervent fans. But training is only training. On May 11, Sugar Ray Leonard, once again in his phenomenal career, was facing the moment of truth.

His opponent was Kevin Howard, a good boxer and a hard puncher. It was not going to be a walkover by any means. In the dressing room it was like old times. Everyone was relaxed, especially Ray, but who could really know the pressure the young man was under. Everyone expected so much. I knew that it was going to be hard. After all, Ray had not fought for two years, and that is one hell of a layoff. It wasn't a topic to keep bringing up in conversation. It sounded defeatist, so we didn't talk of it. What the hell, Ray would answer all our doubts and questions when he entered the ring.

From round one onward there was no ignoring the fact that Ray was ring rusty, and there was no ignoring the fact that in patches Ray was simply brilliant. Sure, his timing wasn't as sharp as it had been, but after a few more fights that would have come back. And, sure, he got decked by a punch he would have avoided two years ago. His pride was hurt more than he was, and he got up, didn't he? And he won the fight, didn't he? The referee had to stop the bout in round nine to save Kevin Howard taking any more punishment.

Ray announced his retirement immediately after the fight, without due consideration or time to reflect on his decision. The decision was his and I respect it and agree with it because psychologically he would always be concerned about his eyes and that worry would take away that extra something from his boxing. Nevertheless, I still believe Ray was more than capable of winning back his title, although I am pleased Ray left the game while he was in such good shape and a winner.

As it stands now, Ray Leonard will join that select band of boxers who are known as "all-time greats." Ray can wear that label with pride and justification. Boxing can be proud of Sugar Ray Leonard and will miss his skills, talent, and personal charisma. As for me, it was a privilege and honor to have worked with such a great athlete.

It was time to get back to work with my other fighters. I hoped they didn't feel neglected, but I was aware that when one of my fighters really took off it affected the time I spent with the other guys. It had always been like that, but somehow it seemed to work for me and for the fighters, too. After all, I did have two of my fighters win world titles on one night. Remember? Sugar Ramos and Louis Rodriguez in March 1963. Who knows—it could happen again. Maybe three next time!

My current bunch are young, keen, and promising. Slobodan Kacar won the Olympic gold medal for Yugoslavia in 1980. Lupe Suarez, from Corpus Christi, Texas, is undefeated, and Ruben Castillo, a Californian featherweight, lost a close fight against Juan LaPorte for the world title.

Then there are Chris Silvas, Mike Hutchinson, Alex Williamson, Dick Curry, and Pat Hallacy. Will any of them become champions? Who knows. There are no guarantees in this business.

On paper your guy can look a "sure thing," except that in boxing there is no such thing as a "sure thing."

How about the fight between Sandy Saddler and Willie Pep way back in 1949. They had met before and Saddler had KO'd Willie in the fourth; now they were meeting again over fifteen rounds in Madison Square Garden for the featherweight title. Saddler was at least three inches taller than Pep, and was strong and very clever. Pep had already tasted the power of Saddler's punches and could have felt wary of taking him on again. Saddler was the favorite in the eyes of the bookies, but Willie Pep outpointed Saddler and gave one of the greatest exhibitions of pure boxing skills that I have ever seen.

Another big upset in boxing was the Sugar Ray Robinson fight against Carmen Basilio. Robinson was acclaimed and recognized as one of the greatest boxers of all time and it looked a "sure thing" that he would whip the smaller, less skillful fighter. But on the night of September 23, 1957, Carmen Basilio outboxed, out-gunned, and outpunched the mighty Robinson.

Carmen fought like a man possessed. Perhaps it was the slurs and insults the press leveled against him before the fight: "He's too small," he gets hit "too easily," "it'll be a training session for the champ." It was no training session!

Basilio had Robinson in trouble a couple of times. He pinned him on the ropes, and used both hands to the body with great effect. It was a great fight, and a great upset. Carmen won and became Middleweight Champion of the World. So, don't talk to me about "sure things." Who the heck knows for sure what is going to happen on the night?

When you are working the corner for a boxer, you don't see the fight in the same way as a spectator. The corner man is too busy watching the moves and trying to plot out new ploys to penetrate the opponent's defense to be able to sit back and enjoy the bout. If I did that my concentration would go; I'd have a good time but I wouldn't be of much help to my fighter.

Only once did I get slightly carried away in the fight. Admittedly it was only for moments and it was the round before the final one. The only excuse I can give is that it was one hell of a fight.

Muhammad Ali—Joe Frazier. "The Thrilla from Manilla." Who ever dreamed up that catch phrase was sure on the ball. The fight was a thriller from beginning to end. You had two supremely conditioned athletes going full out from the first moment the bell sounded.

Their stamina, strength, determination were above the call of duty. It was a battle of attrition.

I implored Muhammad to stay away and slow down the pace,

but the two fighters were caught up in this frenzy of fighting and they intended to go on until one of them dropped.

The bell went for the fourteenth round, and I breathed out a sigh of relief because I hadn't been at all sure that Muhammad would not collapse from sheer exhaustion. Now, seconds before the start of the round I detected a change in this remarkable man. Somehow, don't ask me how, he had drawn on a hidden reserve of strength. Deep from within himself he had found more resolve, more determination, and more power.

The bell sounded and the gladiators once again exchanged blows. My concentration momentarily left me as I watched the exhausted boxers defying the laws of nature. I sensed the end was near. I was completely captivated by the fight and I cheered and shouted with the rest of the fans as the fight ended. The brave Joe Frazier was finally vanquished by the remarkable Muhammad Ali.

I salute both men. It was a great fight, an exhibition of courage and skill that I will never forget.

That is the kind of fight that makes boxing such an exciting sport, and in spite of its detractors, it is a great sport. It has its problems, most sports do, and it is dangerous—although an independent study group was of the opinion that amateur boxing was seventeenth in the league of dangerous sports. Strange, you never hear anyone shouting about banning the other sixteen!

Boxing must improve its image and must take better care of its participants, because without the fighters there isn't anything.

I believe that boxing will improve its protective practices. There should be stricter physicals, before and after fights, and the rating system must be improved. Mismatches are one of the worst aspects in the game, and the WBC and WBA must take the responsibility, as must the newly formed IBF.

I am going to quote Marc Maturo, president of the International Boxing Writer's Association: "Perhaps it is time for an independent body of concerned and knowledgeable men to make the ratings."

Change doesn't necessarily equate to improvement. For instance, I don't like the thumbless glove. The idea is that it would prevent a fighter from having a thumb stuck in his eye either accidentally or on purpose. That is true, but I think that a glove without a thumb is unnatural, and will affect the fighter's reflexes and diminish his punching power. It could also result in hand damage, which happened to Sugar Ray Leonard in his last fight. I am in favor of the glove with an attached thumb. This will give the fighters exactly the same feel as an unattached thumb, but will prevent the thumb damaging an opponent's eye.

New safety measures will come into the game, in the same way as we moved from bare-fisted fighting to the wearing of gloves. Managers, officials, and promoters come and go; those who have been only takers and didn't put anything back into the game are best forgotten. Boxing will survive and I hope that I will be remembered as a man who did what he could for the betterment of the sport.

CHAPTER TWENTY-ONE

THE PERFECT 10

"I've called this book I Only Talk Winning for a reason. In life, there are positive and negative thoughts. And hey, it doesn't cost you a cent more to think positively."

What do I look for in a fighter? What makes a champion? Because I'm always looking and hoping that my fighter is going to become a champion, I'm always looking for the same ingredients. The boxer must be A1 physically and have the tenacity and determination needed to persevere in the training regimens. Balance is a must; so is great coordination of hands, feet, and body. His outside activities must be compatible with his career, and he must have self-discipline to avoid the pitfalls of booze, drugs, and late nights.

Of course, the boxer's weight division makes some difference. As a rule, I have found heavyweights to be late bloomers, and the lighter weights seem to develop earlier. I do not like overmuscular boxers; bulky shoulders and muscles are not plusses for me. Boxers must be able to throw straight punches from all angles; the body muscles must be attuned to this and are best left to develop naturally. Training achieves this, but I guess the most important ingredient is desire: the desire to be a fighter, the desire to win, and the desire to be the best there is.

A lot of people have asked me for my personal Boxer's Hall of Fame and I've always tried to steer clear of trying to rate boxers. I'm not into that who-was-better-than-who business, but I don't think anyone can argue that the following fighters must rate as some of the cream of the crop: Muhammad Ali, Sugar Ray

270

Robinson, Sugar Ray Leonard, Tony Canzoneri, Joe Louis, Henry Armstrong, Willie Pep, and Rocky Marciano.

I have seen those guys fight and I know they are all-time greats, but there are others who I never saw applying their art. If what my older friends told me way back when I started out is true, and I believe it is, Abe Attell, Mickey Walker, Benny Leonard, Ted (Kid) Lewis, Harry Greb, and Jack Dempsey must have been something special.

I have left out so many great fighers. Larry Holmes, Carmen Basilio, Sugar Ramos, Alexis Arguello, certainly must be considered. And what about Duran, Pedroza, Monzon, Griffith, Hagler? All great fighters.

The list could go on. There have been many great boxers but as someone once said, "comparisons are odious." (Remember, it isn't easy to judge a fighter by television coverage—you have to see them live. I mean you have to be at the fights, and let your own eyes be the camera.)

I tell you, every fighter I ever worked with had something special, but some have more that is special than others.

I don't think I would be shooting off my mouth by saying that I have been a decisive factor in the development of nine World Champions. I was lucky to have been around at the right time, and allowed to contribute to their success. I guess I'm the only guy in boxing to have had two consecutive World Heavyweight Champions—Muhammad Ali and then Jimmy Ellis. That's not bad for a kid from South Philly who only got into boxing by default.

My brother Jimmy always said that I would make it in the fight game. The year before he died—it was around the time I was having contractual problems with Mike Trainer—Jimmy told me not to worry and that I'd find another champion. "You'll be a perfect ten, Ang. It'll happen, don't doubt it," he said. I reached the summer of 1984 confident that one day I would find the fighter who would become my tenth champion.

It was way back in 1979 that this fighter first called me. He wanted to know if I was interested in representing him. The kid had had only five pro fights, but I'd seen him in action; he looked promising. I would have been interested, but the fighter had some kind of a management deal with a pal of mine. I let the offer pass.

Let me tell you a little about the fighter. His name, Pinklon Thomas. At the age of twelve he was on drugs; by the time he was fourteen he was a heroin addict. He was snorting raw heroin and then shooting it. He took two trips to the detoxification center, but he got hooked on methadone, the drug they had given him to beat the habit.

He was a well-built kid who hung out with the older boys; maybe that's why he did heavy drugs, he wanted to look a big man. The integration standards of Pontiac, Michigan, where Pinklon lived, demanded that he be bussed out of his neighborhood, and Pinklon found himself in a strange school with no friends. Drugs were his closest companions.

He quit school and for a while he concentrated on being a dope addict. He learned all the tricks. Robbing the bread man, the beer man, strong-arming people. All the antisocial acts required to find money to feed his habit. Throughout this bad period, his girlfriend Kathy stuck with him trying to get him to clean up his act. She saw beneath his drug-infected surface. When they both turned seventeen, they were married.

That same week, Kathy joined the Army, and before Pinklon could say Thomas his new wife was in Fort Jackson, South Carolina, and he was living on the base. In that environment, without the outside pressures, Pinklon successfully broke the habit. It wasn't easy. He wound up physically and emotionally drained. Unfortunately, Kathy was transferred to Seattle and somehow the move unsettled Pinklon. Before long he was back on heroin.

It seemed as if this story was doomed to have an unhappy ending, but Kathy gave birth to a baby boy, and the proud father, Pinklon, determined to cut out drugs from his life for good. He went "cold turkey" and this time his determination paid off. He was only nineteen years of age.

Boxing looked a quick and easy way to make a few bucks, but Pinklon soon found out that the fight game was tough, unrelenting, and not for the fainthearted. Pinklon was far from that, and he began to make a mark for himself. Hell, any guy that could quit dope cold turkey could do anything.

I met up with Pinklon in March 1982. He had been called in to fight Jim Tillis on two days' notice, and I figured it would be a fight Tillis, a title contender, should win. Obviously, Pinklon didn't agree with me because he KO'd Tillis in the eighth round. Sure things in boxing? Don't make me laugh!

For two years Pinklon and I went our separate ways but I followed Pinklon's career with interest. He didn't exactly forget me either because in June 1984 I received a call from Pinklon's close friend, Lloyd Peterson, inquiring if I was interested in working with Thomas in his upcoming title fight against Tim Witherspoon. Pinklon no longer had a manager, so I was interested—but not in a one-fight deal; I wanted a long-term relationship.

Lloyd wrote me a couple of letters, and we talked over the phone. I talked with Pinklon too. We reached an arrangement, and I went to Las Vegas to work with him on preparation for his title shot.

We only had three weeks before the fight, and Witherspoon was a good, tough opponent. He had beaten Greg Page for the WBC title which had been left vacant when Larry Holmes was stripped of his title for not defending it against the number one contender. I won't go into the rights and wrongs of that, except to say I believe that a boxer should be the one to accept or refuse an offer if the money isn't what he wants. Larry Holmes decided not to accept the money offered for his title defense and therefore had his title taken away. He became champion of the newly formed boxing federation, the IBF (International Boxing Federation), and the fight game became even more complicated than it already was.

That wasn't my worry—I was more concerned about Thomas beating Witherspoon. I knew how Pinklon could handle it, but rather than going into details I'll quote Pinklon: "Ang joined me in Vegas and every step of the way out there he kept me laughing. Maybe that's why I was so relaxed the night of the fight. He showed me where Witherspoon was vulnerable and I was able to pick him apart."

I've got to say, Pinklon learned fast. I began calling him Methuselah, because he was so sharp and wise. I soon realized that he was a better boxer than I had thought. And when the bell sounded for the start of the fight I was full of confidence.

It wasn't a very exciting fight, except perhaps for the purists, because they must have enjoyed Pinklon Thomas's display of how to execute a left jab. He stuck it in Witherspoon's face throughout the fight. Sometimes it would be a straight jab, hard and accurate, keeping Witherspoon off-balance as we had planned; or, at other times, Pinklon would flick up his left hand from knee height, still catching his bemused opponent. It was reminiscent of Sonny Liston at his best. Pinklon also showed his skill in slipping and weaving away from blows. For a big man (he weighs 216 pounds) he had extraordinary upper torso flexibility.

We reached the last round. I wiped the sweat from his eyes, slapped him on the legs. "This is it. Only three minutes to go. This is what we're here for. Let's go and do it," I said.

We waited for the decision. I could see the anxiety on his face. Unless the judges had been blind the decision could only go one way. The winner was announced: it was Pinklon by a majority decision. One judge scored it even—he must have slept through the fight! I rushed over to Pinklon and gave him a hug. He was the new Heavyweight World Champion.

A feeling of elation washed over me. I said a silent prayer to my brother Jimmy. It was August 31 and I had become a perfect ten. It was also my brother Jimmy's birthday.

Another night of success to counterbalance the nights of defeat, and my life has had its share of both. I look forward to working with Pinklon, watching him improve—and he will—and hopefully he will be the boxer to unify all the boxing federations. He will become the undisputed heavyweight champion of the world—at least I hope so, it will be so good for boxing. Yes, life looks kind of exciting right now and that's the way I like it.

I've called this book *I Only Talk Winning* for a reason. In life, there are positive and negative thoughts. And hey, it doesn't cost you a cent more to think positively. *I Only Talk Winning* stands for "don't be afraid of losing." Losing is nothing. There is no such thing as failure, only learning how.

INDEX